The City of Tempe
the Tempe Chamber of Commerce
and
the Tempe Convention & Visitors Bureau
express their thanks
to the community-dedicated corporations
which made possible this
City of Tempe Edition
and to
Bridgewood Press
the Valley of the Sun art book publisher
who initiated
and coordinated this effort.

Bridgewood Press
art book publisher
and
Michel F. Sarda
photographer
are pleased to present
the communities of
the Valley of the Sun
in full-color
large format publications.

(top)
*Rain-in-the-face*, a polychrome bronze
by artist Dave McGary **
(center)
Man and horse in Scottsdale **
(right)
Hayden Square in Tempe *

* from *Phoenix – from legend to reality*
Clothbound, 136 pages, 115 color plates, captions in 4 languages

** from *Scottsdale – a portrait in color*
Clothbound, 136 pages, 115 color plates, captions in 4 languages

**Bridgewood Press**
4610 North 40th Street, Phoenix, Arizona 85018
Tel / Fax (602) 954-6573

**Bridgewood Press**
Phoenix

# AlliedSignal Salutes Tempe — Our Partner for the Future.

Together we will:

Promote economic growth
for our city and state

Enhance quality of life for citizens
and our employees

Strengthen Tempe schools
and neighborhoods

Protect and improve
the environment

**AlliedSignal**
AEROSPACE

**MOTOROLA**
*Semiconductor Products Sector*
*Tempe Site*

Motorolans are proud of the roles we play as employer, employees and corporate citizen in the progressive city of Tempe. We are a technology center with the Tempe Site as a major sector facility housing the following organizations:

Bipolar Analog Division
Military Products Operation
Sector Finance and MIS
Phoenix Coporate Research Lab
LATG Final Manufacturing
   & Advanced Technology
Semiconductor Systems
   Design Technology
Compound Semiconductor - 1
World Marketing organizations
Purchasing and support
Discrete Equipment Engineering
   & RF IC Operations

AMERICA'S BUILDER
OF LUXURY HOMES

**UDC HOMES**
Listed on the New York Stock Exchange

National Headquarters
Tempe, Arizona

# CONGRATULATIONS, TEMPE!

Radisson
Tempe Mission Palms

The Buttes

Fiesta Inn

Congratulations, Tempe! The management and staff of The Radisson Tempe Mission Palms, The Buttes and The Fiesta Inn, three of the finest hotel properties in the Valley of the Sun, salute you. We are proud to be a part of all you have become – one of the most dynamic and diverse cities in the southwest.

Forever Living Products started in Arizona in 1978 as a network marketing company devoted to the goal that people everywhere needed an opportunity to make a living that was accessible and entrepreneurial in spirit. Starting with a small product line, the company launched what has become one of Tempe's greatest business success stories. Rex Maughan is Chairman of the Board and President of Forever Living Products International. He graduated from Arizona State University with a B.S. degree in Business Administration. His incredible energy and commitment to Forever Living Products and his generous leadership has resulted in his employees and Distributors rallying behind him to make Forever Living what it is today.

Location is critical for success in any business. In 1981 Forever Living Products International, today's largest grower, producer and distributor of Aloe Vera products, purchased its first International Headquarters located in Tempe. Company growth was so dynamic, a larger facility was soon required and was purchased on Priest Road between University and Broadway. With over $637,000,000 in retail sales in 1992 and being named Arizona's largest privately held corporation, Forever Living Products is now worldwide with 3,000,000 Distributors marketing its products in over 26 foreign countries.

As more and more people found success in building their own "Forever business," they experienced the miracle of Aloe Vera by using the finest stabilized Aloe Vera products on the market–products recognized for their purity and consistency by the International Aloe Science Council, who awarded Forever Living the first Seal of Approval. These products worked so well that sales soared as people everywhere were seeking natural products that made them feel better and look younger and more beautiful!

In the following years, Forever Living added a sister entity, also located in Tempe. Forever Resorts owns and operates various recreational properties, including Callville Bay Marina on Lake Mead and down the Colorado River is Cottonwood Cove Marina on Lake Mohave, both in Nevada, the Holiday Inn of Estes Park, For the Nineties and Rocky Mountain Park Company in Colorado; Florida Houseboat Vacations on the St. John's River; Fun Country Marine Industries in Indiana; Lake Cumberland Houseboat Rentals in Kentucky; Lake of the Ozarks Marina in Missouri; Signal Mountain Lodge in Wyoming and Lake Amistad Marina, Padre Island Park Company and Southfork Ranch in Texas.

Tempe based Forever Living Products International is a dream come true for Distributors and customers worldwide, providing opportunities for achieving financial freedom, a healthier lifestyle and a chance for quality recreation.

A 110-bed acute care and surgical hospital near Arizona State University, Tempe's only hospital has served East and Southeast Valley residents for more than 40 years.

Tempe St. Luke's provides comprehensive emergency services, inpatient and outpatient diagnostic treatment programs, a chemical dependency detoxification unit and obstetrical and pediatric care.

Tempe St. Luke's newly renovated and expanded emergency department provides a larger, more comfortable area to deliver quality patient care. Designated as a Level II Emergency Department, Tempe St. Luke's treats thousands of Arizona State University students and East Valley residents annually.

The hospital's sleek, new Family Care Center offers the latest in obstetrical and pediatric care. Maternity care at the Center is comprehensive, concentrating on the social, economic and psychological dimensions of birth - as well as the physical experiences.

*In a healthcare climate where machines are replacing human contact, Tempe St. Luke's offers personalized care, while providing state-of-the-art equipment.*

# Tempe St. Luke's Hospital

SW Ambulance has served Arizona for over ten years, providing Basic and Advanced Life Support in Maricopa County.

We are particularly proud of our relationship with Tempe, the All American City, where we work hand-in-hand with the Tempe Fire Department to bring you 911 emergency ambulance services.

Southwest Ambulance, which was founded locally by Bob Ramsey, is a private, employee-owned company whose goal is to provide Arizonans with the best emergency

**Partnerships.**
**Progress.**
**Prosperity.**
**Responsibility.**
**Leadership.**
**Vision.**

These are the principles upon which Salt River Project (SRP) was founded. Established in 1903 as the nation's first multi-purpose reclamation project, SRP today is the nation's third-largest public power utility and the state's major water supplier.

We provide power to more than 550,000 customers throughout central Arizona. We administer water rights in a 240,000-acre area, and operate a system of dams and canals that deliver water to the area. We employ nearly 4,700 people and generate annual revenues of $1.1 billion.

As we celebrate our 90th Anniversary, we recommit ourselves to these principles, our customers and the community. In doing so, we honor our past and prepare for a future filled with possibilities.

**SRP**
**SALT RIVER PROJECT**

**90 YEARS** *MAKING A DIFFERENCE 1903-1993*

## BLACK&DECKER®
### HOME IMPROVEMENT LIBRARY™

# Building Projects for the Home

Cy DeCosse Incorporated
Minnetonka, Minnesota

# Contents

**Introduction . . . . . . . . . . . . . . . . . . . . . . . . . . . . 5**

**Tools & Materials . . . . . . . . . . . . . . . . . . . . . . 7**

**Planning Major Projects . . . . . . . . . . . . . . . . . 77**

**Remodeling Projects . . . . . . . . . . . . . . . . . . . . 97**

Copyright © 1994
Cy DeCosse Incorporated
5900 Green Oak Drive
Minnetonka, Minnesota 55343
1-800-328-3895
All rights reserved
Printed in U.S.A.

CY DeCOSSE INCORPORATED
*Chairman:* Bruce Barnet
*Chairman Emeritus:* Cy DeCosse
*CEO/President:* James B. Maus
*Executive Vice President:* William B. Jones

Library of Congress
Cataloging-in-Publication Data

Building projects for the home

p. cm.—(Black & Decker home improvement library)
Includes index.
ISBN   0-86573-925-0
1. Dwellings—Remodeling—Amateurs' manuals.
I. Cy DeCosse Incorporated.
II. Black & Decker Corporation (Towson, Md.)
TH4816.B84   1994                    94-12578
643'.7—dc20

## Landscape Construction Projects . . . . . . . . . . 204

## Building Decks . . . . . . . . . . . . . . . . . . . . . . . . 299

## Feature Decks . . . . . . . . . . . . . . . . . . . . . . . . 379

## Deck Finishing & Repair. . . . . . . . . . . . . . . . . 399

Created by: The editors of Cy DeCosse Incorporated, in cooperation with Black & Decker. *BLACK&DECKER* is a trademark of the Black & Decker Corporation and is used under license.

Also available from the publisher:
*Everyday Home Repairs, Decorating With Paint & Wallcovering, Kitchen Remodeling, Home Plumbing Projects & Repairs, Basic Wiring & Electrical Repairs, Workshop Tips & Techniques, Advanced Home Wiring, Bathroom Remodeling, Built-in Projects for the Home*

*Creative Director:* William B. Jones
*Project Director:* Paul Currie
*Art Directors:* Tim Himsel, Gina Seeling
*Project Manager:* Diane Dreon
*Copy Editor:* Janice Cauley
*Production Staff:* Carol Harvatin, Tracy Stanley, Julie Sutphen
*Print Production Coordinator:* Linda Halls

*Printed on American paper by:* R. R. Donnelley & Sons Co. (0894)

# Introduction

One of the many joys of owning your home is in building projects that will improve your house and make it meet your specific needs. You can add space as your family grows, convert space when needs change and create specialty areas that match your activities. And these projects can add to the value of your home, particularly when you do all, or even some, of the work yourself.

*Building Projects for the Home* contains all you need to know to complete major projects that can make your home complete. Building a deck, porch or patio; creating additional bedroom space; converting existing small rooms into larger living areas; adding doors and windows; or adding trellises, arbors, paths and planters that turn your yard into a beautiful and enjoyable landscape—all of these projects and more are here to satisfy your home improvement desires.

Every home how-to material, technique and project shown comes from professional builders and designers. Your projects will have a professional-quality look at a fraction of the cost. And if you will be working with professionals on any portion of your project, this book will give you the knowledge to deal with them effectively, and get the most for your money. It will help you design and plan a project, as well as build it yourself.

The first section of the book, Tools & Materials, is a primer for all the basic tools and materials your projects will require. You will see which tools should be part of your essential tool box and how to create useful workshop space and basic workbench and shelving projects. This section also contains all the information you need to choose lumber, plywood and other sheet goods and fasteners.

This is followed by Planning Major Projects, where you will find everything you need to know about designing and planning major remodeling projects. This section shows you how your house is constructed and how to make remodeling modifications, draw plans and get the proper building permits. In addition, you will learn how to choose from the wide range of window and door styles available, and how to plan the openings for them.

The Remodeling Projects section contains all the how-to techniques and step-by-step methods to do major home remodeling projects on the inside of your house. You learn how to prepare the work area and protect the rest of your home from dust and debris. You see how to remove existing wall, floor and ceiling surfaces so you can make the

changes your project requires. Building and removing walls, installing new doors, windows, skylights, patio doors, bay windows and other projects are all completely covered.

Landscape Construction Projects shows you how to "remodel" your yard. You learn how to design, plan and build patios, freestanding and retaining walls, garden steps, walkways, arbors and trellises, fences and garden ponds. You also see how to grade and contour your yard and deal with drainage problems. Included is all the information about tools, choosing materials and building techniques you will need to transform your yard into a beautiful landscape.

Finally, the last three sections are a complete manual for designing, planning and building a deck. Whether you attach it to your house or build a free-standing unit, you will find everything you need to know about the necessary tools, best materials and professional building tips and techniques. You also learn about deck maintenance and repair methods.

*Building Projects for the Home* is a how-to manual you will want to take to your project site. The step-by-step illustrated instructions are easy to follow and will help give your projects professional-looking results.

Framing square

C-clamp

16-oz. claw hammer

Phillips screwdriver

Standard screwdriver

Sanding
block

Plumb bob/
chalk line

Nail
sets

Mallet

2' carpenter's level

STUDSENSOR II

3/8'' power
drill

Electronic
stud
finder

Chisel

Utility
knife

Putty
knife

Drill bits

T-bevel

Cordless
screwdriver

Combination
square

12' tape
measure

Wonderbar®

Cat's
paw

STANLEY
Dry Wall Saw
No.15-207  5 1/2POINTS
U.S.A.

STANLEY

Crosscut
saw

Wallboard
saw

**Starter tool set** should include a generous selection of hand tools, plus a ³⁄₈-inch power drill and a cordless screwdriver. Inspect the finish on hand tools. Quality hand tools made of high-carbon steel are machined with clean-cut metal surfaces. Tool handles should be tight and comfortably molded.

# Tool Basics

A quality tool collection does not require a large initial investment. A home owner can build a tool collection by buying tools as they are needed for each carpentry project. Invest in top-grade tools made by reputable manufacturers. A quality tool always carries a full parts and labor warranty.

Read power tool specifications to compare features like horsepower, motor speed and cutting capacity. Better-quality tools also have roller or ball bearings instead of sleeve bearings, reinforced power cords, and heavy-duty trigger switches.

**Intermediate tool collection** includes additional power tools and special-purpose hand tools. Replace blades or resharpen cutting tools whenever they become dull.

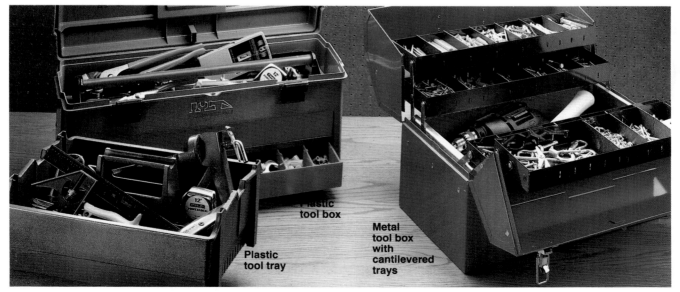

**Tool boxes** made of plastic or metal are lightweight and durable. Tool boxes with cantilevered trays and divided compartments keep tools and materials organized.

# Measuring & Layout Tools

An important first step in every carpentry project is measuring distances and angles accurately. Buy a steel tape measure with a ¾-inch-wide blade for general home use.

A combination square is a compact tool used to measure and mark 45° and 90° angles. Use a framing square to lay out 90° angles. Choose a T-bevel with a locking handle to measure and transfer any angle.

To check surfaces for plumb and level, buy a quality 2-foot carpenter's level made of metal or wood. Select a level with screw-in bubble vials that can be replaced if they are damaged. Also buy a string chalk line to lay out long, straight lines.

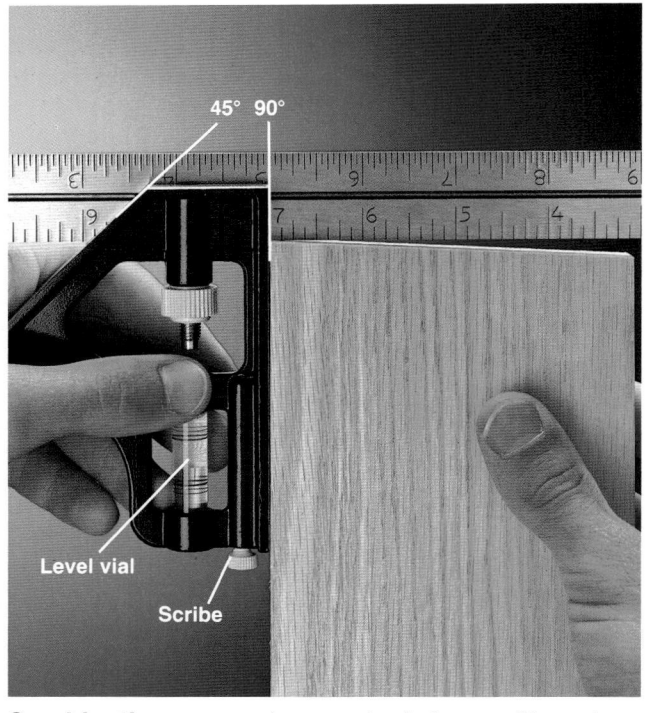

45° 90°

Level vial

Scribe

**Steel tape measure** with ¾-inch-wide blade is good for general-purpose home use. Choose a tape with blade marked every 16" for easy layout of stud or joist locations.

**Combination square** is many tools in one. The adjustable handle has two straight surfaces for marking 90° and 45° angles. The square also has a built-in level. Some squares include a pointed metal scribe to mark work for cutting.

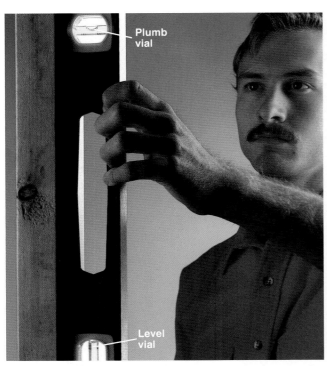

**Two-foot carpenter's level** has plumb vial for checking vertical surfaces and a level vial for checking horizontal surfaces. Level shows correct position when bubble is exactly between the line markings.

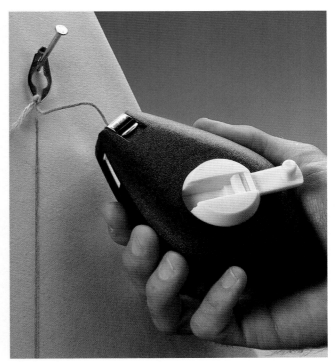

**Chalk line** marks long lines needed for large layout jobs. Hold string taut at both ends, and snap firmly to mark surface. Chalk line can also be used as a plumb bob for laying out stud walls.

## How to Duplicate Angles with a T-bevel

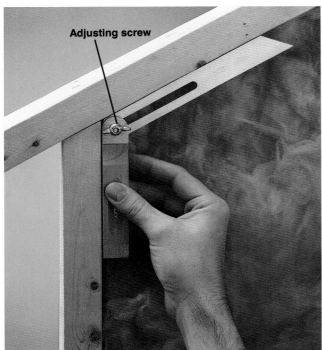

**1** Loosen the T-bevel adjusting screw and adjust the arms to match the angle to be copied. Tighten the adjusting screw.

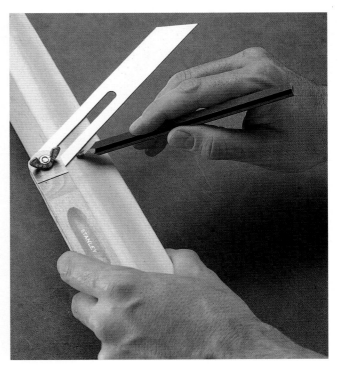

**2** Move the T-bevel to the workpiece, and mark the profile of the angle. Cut the workpiece to match the angle.

Labels on the main photograph:

**Hacksaw**

**Coping saw**

**Crosscut saw**

**Backsaw**

# Handsaws

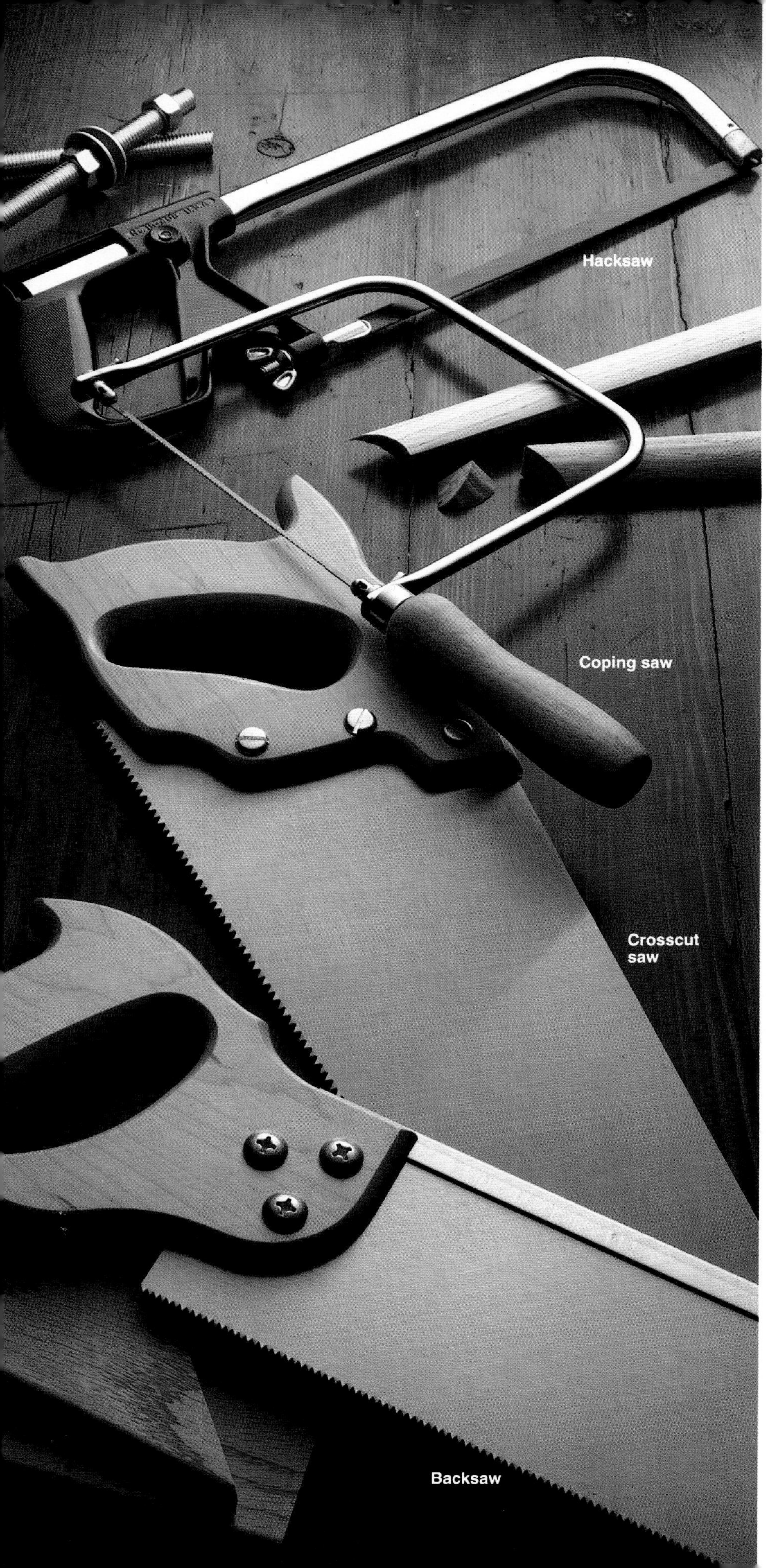

Handsaws can be more practical than portable power saws for small jobs and occasional use.

The crosscut saw is a standard cutting tool designed to cut across the wood grain. A crosscut saw may also be used for occasional "rip" cuts parallel to the wood grain. A crosscut saw with 10 teeth per inch is a good choice for general-purpose cutting.

A backsaw and miter box makes straight cuts. The reinforced spine keeps the backsaw blade from flexing. The miter box locks at any angle for cutting precise miters and bevels.

A coping saw makes curved cuts on materials like wood molding. The coping saw has a very narrow, flexible blade held taut by a C-shaped spring frame. To adjust blade position for scroll cuts, rotate the spigots holding the blade.

Hacksaws are designed to cut metal. Like a coping saw, a hacksaw has a fine, flexible blade that can be replaced when it becomes dull.

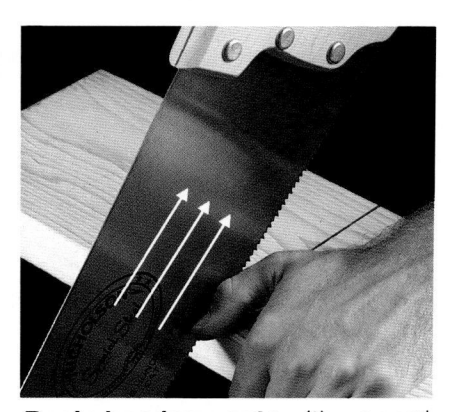

**Begin handsaw cuts** with upward strokes to establish the cut line, then make long, smooth strokes with blade at 45° angle to workpiece. Guide the saw at the beginning of a cut by supporting the edge with the side of your thumb.

**Crosscut saw** is a standard carpenter's tool. At end of cut, saw slowly and support waste material with a free hand to prevent the wood from splintering.

**Backsaw with miter box** cuts precise angles. Clamp or hold workpiece in miter box. Make certain that miter box is securely fastened to work surface.

**Coping saw** has a thin, flexible blade designed to cut curves. It is a necessary tool for cutting and fitting wood moldings.

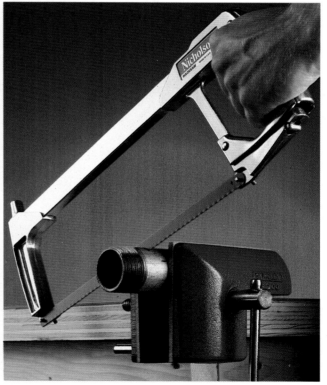

**Hacksaw** has a flexible, fine-tooth blade designed to cut metal. Blade must be stretched tightly in frame.

# Circular Saw

The power circular saw is ideal for making fast, straight cuts in wood. Special-purpose saw blades make it possible to cut metal, plaster or even concrete with a circular saw. The locking baseplate pivots to adjust blade depth, and rotates for bevel cuts.

Choose a saw with blade size of at least 7¼ inches. A smaller saw may not cut through 2-inch lumber, especially when set at a bevel position. Select a saw with a motor rated at 2 horsepower or more.

Because a circular saw blade cuts as it rotates upward, the top face of the workpiece may splinter. To protect the finished side of the workpiece, mark measurements on back side of workpiece. Place the good side down, or facing away from the baseplate, when cutting.

**Check the cutting angle** of circular saw with a T-bevel or square. Make test cuts on scrap wood. If bevel scale is inaccurate, adjust the baseplate to compensate (page opposite).

**Use an edge guide** for straight, long cuts. Clamp a straightedge on the workpiece. Keep baseplate tight against edge guide and move the saw smoothly.

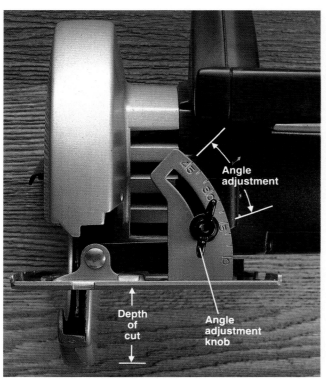

**Set blade angle** by loosening the adjustment knob. Set blade depth by loosening adjustment knob at rear of saw. For safety, set the blade so that it projects through bottom of workpiece by no more than the length of one saw tooth. Tighten knobs firmly.

Panel blade for smooth cuts in plywood

Hollow ground planer blade for fine woodworking

Carbide-tipped combination blade

Masonry blade

Metal-cutting blade

Precisio
Saw Blade

BLACK & D
Chro
Plated Saw

BLACK & DECKER

Piranl
Carbide-Tooth Sa

BLACK
Abr
Saw

BLACK & DEC
Abrasi
Saw Blade

**Circular saw blades** include: carbide-tipped combination blade for general use; panel blade with small teeth which do not chip thin veneer layers in plywood; hollow-ground planer blade with tapered surface that reduces friction, used for fine woodworking; abrasive blades used to cut metal or masonry.

# Jig Saw

The jig saw is the best choice for cutting curves. The cutting capacity of a jig saw depends on its power and the length of its blade stroke. Choose a saw rated to cut 2-inch-thick softwood and ¾-inch-thick hardwood stock. Some jig saws have a pivoting baseplate that can be locked to make bevel cuts.

Select a variable-speed jig saw, because different blade styles may require different cutting speeds for best results. In general, use faster blade speeds when cutting with coarse-tooth blades and slower speeds with fine-tooth blades.

A jig saw tends to vibrate because of the up-and-down blade action. A quality jig saw has a heavy-gauge steel baseplate that reduces vibration. To further minimize vibration, hold the saw tightly against the workpiece, and move the saw slowly so the blade does not bend.

Because jig saw blades cut on the upward stroke, the top side of the workpiece may splinter. If the wood has a good side to protect, cut with this surface facing downward.

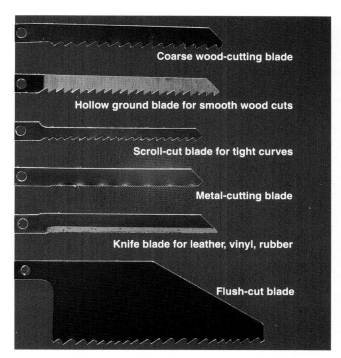

Coarse wood-cutting blade

Hollow ground blade for smooth wood cuts

Scroll-cut blade for tight curves

Metal-cutting blade

Knife blade for leather, vinyl, rubber

Flush-cut blade

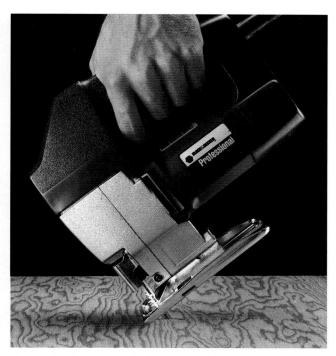

**Jig saw blades** come in different designs for cutting different materials. Choose a blade that is correct for the job. With fine-tooth blades that have 14 or more teeth per inch, set saw at low blade speed. Coarse blades require faster blade speeds.

**Plunge cuts** are made by tipping the saw so front edge of the baseplate is held firmly against workpiece. Start saw, and slowly lower it to a horizontal position, letting blade gradually cut through workpiece.

Scrolling knob

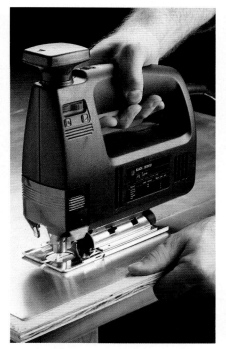

**Scroll or curved cuts** are made with a narrow blade. Move saw slowly to avoid bending the blade. Some jig saws have a scrolling knob that allows the blade to be turned without turning the saw.

**Cut metals** with a fine-tooth metal-cutting blade and select a slow blade speed. Support sheet metals with thin plywood to eliminate vibration. Use emery paper or a file to smooth burred edges left by jig saw blade.

**Do not force blades.** Jig saw blades are flexible and may break if forced. Move saw slowly when cutting bevels or tough materials like knots in wood.

# Hammers

Hammers are made in a wide variety of sizes and shapes. Choose a hammer with a smoothly finished, high-carbon steel head and a quality handle made of hickory, fiberglass, or solid steel.

The 16-ounce curved claw hammer is the most frequently used hammer for carpentry. It is designed only for driving, setting, or pulling nails. For all other striking jobs, use a specialty hammer. A tack hammer with a magnetic head drives nails and tacks that are too small to hold. A rubber- or plastic-head mallet drives wood chisels. Select a ball peen hammer to pound hardened metal tools, like masonry chisels or pry bars, because it has a heat-treated steel head that resists chipping.

Use a nail set to drive nail heads below the work surface without damaging the wood.

**Tack hammer**

**Rubber-head mallet**

**Ball peen hammer**

**Claw hammer**

**Nail set**

**Clean hammer face** periodically with fine sandpaper. Wood resins and nail coatings may build up on the face, causing the hammer to slip and mar the work surface or bend the nail.

# Hammering Tips

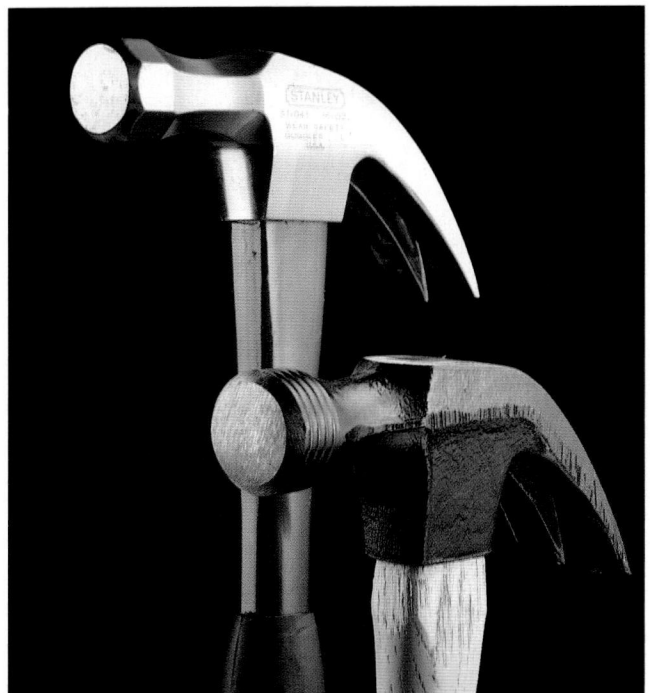

**Claw hammer** drives and pulls nails. Choose a quality hammer (left) with a 16-ounce head. Look for a smoothly finished, high-carbon steel head. Bargain tool (right) has rougher, painted finish with visible cast marks.

**Tack hammer** with magnetic head drives small nails or brads that are difficult to hold by hand.

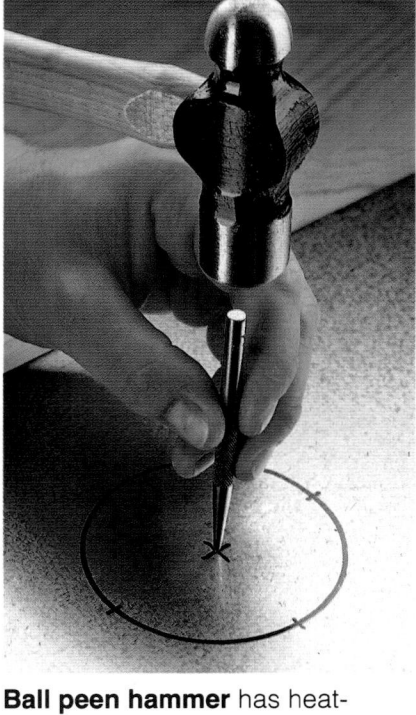

**Mallet with rubber** or plastic head drives woodworking chisels. Soft mallet face will not damage fine woodworking tools.

**Ball peen hammer** has heat-treated steel head that resists chipping when driving hardened steel tools or pry bars.

**Nail set** drives heads of finish and casing nails below wood surface. Choose a nail set with tip that is slightly smaller than nail head.

# Nails

The wide variety of nail styles and sizes makes it possible to choose exactly the right fastener for the job. Use either common or box nails for general framing work. Box nails are smaller in diameter, which makes them less likely to split wood. Most common and box nails have a cement or vinyl coating that improves their holding power.

Finish and casing nails have small heads and are driven just below the work surface with a nail set, for projects like nailing wood trim. Casing nails have a slightly larger head than finish nails for better holding power. Galvanized nails have a zinc coating that resists rusting, and are used for outdoor projects.

Other specialty nails are identified by their intended function, like wallboard nails, siding nails, masonry nails, or flooring nails.

Nail lengths are identified by numbers from 4 to 60 followed by the letter "d," which stands for "penny." Some specialty nails are identified by either length or gauge.

## Nail Sizes

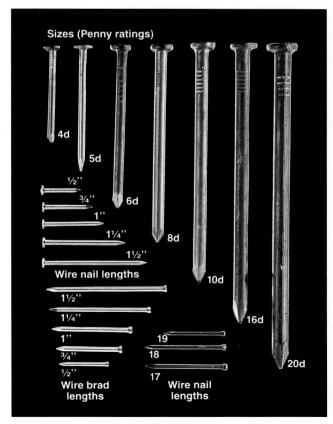

Sizes (Penny ratings)

4d
5d
½"
¾"
1"
1¼"
6d
1½"
8d
**Wire nail lengths**
10d
1½"
1¼"
16d
1"
19
¾"
18
½"
17
20d
**Wire brad lengths**
**Wire nail lengths**

## Types of Nails

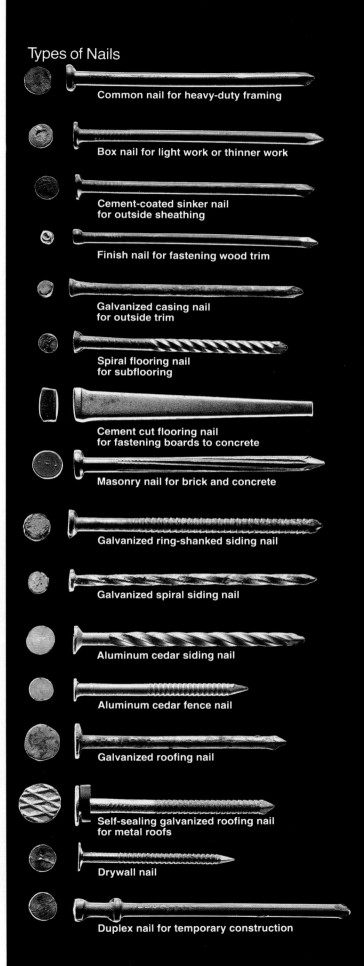

Common nail for heavy-duty framing

Box nail for light work or thinner work

Cement-coated sinker nail for outside sheathing

Finish nail for fastening wood trim

Galvanized casing nail for outside trim

Spiral flooring nail for subflooring

Cement cut flooring nail for fastening boards to concrete

Masonry nail for brick and concrete

Galvanized ring-shanked siding nail

Galvanized spiral siding nail

Aluminum cedar siding nail

Aluminum cedar fence nail

Galvanized roofing nail

Self-sealing galvanized roofing nail for metal roofs

Drywall nail

Duplex nail for temporary construction

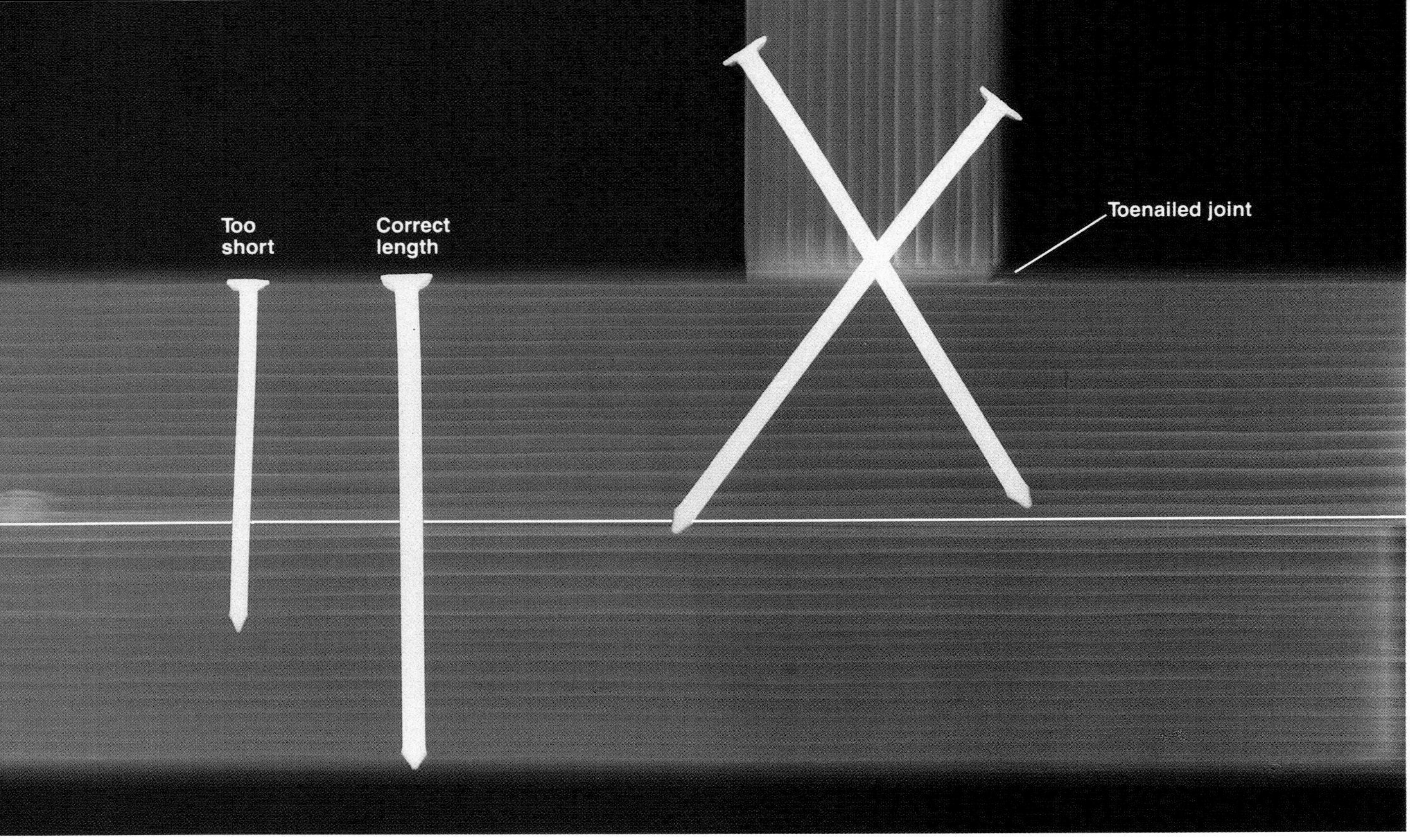

**Too short**  **Correct length**  Toenailed joint

**X-ray view** shows how nails penetrate wood. Longer nail that fully penetrates second 2 × 4 has greater holding power than short nail. Use toenailing (right) when nails cannot be driven from the outside surface. Drive nails at opposing 45° angles. Offset nail positions so that nails do not hit each other.

## Tips for Nailing

**Drive flat concrete nails** into the mortar joints instead of the concrete blocks. Mortar is easier to penetrate.

**Metal connectors** help join wood with ease and speed, and are often used to connect studs to sole and top plates.

## How to Fasten Wood to a Steel Beam

**1** Coat the top of 2 × 4 with a generous application of construction adhesive. Clamp 2 × 4 to bottom of I-beam.

**2** Drill holes spaced 16" on-center through 2 × 4 and base of I-beam, using $^9/_{64}$-inch twist bit. Use low speed when drilling metal. Drive 16d common nails through holes and clinch them on base of I-beam.

**Clinch nails** for extra holding power. Bend the nail over slightly, then drive it flush to the surface with a hammer.

**Use finish nail** in electric drill to bore a pilot hole in hardwood. Tighten drill chuck securely on nail.

# Prying Tools

Quality pry bars are made of high-carbon steel, and are available in many sizes. Choose tools forged in a single piece. Tools made from welded parts are not as strong as those that are forged.

Most pry bars have a curved claw at one end for pulling nails and a chisel-shaped tip at the opposite end for other prying jobs. Improve leverage by placing a wood block under the head of pry tools.

**Wonderbar®** is a slightly flexible tool made of flattened steel. This tool is useful for a variety of prying and wrecking jobs. Both ends can be used for pulling nails.

**Prying tools** include wrecking bars for heavy demolition work, cat's paws for removing nails, and brad pullers. Wonderbars are made of flattened steel and come in a variety of sizes for light and heavy use.

**Wrecking bar,** sometimes called a crowbar, is a rigid, heavy-use tool for demolition and heavy prying jobs. Use scrap wood under the bar to protect surfaces.

**Cat's paw** has a sharpened claw. To extract nails, drive the claw into the wood under the nail head with a hammer.

# Drills

Most drilling jobs can be done easily with a power drill. Power drills are commonly available in ¼-, ⅜- and ½-inch sizes. The number refers to the largest bit shank diameter that fits the drill chuck. A ⅜-inch drill is a good choice because it accepts a wide range of bits and accessories. A variable-speed reversing (VSR) drill will adapt to many uses, like drilling masonry, or driving and removing wallboard screws. A cordless drill offers freedom from extension cords.

When choosing a drill, look for quality features like an extra-long power cord with reinforced cord protector, and a sealed switch that prevents dirt from entering the trigger. A drill that uses top-quality materials may actually be smaller, lighter, and easier to handle than a cheaper drill.

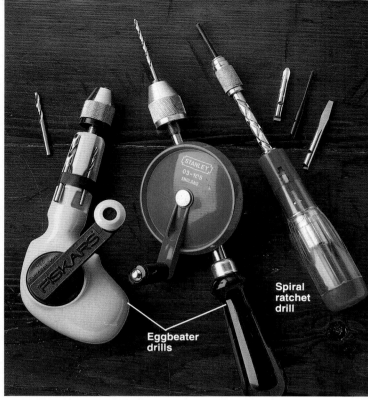

**Hand drills** include eggbeater and spiral ratchet styles. Hand drills are often used in fine woodworking, or for carpentry jobs where a power drill is not convenient.

Spiral ratchet drill

Eggbeater drills

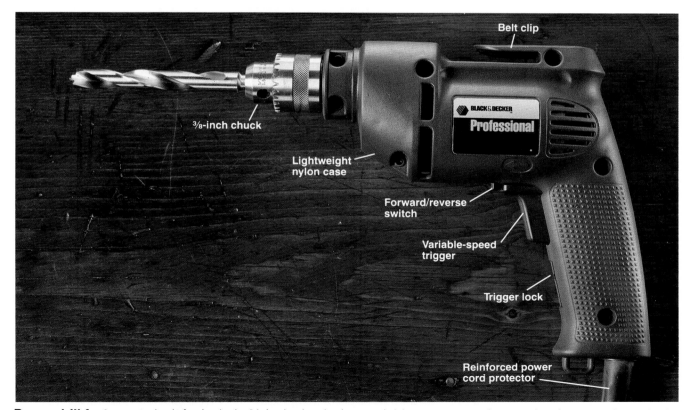

Belt clip

⅜-inch chuck

Lightweight nylon case

Forward/reverse switch

Variable-speed trigger

Trigger lock

Reinforced power cord protector

**Power drill features** to look for include ⅜-inch chuck size, variable motor speed, reversing feature, trigger lock to set a constant speed, a heavy power cord with reinforced protector, a tough lightweight nylon case, and a molded clip that allows the tool to be hung from a belt or pants pocket.

# Drill Bits

Twist bits can be used to bore in both metal and wood. They come in many sizes, ranging from wire gauge to more than ½ inch wide. Some self-piloting bits have a special point for accurate drilling. Most twist bits are made from high-speed or carbon steel. For drilling stainless steel and other hard metals, choose a titanium or cobalt bit.

Spade bits have a long point and flat-edged cutters and are used to cut holes in wood quickly and accurately. Other types of drill bits are available for special applications, like drilling extra-large holes for a lockset, or boring into concrete. Store drill bits so they do not bump against each other, and clean them with linseed oil to prevent rust.

**Twist bit** can be used in wood or metal. Drill wood at high speeds, metal at low drill speeds.

Pilot tip

**Self-piloting** bit requires no center punch. Special tip reduces splintering in wood, and prevents bit from binding when drilling metal.

**Carbide-tipped masonry** bit can drill in concrete, cinder block or brickwork. Use low drill speed, and lubricate drill hole with water to prevent overheating.

**Glass & tile** bit drills smooth holes in smooth, brittle surfaces. Use low drill speed, and wear gloves and eye protection.

**Drill saw** has twist tip to cut entry hole, and side-cutting rasp teeth for reaming cuts in wood, plastic or light-gauge metals.

**Spade bit** is used to drill wood. Long tip anchors bit before the cutting edges enter the wood. Begin at low speed, gradually increasing as bit enters wood.

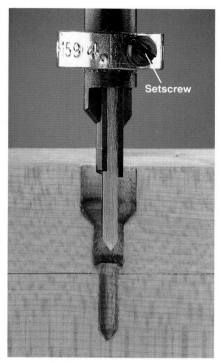

**Adjustable counterbore** bit drills screw pilot, countersink and counterbore holes with one action. Loosen setscrew to adjust bit to match length and shape of screw.

**Plug cutter** cuts circular wood plugs used to fill screw counterbore holes.

**Hole saw** with mandrel pilot bit cuts smooth holes in wood, like those used to mount door locksets.

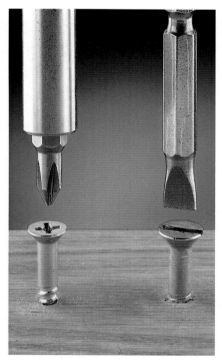

**Screwdriver bits,** available in many styles, convert a variable-speed drill into a screwgun.

**Extractor bit** removes screws with worn or broken heads. Drill a pilot hole into top of screw with twist bit, then use extractor and reverse drill setting to remove screw.

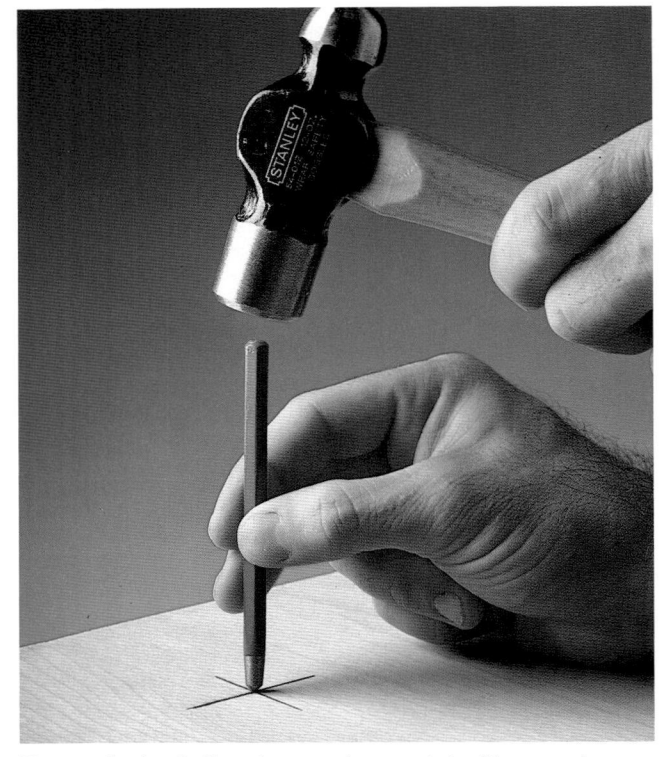

**Tap an indentation** in wood or metal with a center punch. Starting point keeps drill bit from wandering.

**Cover drilling area** on glass or ceramic with masking tape. Tape keeps bit from wandering on smooth surface.

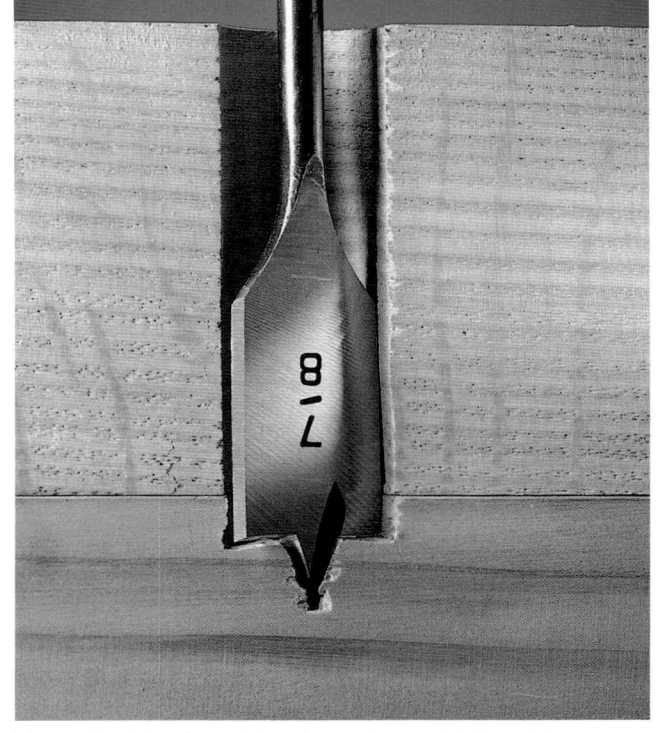

**Use a backer** board underneath workpiece to prevent splintering when drill bit breaks through.

**Wrap masking tape** around drill bit to control depth of hole. Drill until bottom of tape is even with top of workpiece surface.

**Lubricate metal** with cutting oil while drilling. Oil prevents bit from overheating. Use low speed when drilling metal.

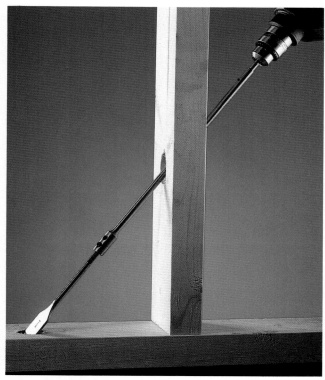

**Use bit extension** to drill deep or inaccessible holes. Drill at low speed until bit is fully engaged.

**Prebore holes** in hardwood and metal with a small bit. Preboring prevents bit from binding and wood from splintering.

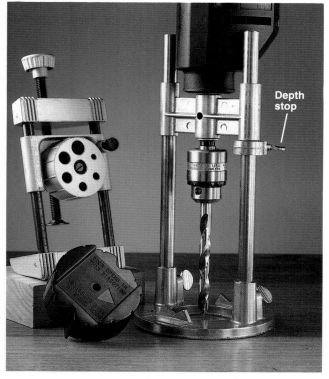

**Guide accessories** control drilling angles for precise perpendicular holes. Drill guide (right) has adjustable depth stop that controls drilling depth.

# Screwdrivers & Screws

Make sure you have several hand screwdrivers, both phillips and slot types. Quality screwdrivers have hardened-steel blades and wide handles that are easy to grip.

For general use, a cordless power screwdriver saves time and effort. For frequent use, or for large jobs like installing wallboard panels, choose a power screwgun with an adjustable clutch to set screws at different depths.

Screws are categorized according to length, slot style, head shape and gauge. The thickness of the screw body is indicated by the gauge number, from 0 to 24. The larger the gauge number, the larger the screw. Large screws provide extra holding power, while small screws are less likely to split a workpiece. When joining two pieces of wood, choose a screw length so that the entire threaded portion will extend into base piece.

Where appearance is important, use countersink or counterbore bits to drill a recessed hole that will hide the screw head. A countersink bit lets you drive a flat-head screw flush with the wood surface, while a counterbore bit lets you recess the screw head to hide the location with a wood plug.

**Common screwdrivers** include (from top): stubby model for use in cramped areas, adjustable-clutch screwgun for fastening wallboard, ratchet hand screwdriver with interchangeable bits, cordless power screwdriver with locking spindle, slot screwdriver.

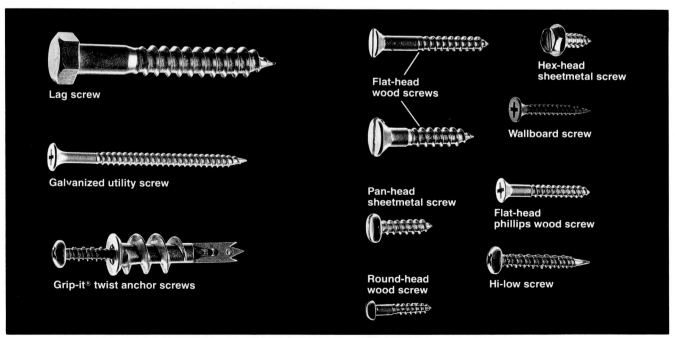

**Types of screws:** lag screw, galvanized utility screw, Grip-It® twist anchor screws, flat-head wood screws, pan-head sheetmetal screw, oval-head screw, hex- head sheetmetal screw, wallboard screw, flat-head phillips wood screw, hi-low screw.

## Tips for Driving Screws

**Lubricate screws** with beeswax to make driving easier. Do not use soap, oil or grease to lubricate, because they can stain wood and corrode screws.

**Pilot hole** keeps wood from splitting when screw is driven. Use a twist bit with diameter that is slightly less than diameter of threaded portion of screw.

**To install a wall anchor,** drill a pilot hole in wall equal in diameter to plastic anchor. Insert anchor and drive it flush with wall. Inserted screw will expand anchor for strong, durable hold.

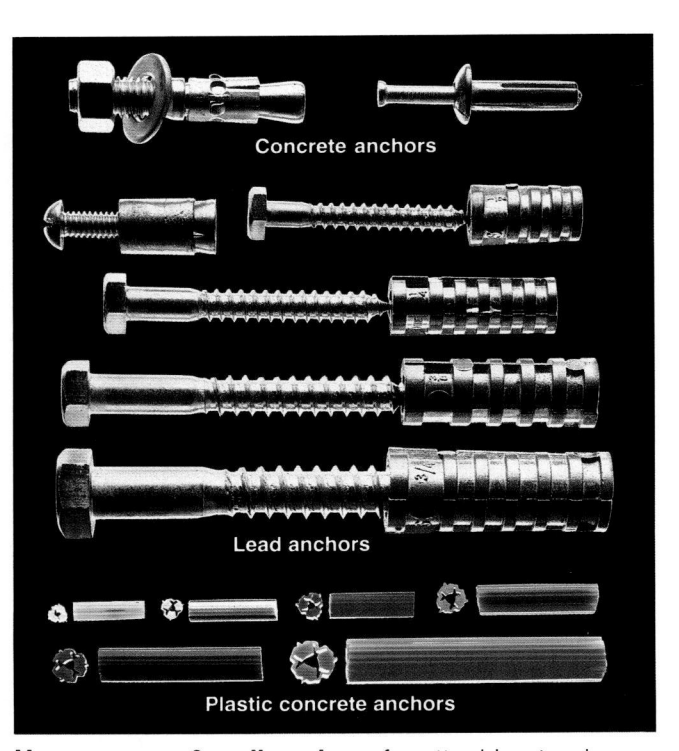

**Use masonry & wall anchors** for attaching to plaster, concrete or brick. Choose an anchor that is equal in length to the thickness of the wall surface.

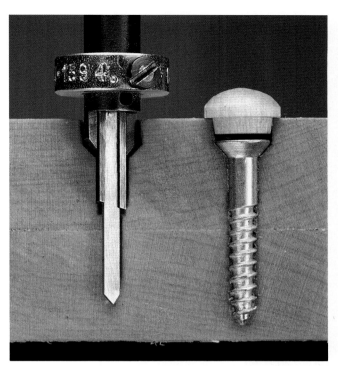

**Drill counterbore pilot** holes with adjustable counterbore bit. Loosen setscrew and set bit to match length and shape of wood screw. Tighten setscrew and drill until collar reaches surface of workpiece. After driving screw, cover hole with wood plug or putty.

**Utility wallboard screws** have wedge-shaped heads that are self-countersinking. Wallboard screws are designed so they will not split wood. Use black screws for inside jobs, and galvanized screws for exterior work.

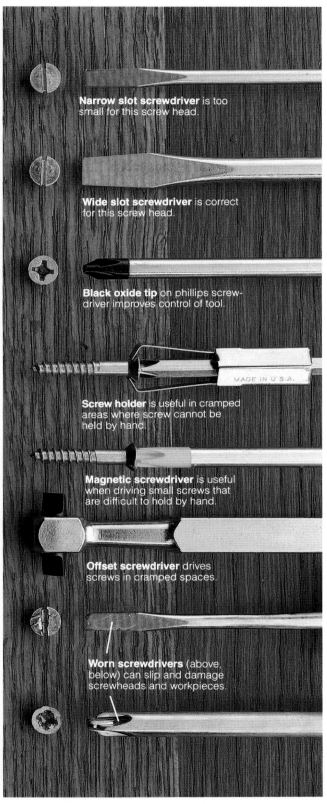

**Narrow slot screwdriver** is too small for this screw head.

**Wide slot screwdriver** is correct for this screw head.

**Black oxide tip** on phillips screwdriver improves control of tool.

**Screw holder** is useful in cramped areas where screw cannot be held by hand.

**Magnetic screwdriver** is useful when driving small screws that are difficult to hold by hand.

**Offset screwdriver** drives screws in cramped spaces.

**Worn screwdrivers** (above, below) can slip and damage screwheads and workpieces.

**Choose proper screwdriver** for the job. Screwdriver should fit slot tightly. Common types of screwdrivers include: slot, phillips, phillips with black oxide tip, screw holder, magnetic, and offset screwdrivers.

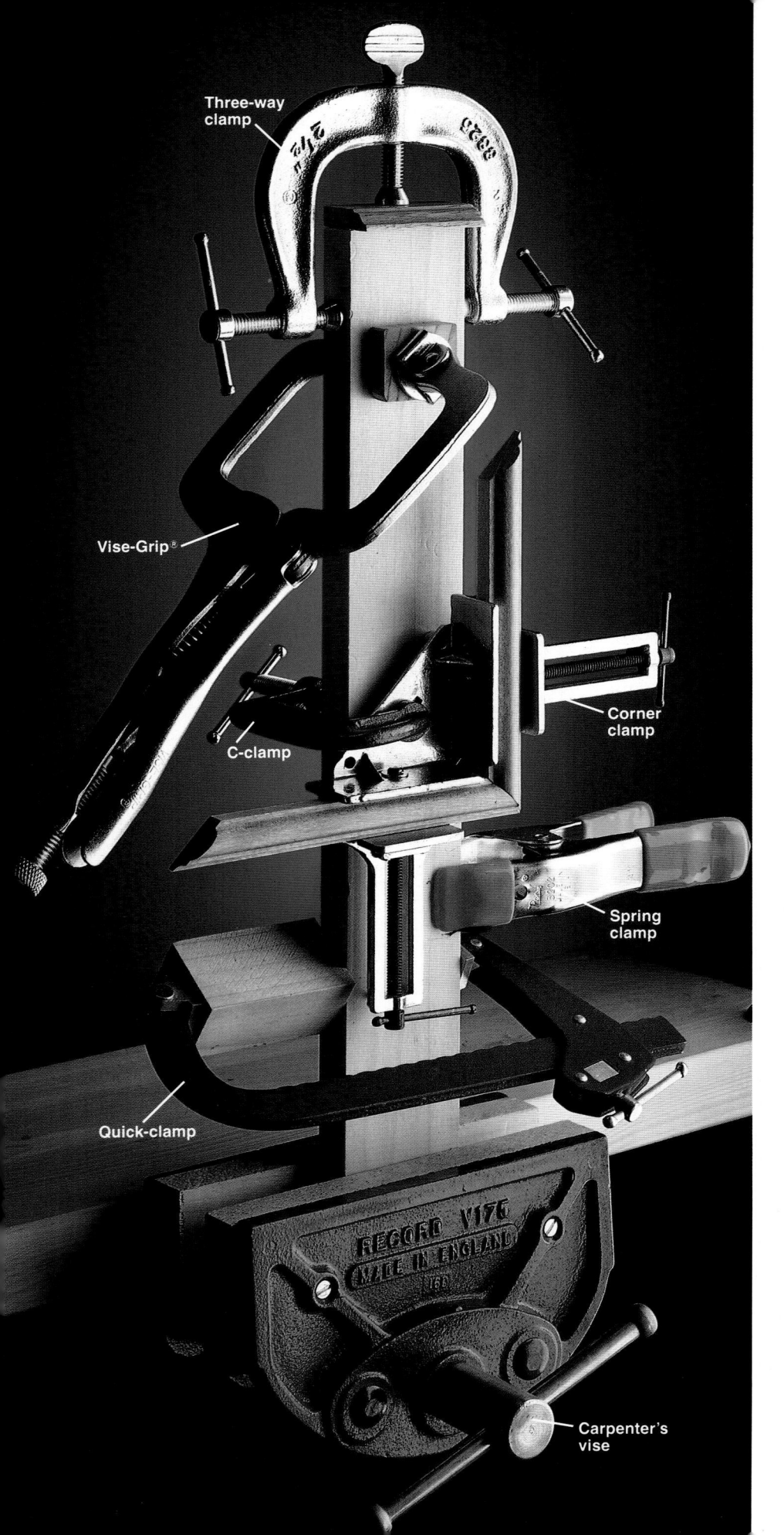

Three-way clamp

Vise-Grip®

C-clamp

Corner clamp

Quick-clamp

Spring clamp

Carpenter's vise

# Clamps, Vises & Adhesives

Use vises and clamps to hold materials in place while working. Equip a workbench with a heavy-duty carpenter's vise. Clamps for small jobs include C-clamps, Vise-Grip® clamps, handscrews, and quick clamps. Clamps with metal jaws can damage a workpiece, so use scrap wood blocks between the workpiece and the clamp jaws.

For wide clamping jobs, use pipe clamps or bar clamps. The jaws of pipe clamps are connected by ordinary steel pipe. The distance between the jaws is limited only by the length of the pipe.

Adhesives bond many materials that cannot easily be nailed or screwed together, like concrete or steel. They also can reduce the number of fasteners needed to install wallboard or paneling. Many new adhesives are resistant to moisture and temperature changes, making them suitable for exterior use.

**Common adhesives** include (clockwise from top right): clear adhesive caulk for sealing cracks in damp areas, waterproof construction adhesive, multi-purpose adhesive, electric hot glue gun with glue sticks, yellow wood glue, white wood glue, and white all-purpose glue.

**Joist & deck adhesive** makes for a stronger, squeak-free floor or deck. Make sure that adhesive is waterproof for outdoor applications.

**Carpenter's vise** attaches to workbench to hold materials for cutting, shaping or sanding. Cover the broad jaws with hardwood to protect workpieces.

**Electric hot glue gun** melts glue sticks for both temporary and permanent bonding of wood and a variety of other materials.

# Tips for Gluing & Clamping

**Handscrews** are wooden clamps with two adjusting screws. Handscrews are used to hold materials together while gluing. The wide wooden jaws will not damage workpiece surfaces. Handscrews adjust to fit angled workpieces.

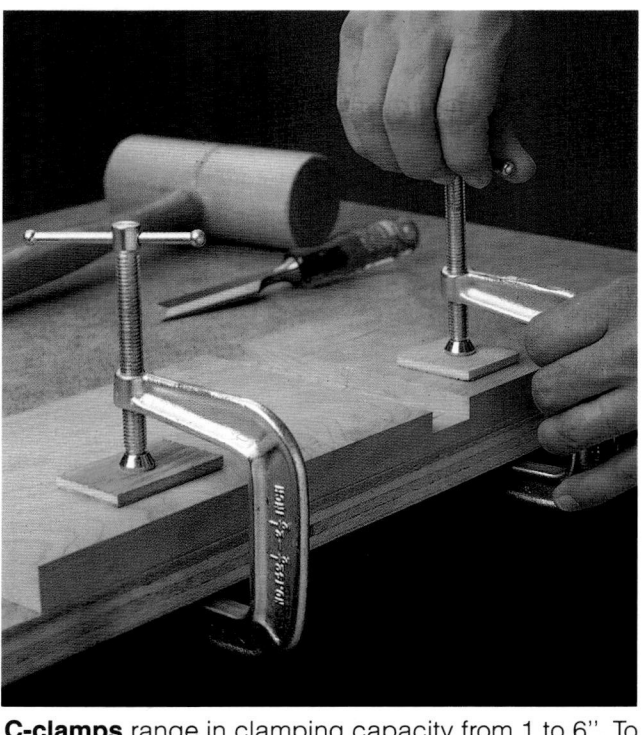

**C-clamps** range in clamping capacity from 1 to 6". To protect the workpiece, place scrap wood blocks between the jaws and the workpiece surface.

**Corner clamp** holds mitered corners when gluing picture frame moldings. Glue and clamp opposite corners, and let them dry before gluing the remaining corners.

**Three-way clamp** has three thumbscrews, and is used to hold edge moldings to the side of a shelf, tabletop or other flat surface. Use scraps of wood to protect workpiece surfaces.

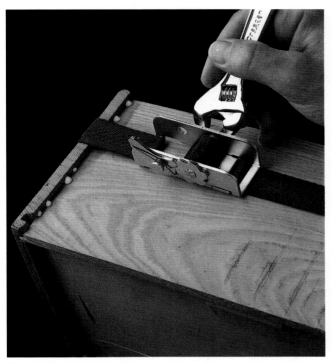

**Strap clamp** and white carpenter's glue are used for gluing furniture and other wood projects. Use yellow glue for exterior projects. Clamp the pieces together until the glue dries.

**Pipe clamps** or bar clamps hold large workpieces. Buy pipe clamp jaws in pairs to fit either ½-inch or ¾-inch diameter pipe. Clamping irregular shapes may require clamping jigs made from scrap lumber.

**Workmate®** portable gripping bench has a jointed, adjustable table that tightens to clamp a workpiece. Accessories, like bench stops, increase the gripping bench's versatility.

**Vise-Grip®** clamps provide good holding power and are easily adjusted. The hand-grip closing action makes these clamps quicker to use than traditional C-clamps.

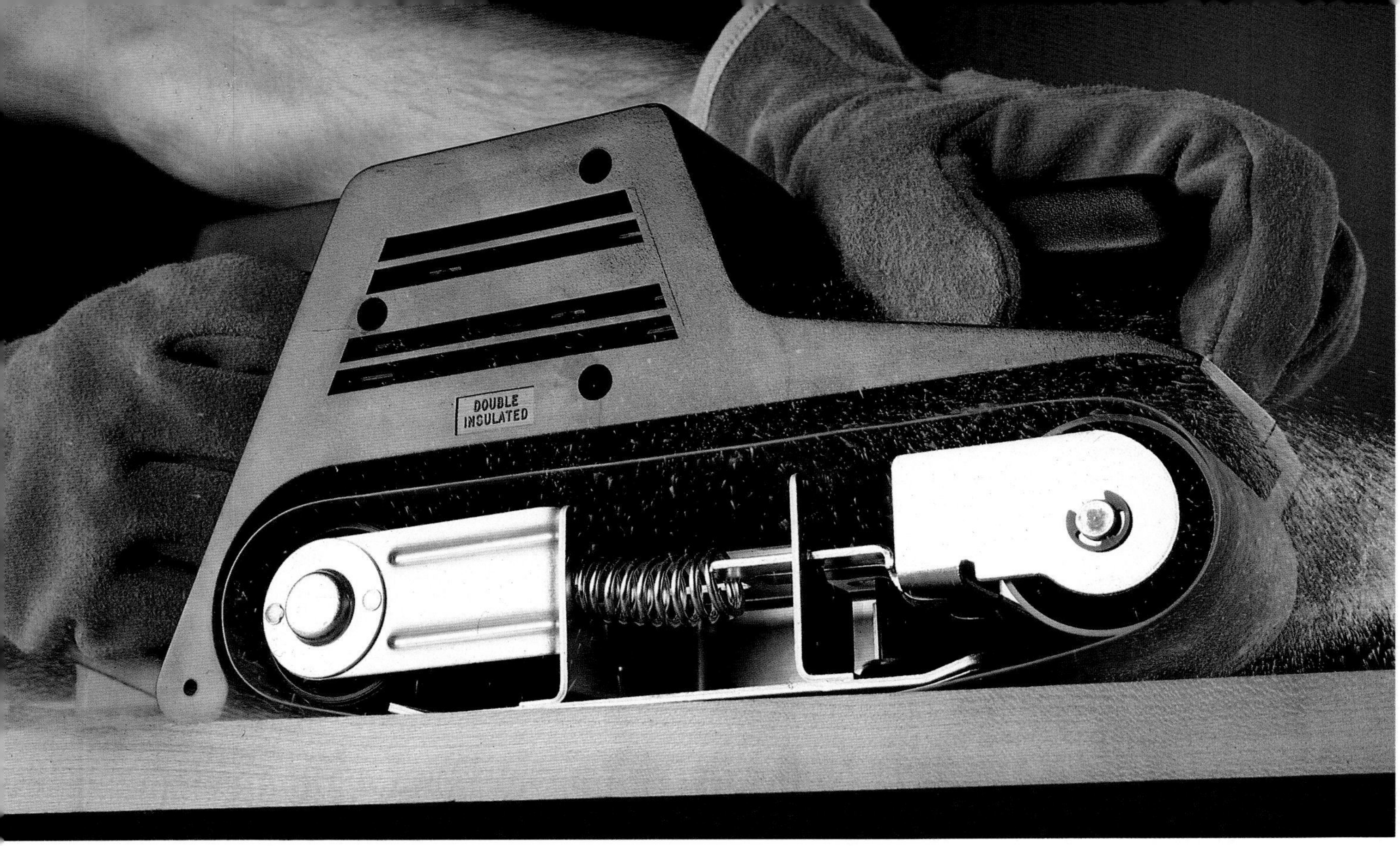

**Sand large areas** quickly with a belt sander. Disposable belts are available in grits ranging from 36 (extra-coarse) to 100 (fine).

# Sanding

Power sanding tools and sandpaper shape and smooth wood and other building materials. For very large areas, like hardwood floors, use a high-speed floor belt sander. Portable belt sanders are suitable for most work involving rough, fast removal of material. Finishing sanders, sometimes called orbital sanders, are best for light to medium removal of material. For very small, intricate, or contoured areas, sand by hand with folded sandpaper or a sanding block.

Sanders come in several sizes and speed ranges. Small "quarter-sheet" sanders are compact and easy to handle. Larger "half-sheet" sanders are better for sanding large areas. High-speed sanders are best for removing large amounts of material, while lower-speed tools create a fine, smooth finish. Variable-speed sanders offer the greatest flexibility for different applications.

Sandpaper is available in a wide range of grits. The lower the grit number, the coarser the grit. Sanding is usually done in steps, proceeding from coarse-grit sandpaper to finer grits.

**Hand sanding block** is helpful for small surfaces. For curved areas, wrap sandpaper around a folded piece of scrap carpeting. Sandpaper conforms to shape of workpiece.

**60-grit coarse** sandpaper is used on hardwood flooring and to grind down badly scratched surfaces. Move sander across the grain for quickest removal.

**100-grit medium** sandpaper is best used for initial smoothing of wood. Move sander in direction of wood grain for smoothest surface.

**150-grit fine** sandpaper puts finish smoothness on wood surfaces. Use fine sandpaper to prepare wood surfaces for staining, or to smooth wallboard joints.

**220-grit extra-fine** sandpaper is used to smooth stained wood before varnishing, or between coats of varnish.

**Quality finishing sanders** have high-speed motors and orbital action, and can flush-sand in tight work areas. For rough-sanding, move tool across the wood grain. For smooth-finishing, move sander in same direction as wood grain.

**Sanding accessories** for power drills include (clockwise from top right): disc sander for fast sanding, sanding drums and flap sander to smooth contoured surfaces, and sanding drum on drill attachment.

# Planes & Chisels

Shave and smooth wood with a hand plane. A hand plane has a flat cutting blade set in a steel base and is used to smooth rough surfaces or reduce the width of a piece of wood.

A wood chisel has a flat steel blade set in a handle. It cuts with light hand pressure, or by tapping the end of its handle with a mallet. A wood chisel is often used to cut hinge and lock mortises.

For best results with any shaping tool, make several shallow cuts instead of one deep cut. Forcing a tool to make deep cuts may ruin both the tool and the workpiece.

**Before You Start:**
Tip: For safety and ease of use, keep shaping tools sharp by honing them on an oilstone or waterstone. Choose a combination stone that has both a coarse and fine face. The stone must be soaked in water or light oil to prevent damage to the tempered metal.

## How to Plane a Rough Edge

**Clamp workpiece** into vise. Operate plane so wood grain runs "uphill" ahead of plane. Grip toe knob and handle firmly, and plane with long, smooth strokes. To prevent dipping (overplaning at beginning and end of board), press down on toe of plane at beginning of stroke, and bear down on heel at end of stroke.

## How to Chisel a Mortise

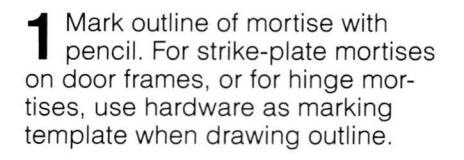

**1** Mark outline of mortise with pencil. For strike-plate mortises on door frames, or for hinge mortises, use hardware as marking template when drawing outline.

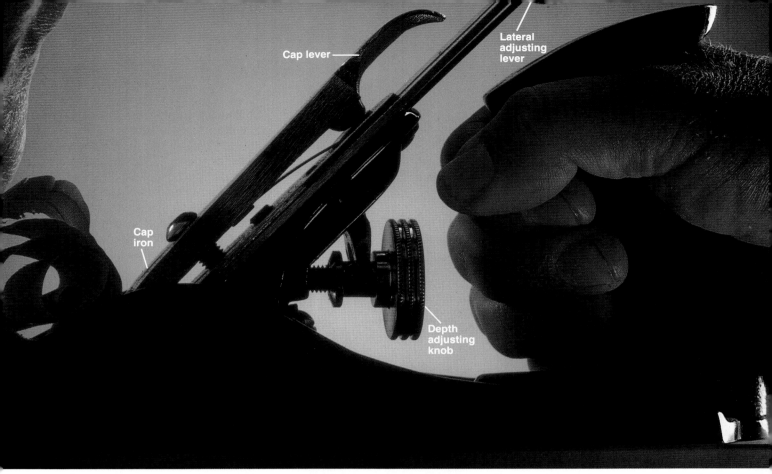

Cap lever

Lateral adjusting lever

Cap iron

Depth adjusting knob

**Set plane blade depth** with adjusting knob. Properly set cutter will remove wood shavings that are paper-thin. Plane may jam or gouge wood if cutter is set too deep. Use lateral adjusting lever to align cutter for an even cut. If edge of cutter leaves a score mark on wood, check lateral adjustment. Loosen the cap lever to set the cap iron 1/16" back from tip of blade.

**2** Cut outline of mortise. Hold chisel with bevel-side in, and tap butt end lightly with mallet until cut is at proper depth.

**3** Make a series of parallel depth cuts 1/4" apart across mortise, with chisel held at 45° angle. Drive chisel with light mallet blows to butt end of chisel.

**4** Lever out waste chips by holding chisel at a low angle with bevel-side toward work surface. Drive chisel by light hand pressure.

# Router

Cut decorative shapes, make grooves, and trim laminates with a router. A router is a high-speed power tool that uses changeable bits to perform a variety of cutting and shaping tasks. Because a router runs at speeds up to 25,000 revolutions per minute, it can make very smooth cuts in even the hardest woods.

For best results, make a series of routing passes, gradually extending the bit until cut reaches the correct depth. Experiment to find the proper speed for moving the router. Pushing the tool too fast slows the motor, causing the wood to chip and splinter. Moving it too slowly can scorch the wood.

Choose a router with a motor rated at 1 horsepower or more. Safety features may include a conveniently placed ON/OFF trigger switch, clear plastic chip guard, and a built-in work light.

Tip: Router bits spin in a clockwise direction, so the tool has a tendency to drift to the left. For best control, feed the router from left to right so that the cutting edge of the bit feeds into the wood.

**Pilot**

**Decorative edging** is usually made with a bit that has a pilot at the tip. The round pilot rides against the edge of the workpiece to control the cut.

# Common Router Bits

**Corner rounding** bit makes simple finish edges on furniture and wood moldings.

**Ogee** bit cuts a traditional, decorative shape in wood. Ogee bits are often used to create wood moldings and to shape the edges of furniture components.

**Rabbet** bit makes step-cut edges. Rabbeted edges are often used for woodworking joints and for picture frame moldings.

Ball-bearing pilot

**Laminate trimmer** bit cuts a finished edge on plastic laminate installations. Ball-bearing pilot prevents bit from scorching face of laminate.

**Straight** bit cuts a square, flat-bottomed groove. Use it to make woodworking joints, or for free-hand routing.

**Dovetail** bit cuts wedge-shaped grooves used to make interlocking joints for furniture construction and cabinetwork.

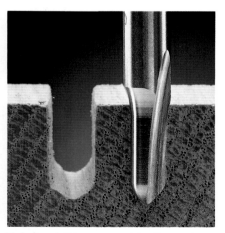

**Veining** bit is a round-bottomed cutter used for free-hand decorative carving and lettering.

# Accessories

A few common accessories can make your work quicker and easier. A tabletop bench grinder with abrasive wheels helps clean and sharpen tools. A tool belt with pockets keeps tools and materials handy. An extension cord with multiple receptacles extends the mobility of your power tools.

A small portable tool table can make a jig saw or router more convenient to use. The tool table lets you securely mount a router or jig saw upside down, and has an adjustable edge fence and a miter guide to improve the accuracy of the tools.

**Bench grinder** accepts different abrasive wheels for grinding, polishing, or sharpening tools. Keep eye shields in place and wear additional eye protection when using bench grinder.

**Electronic stud finder** detects studs inside wall, and pinpoints both edges of the framing member. Red light comes on when the tool senses changes in wall density caused by underlying stud.

**Multi-receptacle extension cord** lets you plug in several power tools at the same location. To prevent electrical shock, use an extension cord that has a ground-fault circuit interrupter (GFCI).

**Tool belt** with pockets and hammer hook keeps nails, screws and small tools handy. Wide, web belt is most comfortable for extended wear.

**Portable tool table** makes a jig saw or router more stable. The adjustable edge fence improves control of shaping cuts. Make sure tool table is held firmly to tabletop or workbench.

**Hammer drill** combines impact action with rotary motion for quick boring in concrete and masonry. To minimize dust and to keep bits from overheating, lubricate the drill site with water. A hammer drill can also be used for conventional drilling when the motor is set for rotary action only.

# Tools for Special Jobs

For one-time jobs or large projects, you may be able to rent or borrow special tools to make the work easier. For example, to frame a room addition or storage shed, rent an air-powered nailer that sinks framing nails with a squeeze of the trigger. Tool rental costs only a few dollars an hour, and can save hours of effort.

If you regularly work on a variety of home carpentry projects, consider buying additional power tools. For the home remodeler, a reciprocating saw is often useful. For fine woodworking and finish carpentry, a power miter box cuts angles quickly and accurately. For all-around carpentry and frequent use, invest in a table saw.

**Stud driver** fires a small gunpowder charge that propels masonry nails into concrete or brick. Use a stud driver to anchor a sole plate to a concrete floor.

**Table saw** and other stationary power tools provide greater capacity and accuracy for frequent carpentry and woodworking projects.

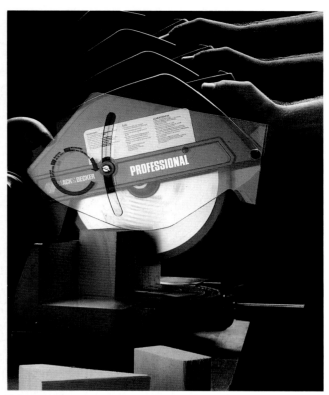

**Power miter box** cuts trim molding quickly and accurately. Locking motor assembly rotates up to 47° in both directions.

**Air-powered nailer** or stapler is attached to an air compressor. Tool trigger releases a burst of air to drive nails or staples into wood.

**Reciprocating saw** can be used for making cutouts in walls or floors, where a circular saw will not work, or for cutting metals like cast-iron plumbing pipes.

**Check lumber** visually before using it. Stored lumber can warp from temperature and humidity changes.

# Lumber

Lumber for construction is usually milled from strong softwoods and is categorized by grade, moisture content, and dimension.

**Grade:** Characteristics such as knots, splits, and slope of the grain affect the strength of the lumber and determine the grade.

## Lumber Grading Chart

| Grade | Description, uses |
|-------|-------------------|
| SEL STR or select structural 1,2,3 | Good appearance, strength and stiffness. 1,2,3 grades indicate knot size |
| CONST or Construction STAND or Standard | Both grades used for general framing, good strength and serviceability |
| STUD or Stud | Special designation used in any stud application, including load-bearing walls |
| UTIL or Utility | Used for economy in blocking and bracing |

**Moisture content:** Lumber is also categorized by moisture content. S-DRY (surfaced dry) is the designation for lumber with a moisture content of 19% or less. S-DRY lumber is the least likely to warp or shrink and is a good choice for framing walls. S-GRN (surfaced green) means the lumber contains a moisture content of 19% or more.

**Exterior lumber:** Lumber milled from redwood or cedar is naturally resistant to decay and insect attack, and makes a good choice for exterior applications. The most durable part of a tree is the heartwood, so specify heartwood for wood that will be in contact with the ground.

Lumber injected with chemicals under pressure is resistant to decay. Pressure-treated lumber is generally less expensive than redwood or cedar. For outdoor structures like decks, use pressure-treated

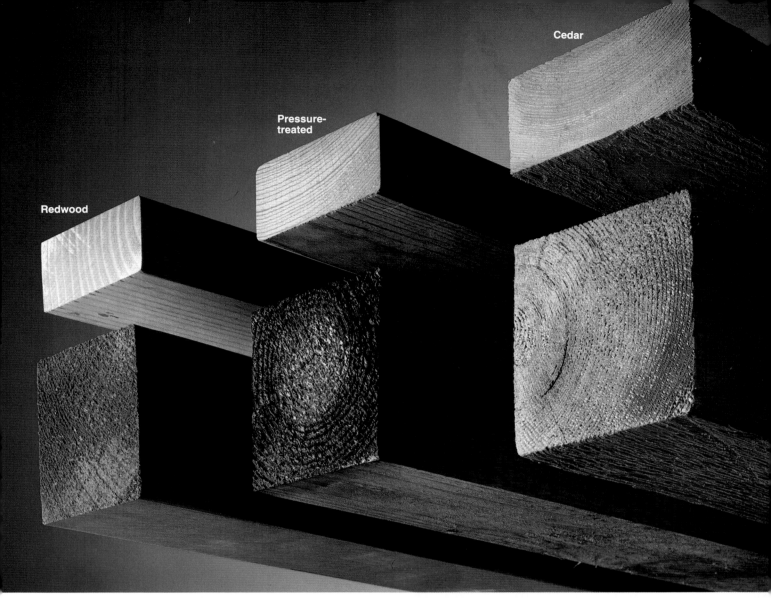

**Build longer-lasting** outdoor structures by using redwood, pressure-treated lumber or cedar. Redwood and cedar are more attractive, but pressure-treated lumber is less expensive. All are available in common lumber dimensions. Pressure-treated lumber contains toxic chemicals, so wear gloves and a protective particle mask when working with these products.

lumber for posts and joists, and more attractive redwood or cedar for decks and railings.

**Dimension:** Lumber is sold according to nominal sizes common throughout the industry, such as 2 × 4 and 2 × 6. The actual size of the lumber is smaller than the nominal size.

## Nominal vs. Actual Lumber Dimensions

| Nominal | Actual |
|---------|--------|
| 1 × 4 | ¾" × 3½" |
| 1 × 6 | ¾" × 5½" |
| 1 × 8 | ¾" × 7½" |
| 2 × 4 | 1½" × 3½" |
| 2 × 6 | 1½" × 5½" |
| 2 × 8 | 1½" × 7½" |

## How to Read Lumber Markings

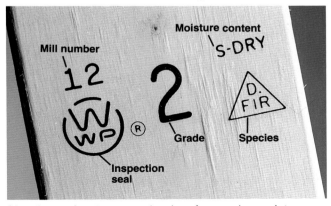

**Check grade stamp** on lumber for grade, moisture content and species.

51

# Plywood & Sheet Goods

Plywood is a versatile building material made by laminating thin layers or "plies" of wood together and forming them into panels. Plywood is available in thicknesses ranging from ³⁄₁₆ to ¾ inch.

Plywood is graded A through D, according to the quality of the wood used on its outer plies. It is also graded for interior or exterior usage. Plywood is classified by group numbers, based on the wood species used for the face and back veneers. Group 1 species are the strongest and stiffest, Group 2 the next strongest.

**Finish plywood** may have a quality wood veneer on one side and a utility-grade ply on the other side. This will be graded A-C. If it has a quality veneer on *both* sides, the grade will be A-A.

**Sheathing plywood** is for structural use. It may have large knotholes that make it unsuitable for finish purposes. Sheathing plywood is rated for thickness, and is graded C-D with two rough sides. Sheathing plywood has a waterproof bond. Plywood rated EXPOSURE 1 is for use where some moisture is present. Plywood rated EXTERIOR is used in applications that are permanently exposed to weather. Sheathing plywood also carries a thickness rating and a roof and floor span index, which

### How to Read Finish Plywood Markings

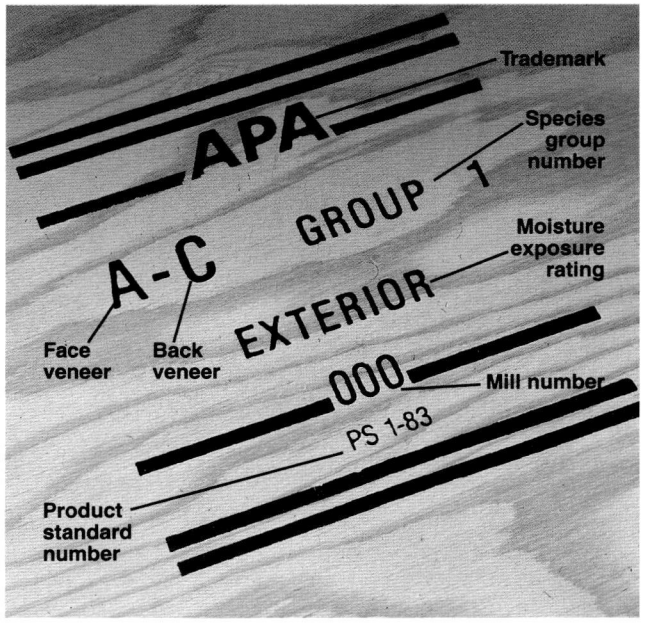

**Finish plywood grading stamp** shows the grade of face and back veneers, species group number, and a moisture exposure rating. Mill numbers and product numbers are for manufacturer's use.

appear as two numbers separated by a diagonal slash. The first number, for roofing applications, indicates the widest allowable spacing for rafters. The second number indicates the widest spacing for joists when plywood is used for subflooring.

**Strand-, particle-, and waferboards** are made from waste chips or inexpensive wood species.

**Plastic laminates,** like Formica®, are durable, attractive surfaces for countertops and furniture. Particleboard is strong and dimensionally stable, making it an ideal base for plastic laminates.

**Plastic foam insulating board** is light in weight and provides good insulation for basement walls.

**Water-resistant wallboard** is made for use in high-moisture areas, like behind ceramic wall tiles.

**Wallboard,** also known as drywall, Sheetrock®, and plasterboard, comes in panels 4 feet wide by 8, 10, or 12 feet long, and in ⅜-, ½-, and ⅝-inch thicknesses.

**Pegboards and hardboards** like Masonite® are made from wood fibers and resins bonded together under high pressure.

## How to Read Sheathing Plywood Markings

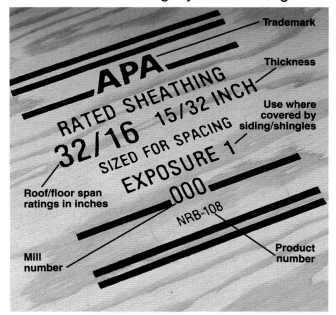

**Sheathing plywood grading stamp** shows thickness, roof or floor span index and exposure rating, in addition to manufacturer's information.

# The Work Area

A good work area is well lighted with 4-foot fluorescent shop lights. The workshop should have an adequate electrical supply, and should have sturdy shelving for storing materials and tools.

Isolate your work area from living areas, so shop noises and debris will not disturb others. Also, work far away from a forced-air furnace, so that dirt or fumes cannot be sucked into the furnace and circulated through the house.

Store hand tools conveniently by mounting a pegboard hanger above your workbench.

**Before You Start:**
Tools & Materials for Pegboard Tool Hanger:
hot glue gun, metal washers, screwgun and wallboard screws (for stud walls), or power drill with masonry bits (for concrete walls), pegboard.

## How to Build a Pegboard Tool Hanger

**1** Use a hot glue gun to attach metal washers over peg holes on back side of pegboard. Space washers across pegboard to match spacing of wall studs (every 16 or 24"). Washers hold pegboard out from wall so tool hooks may be inserted.

Finish washer

**2** Position pegboard on wall so that holes backed by washers are over stud locations. Drive wallboard screws through pegboard and washers into studs. Use finish washers if desired. For concrete walls, attach pegboard with masonry anchors (page 34).

## Tips for Hanging Tools

**Trace tools** with felt-tip pen so that they can be returned to the same location after use.

**Glue hangers** to pegboard with hot glue gun to prevent them from falling out when tools are removed.

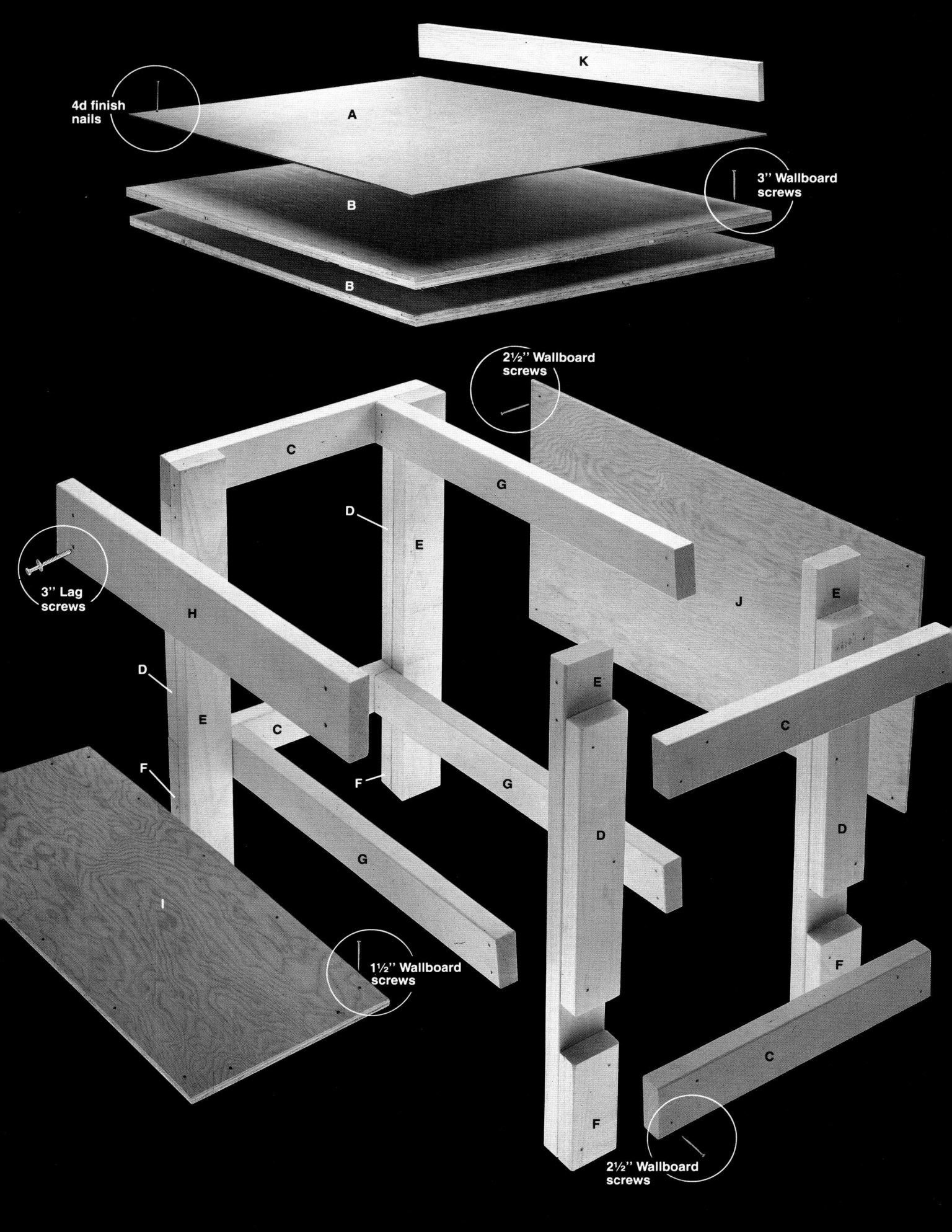

4d finish nails

A

B

B

K

3'' Wallboard screws

2½'' Wallboard screws

C

D

E

G

J

E

H

D

E

C

F

G

F

E

D

C

D

F

G

I

3'' Lag screws

1½'' Wallboard screws

F

C

F

2½'' Wallboard screws

# Building a Workbench

This workbench has heavy-duty legs to support big loads, and a sturdy double-layer top to withstand pounding. Cover the top with a hardboard surface that can be removed when it becomes damaged. Build a shelf below the work surface for storing power tools. If desired, mount an all-purpose vise bolted to the front or top of the workbench.

### Before You Start:
Tools & Materials: circular saw, carpenter's square, wallboard screws (1½-, 2½-, and 3-inch), screwgun or cordless screwdriver, drill and bits, lag screws (1½- and 3-inch), ratchet or adjustable wrench, 4d finish nails, nail set.

Tip: A workbench can be equipped with useful accessories, like pegboard screwed to the bench ends for storing saw blades and small tools, or woodworking vises.

**Lumber List:** six 8-foot 2 × 4s, one 5-foot 2 × 6, one 4 × 8-foot sheet of ¾" plywood, one 4 × 8-foot sheet of ½" plywood, one 4 × 8-foot sheet of ⅛" hardboard. Use a framing square to mark pieces, and cut with circular saw to dimensions indicated below.

| KEY | Pcs | SIZE AND DESCRIPTION |
|-----|-----|----------------------|
| A | 1 | ⅛-inch hardboard top, 24" × 60" |
| B | 2 | ¾-inch plywood top, 24" × 60" |
| C | 4 | 2 × 4 crosspieces, ends, 21" |
| D | 4 | 2 × 4 legs, 19¾" |
| E | 4 | 2 × 4 legs, 34½" |
| F | 4 | 2 × 4 legs, 7¾" |
| G | 3 | 2 × 4 braces, 54" |
| H | 1 | 2 × 6 front (top) brace, 57" |
| I | 1 | ½-inch plywood shelf, 14" × 57" |
| J | 1 | ½-inch plywood shelf back, 19¼" × 57" |
| K | 1 | 1 × 4 backstop, 57" |

## How to Build a Workbench

**1** For each end, cut two each of pieces C, D, E, and F. Assemble with 2½-inch wallboard screws.

**2** Attach both 2 × 4 rear braces (G, G) inside back legs of assembled ends. Use 2½-inch wallboard screws.

**3** Attach 2 × 4 front lower brace (G) inside front legs of assembled ends. Secure bottom shelf (I) and workbench back (J) with 2½-inch wallboard screws to assembled 2 × 4 frame.

**4** Drill pilot holes and join 2 × 6 front upper brace (H) outside front legs with 3-inch lag screws.

**5** Center bottom layer of ¾-inch plywood work surface (B) on top of frame. Align with back edge, and hold in place with 4d nails.

**6** Align bottom and top layers of plywood work surface (B, B). Drive 3-inch wallboard screws through both layers into bench frame.

**7** Nail hardboard work surface covering (A) to plywood substrate (B, B) with 4d finish nails. Set nails below surface.

## How to Mount a Tabletop Bench Vise

**1** Position vise at end of bench. On bench top, mark holes in vise base. Bore ¼-inch holes into bench top to secure vise.

**2** Attach vise with 1½-inch lag screws. Attach backstop (K) to back of bench top, with 2½-inch wallboard screws.

# Sawhorses

Sawhorses are used to support work materials for marking and cutting. They can also form the base for sturdy temporary scaffolding to use while painting or installing wallboard. For scaffolding, place good-quality 2 × 10s or 2 × 12s across two heavy-duty sawhorses. Small break-down sawhorses are a good choice if storage space is limited.

**Before You Start:**
Tools & Materials: four 8-foot 2 × 4s, 2½-inch wallboard screws, circular saw, framing square, screwgun or cordless screwdriver.

### Lumber Cutting List

| KEY | Pcs | SIZE AND DESCRIPTION |
|-----|-----|----------------------|
| A | 2 | Vertical braces, 2 × 4, 15½" |
| B | 2 | Top rails, 2 × 4, 48" |
| C | 1 | Bottom brace, 2 × 4, 48" |
| D | 2 | Horizontal braces, 2 × 4, 11¼" |
| E | 4 | Legs, 2 × 4, 26" |

## Easy-storing Sawhorses

**Fold metal sawhorses** and hang them on the workshop wall when they are not in use.

**Buy brackets** made from fiberglass or metal, and cut a 48-inch top rail and four 26-inch legs from 2 × 4s. Take sawhorses apart for storage.

## How to Build a Heavy-duty Sawhorse

**1** Heavy-duty sawhorse has wide top for supporting large loads. Cut vertical braces (A), top rails (B), and bottom brace (C) to lengths specified in Lumber Cutting List (page opposite).

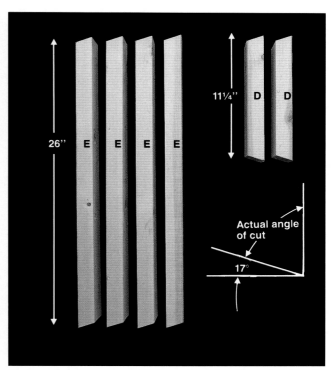

**2** Set circular saw to 17° bevel angle. (Bevel cuts will match angle shown above.) Cut ends of horizontal braces (D) with opposing angles. Cut ends of legs (E) with parallel angles.

**3** Attach top rails (B) to vertical braces (A), as shown, using 2½-inch wallboard screws.

**4** Attach horizontal braces (D) to vertical braces (A), using 2½-inch wallboard screws. Attach legs (E). To complete sawhorse, attach bottom brace (C) to horizontal braces (D).

61

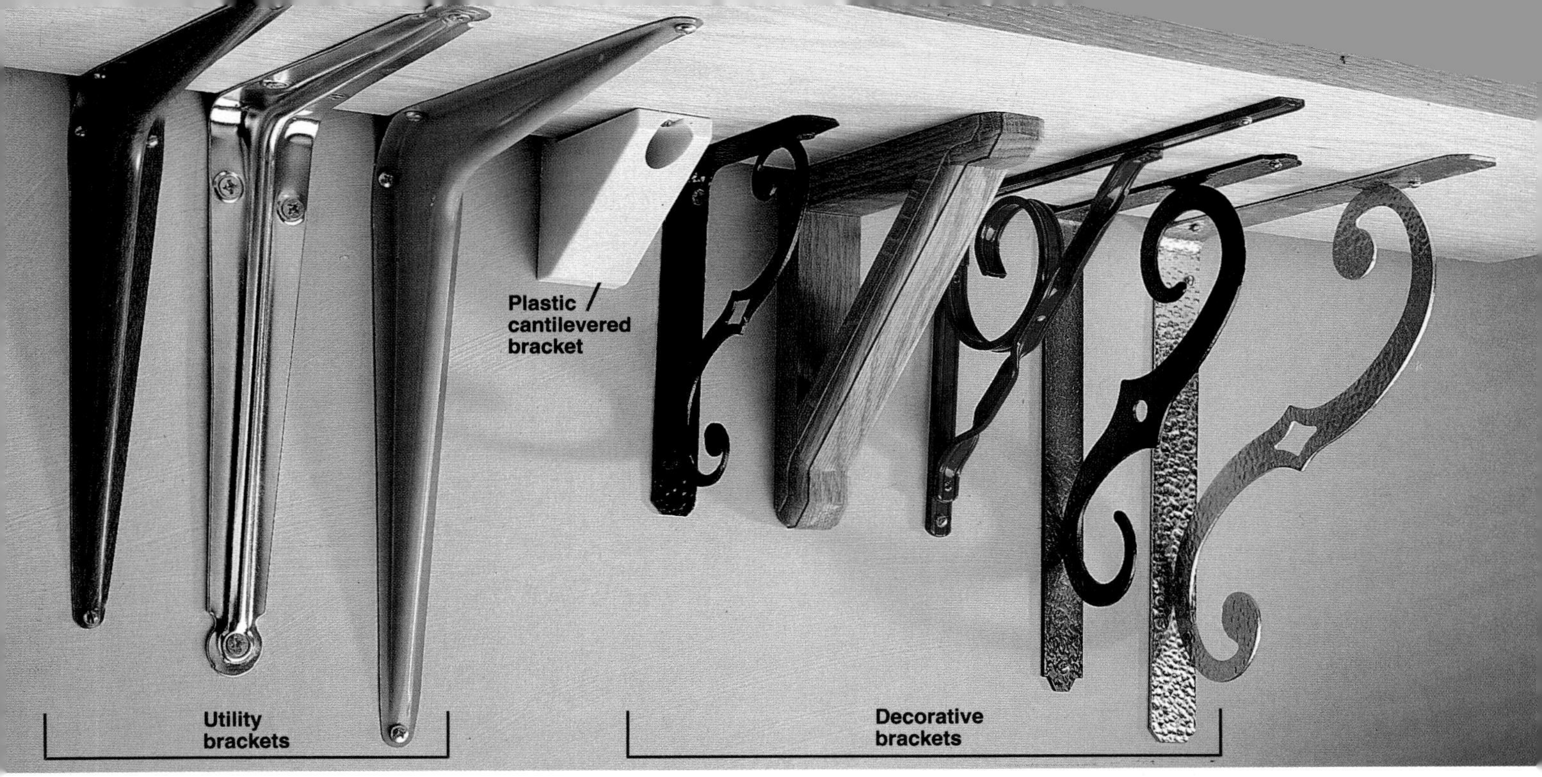

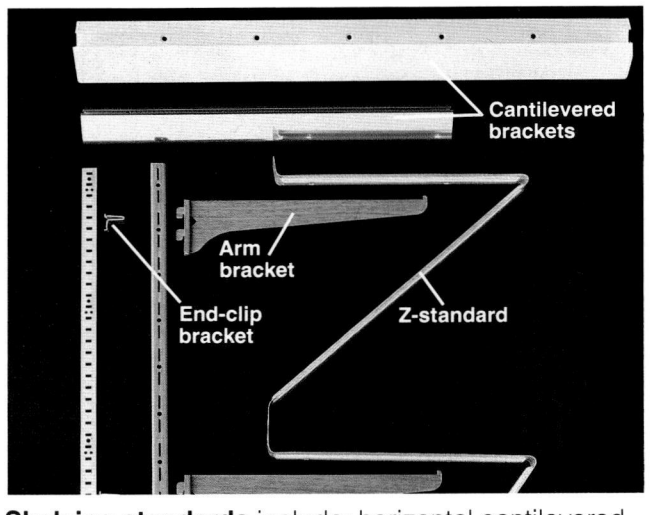

**Stationary brackets** are available in both decorative and utility styles, and come in a wide range of sizes. For greatest strength, choose brackets with diagonal supports. In most applications, attach longer bracket arm to the wall, and shorter arm to the shelf.

# Ready-to-Hang Shelving

Shelves are sturdiest when their supports are anchored directly to wall studs. If brackets must be anchored between studs, use mollies or toggle bolts, and follow manufacturer's weight limits. On cement or brick walls, use masonry anchors to attach shelf supports.

**Before You Start:**

Tools & Materials: stud finder, shelving brackets, drill and bits, screwdriver, carpenter's level.

Tip: To minimize sagging on shelves, mount the brackets at least 6" from the ends of the shelves.

**Shelves** include: 1-inch hardwood cut to size, decorative glass, hardwood board with routed edge, hardwood veneer over processed wood, woodgrain plastic laminate over chipboard, and white plastic laminate.

**Shelving standards** include: horizontal cantilevered brackets, Z-standard for utility shelves, adjustable arm-bracket standard, adjustable end-clip standard.

## How to Hang Shelf Brackets & Standards

**Attach hardware to studs** whenever possible. Use an electronic stud finder to locate studs (page 47). For heavy loads, attach a standard to every stud along span of shelf.

**Molly bolts** (shown) and toggle bolts expand and grip inside wallboard to support loads.

**Molly bolt** before tightening.

**Molly bolt** after tightening.

**Attach hardware between studs** using mollies or toggle bolts. Do not exceed manufacturer's recommended load limits for between-stud installation.

**Attach hardware to masonry** using plastic concrete anchors and screws (page 34). Attach one shelf bracket for every 16 to 24" of shelf span, depending on the intended load weight.

**Level shelf brackets** and standards using a carpenter's level. If necessary, hold the level on a straight 2 × 4 for leveling wide spans.

# Simple Shelving

Sturdy wall shelving can be installed quickly using slotted metal standards and arm brackets. Use a stud finder to locate the wall studs, and attach the shelving standards directly to the studs for the greatest strength. Long wall shelves should be supported by standards every 48 inches.

For more decorative shelving, mortise the metal standards into strips of hardwood (above). Use an electric router to cut grooves into the hardwood strips, then insert the metal standards inside the

grooves and attach them to the wall. A router can also be used to mold a decorative edge on the shelves.

**Before You Start:**
Tools & Materials: saw, 1 × 2 hardwood strips, 1 × 8 hardwood boards, router and straight bit, portable tool table, metal shelving standards, drill and bits, 3-inch wallboard screws.

**1** Cut 1 × 8 hardwood shelves to chosen length. Cut 1 × 2 hardwood strips to same length as metal shelving standards. Position metal standards on hardwood strips, and trace outline on the wood.

**2** Cut groove along center of each strip using a router and straight bit. Mount router in portable tool table for best control. Make several passes until groove is equal in depth and thickness to metal standard.

**3** Insert standards into the routed grooves, then drill pilot holes through the hardwood strips at each screw opening.

**4** Attach standards to wall studs with 3-inch wallboard screws. Use a carpenter's level to make sure standards are plumb and arm brackets will be level. Attach arm brackets and hang shelves.

# Built-in Shelving

Permanent shelves can be built into any space where storage is needed. The space between a door or window and an adjacent wall corner is often used for built-in shelving.

A shelving unit can be built out of any 1-inch lumber except particleboard, which sags under heavy weight. For heavy loads, like books, a shelving unit should be built from 1 × 10- or 1 × 12-inch hardwood boards and should span no more than 48 inches. Shelves can be supported from the ends by pegs or end clips.

**Before You Start:**

Tools & Materials: tape measure, saw, framing square, 1 × 10- or 1 × 12-inch hardwood lumber, 2 × 2 lumber, scrap pegboard, drill and ¼-inch bit, paint or wood stain, hammer, 6d finish nails, 12d common nails, trim moldings, nail set.

Tip: When framing the basic shelving unit, build it 1" shorter than the floor-to-ceiling measurement. This allows you to tilt the unit into position without damaging the ceiling. Trim moldings are used to hide gaps along the ceiling and floor.

## How to Construct a Built-in Shelving Unit

Cut baseboard

Cut baseboard

**1** Measure the height and width of the available space. For easy installation, the basic unit is built 1" shorter than ceiling height. Remove baseboards (page 25), and cut them to fit around shelving unit. Replace baseboards after unit is nailed in place.

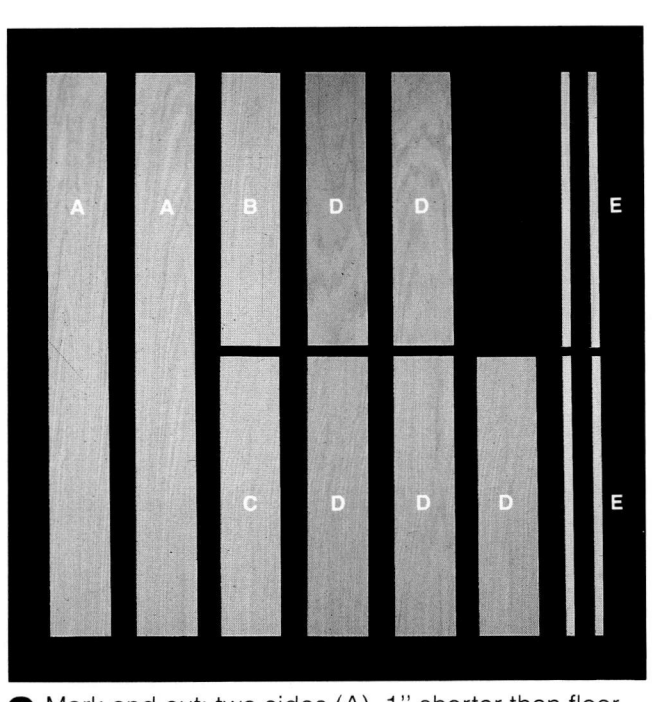

**2** Mark and cut: two sides (A), 1" shorter than floor-to-ceiling measurement; unit top (B), bottom (C), and shelves (D), each 1½" shorter than unit width measurement; four 2 × 2 frame supports (E), 1½" shorter than unit width measurement.

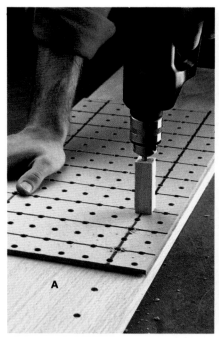

**3** Using scrap pegboard as guide, drill pairs of ¼-inch holes along inside of each side (A), spaced horizontally 9" apart and vertically every 2". Holes should be ⅜" deep. Use scrap wood or bit attachment as depth guide.

**4** Paint or stain wood as desired before assembling unit. Attach sides (A) to ends of frame supports (E). Drive 6d finish nails through sides and into end grain of frame supports.

**5** Tilt unit into position flush against wall. Nail through top rear frame support (E) into wall studs, and through bottom frame supports into floor, using 12d common nails. Replace cut baseboards around bottom of shelving unit.

**6** Attach bottom (C) and top (B) inside shelving unit. Drive 6d finish nails through sides (A) into end grain of top and bottom.

**7** Miter-cut trim molding to fit around top and bottom of shelving unit. Attach trim with 6d finish nails. Use nail set to recess nail heads.

# Closet Organizers

This organizer makes efficient use of space, and can double closet storage capacity. It may cost hundreds of dollars to buy custom-made organizers, but you can build an organizer for a 5-foot closet for the cost of a single sheet of plywood, a clothes pole, and a few feet of 1 × 3 lumber.

**Before You Start:**
Tools & Materials: hammer, finish nails (6d and 8d), 1 × 3 lumber, one 4 × 8-foot sheet of ¾-inch-thick plywood, tape measure, framing square, circular saw, clothes pole, six clothes-pole brackets, screwdriver, paint or wood stain.

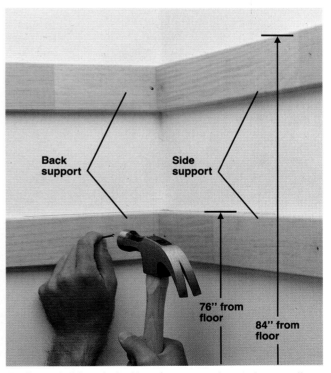

**Single sheet of plywood** yields two 11⅞-inch-wide sides (A), two long 11⅞-inch-wide shelves (B), and six 11⅞-inch-square shelves.

## How to Build a Closet Organizer

**1** Cut 1 × 3 shelf supports to fit back and end walls of the closet. Attach supports to the wall with top edges 84″ above floor, using 8d finish nails driven into the wall studs.

**2** Cut additional shelf supports and attach to wall with top edges 76″ above floor, using 8d finishing nails driven into wall studs.

(continued next page)

# How to Build a Closet Organizer (continued)

**3** Cut two 11⅞-inch-wide shelves (B) from ¾-inch plywood. Cut length of shelves to fit closet width.

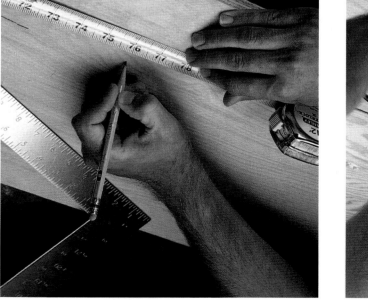

**4** Measure and cut two 11⅞" × 76" shelf unit sides (A) from ¾-inch plywood.

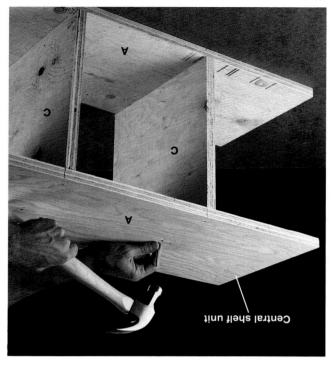

**5** Measure and cut six 11⅞-inch-square shelves (C) from ¾-inch plywood.

**6** Assemble central shelf unit, using 6d finish nails. Space shelves evenly, or according to height of items stored. Leave top of unit open (see Step 8).

Central shelf unit

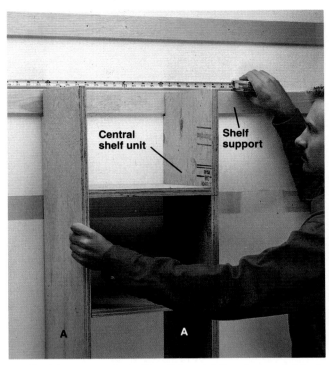

**7** Position central shelf unit in middle of closet. Mark and notch shelf unit sides (A) to fit around lower shelf support.

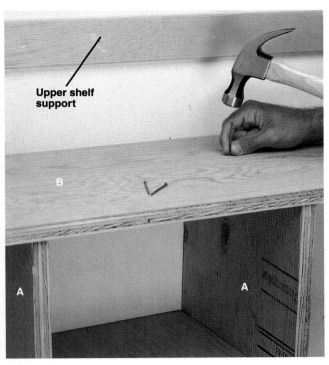

**8** Lay long shelf (B) on lower shelf supports and top of central shelf unit sides (A). Attach with 6d finish nails. Lay remaining long shelf on upper shelf supports and attach with 6d finish nails.

**9** Attach pole bracket to shelf unit side (A), 11" from rear wall and 3" below long shelf. Attach opposite bracket directly to wall stud with a screw or to wallboard using wall anchor (page 34). If desired, install brackets for lower clothes pole 38" above floor.

**Finished closet organizer** allows easy access to stored items. Place shoes, blankets, and other bulky articles in central shelf unit.

71

**U-shaped brackets** keep wood dry and permit air circulation so that lumber stays warp-free.

# Utility Shelves

Building utility shelves is an easy way to organize a workshop, basement, garage, or attic. Use sturdy ladder-shaped brackets for support, and cut the shelves from ½- or ¾-inch plywood. Anchor utility shelving to the wall using wallboard screws or masonry anchors.

To store lumber in the basement or garage, build a hanging storage rack with U-shaped supports made from 1 × 4 lumber. The lumber rack keeps wood dry and flat, and can be suspended in the garage above the hood of your car to make efficient use of empty space.

**Before You Start:**
**Tools & Materials for Utility Shelves:** 2 × 2 lumber, tape measure, saw, carpenter's square, ⅜-inch-thick scrap plywood, carpenter's glue, wallboard screws (1- and 3-inch), screwgun or cordless screwdriver, ½- or ¾-inch-thick plywood.
**Tools & Materials for Lumber Storage Rack:** 1 × 4 lumber, tape measure, saw, metal connectors, 1-inch wallboard screws, screwgun or cordless screwdriver, drill and ¼-inch bit, 1½-inch lag screws.

**Buy preassembled ladder brackets** for convenience when building utility shelves, or build brackets from 2 × 2 lumber (next page).

# How to Build Utility Shelves

**1** To build ladder brackets, cut the legs and cross braces from 2 × 2 lumber. Cross braces should be 3" shorter than width of shelves.

**2** Assemble legs and cross braces with 4½-inch triangular gussets cut from ⅜-inch plywood, or metal connectors. Attach gussets with glue and 1-inch wallboard screws for strong joints.

Gusset 4½"

Leg

Cross bracket

WOOD-WORKERS GLUE

Leg

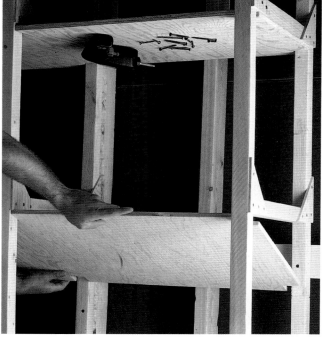

**3** Attach ladder brackets to wall studs, using 3-inch wallboard screws. If attaching to a concrete wall, use masonry anchors (page 34).

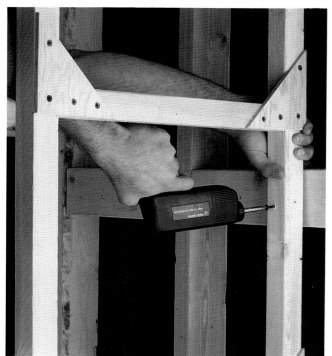

**4** Cut shelves from ½- or ¾-inch plywood. Use a jig saw to cut 1½-inch square notches in shelves to fit around legs of ladder brackets.

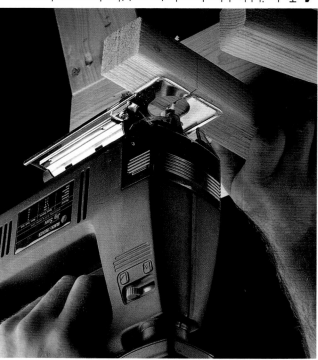

## How to Build a Lumber Storage Rack

**1** Measure height, length and width of rack area. For garage storage, make sure rack will hang above level of car hood. Lumber storage rack requires one U-shaped support every 4'.

**2** From 1 × 4 lumber, cut 2 legs and 1 cross brace for each U-shaped support. Cross brace should be 7" shorter than overall width of storage rack.

**3** Assemble legs and cross braces with metal connectors and 1-inch wallboard screws.

Lag screws

**4** Drill 1/4-inch pilot holes through top of each leg and through ceiling joists. Attach supports to joists with 1 1/2-inch lag screws. On finished ceilings, attach 2 × 4 ceiling plates to ceiling, then attach lumber rack supports to the ceiling plates.

# Planning Major Projects

# Project Planning

When planning a remodeling project, you will need to consider and choose from dozens of design and construction options. Making the proper choices helps ensure that your project will increase both your present enjoyment and the future value of your home.

**Using professionals:** As you plan your remodeling project, consider hiring professionals if you are unsure of your own skills. For example, if you are removing a long load-bearing wall, you may want to hire a builder to install the heavy permanent header, but do all other work yourself. If your project requires changes to the electrical and plumbing systems, you also may want to leave this work to licensed professionals.

Topics covered in this section include:
- The anatomy of your house (pages 79 to 83)
- Code requirements (pages 84 to 85)
- Choosing windows and doors (pages 86 to 91)
- Drawing plans and getting a building permit (pages 92 to 93)
- Tools and materials for remodeling (pages 94 to 95)

## Anatomy of a Platform-framed House

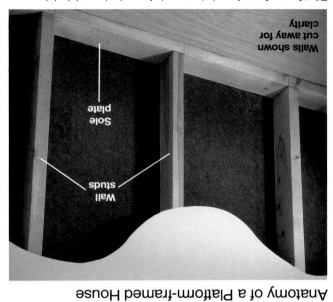

Walls shown cut away for clarity

Sole plate

Wall studs

**Platform framing** (photos, left and above) is identified by the floor-level sole plates and ceiling-level top plates to which the wall studs are attached. Most houses built after 1930 use platform framing. If you do not have access to unfinished areas, you can remove the wall surface at the bottom of a wall to determine what kind of framing was used in your home.

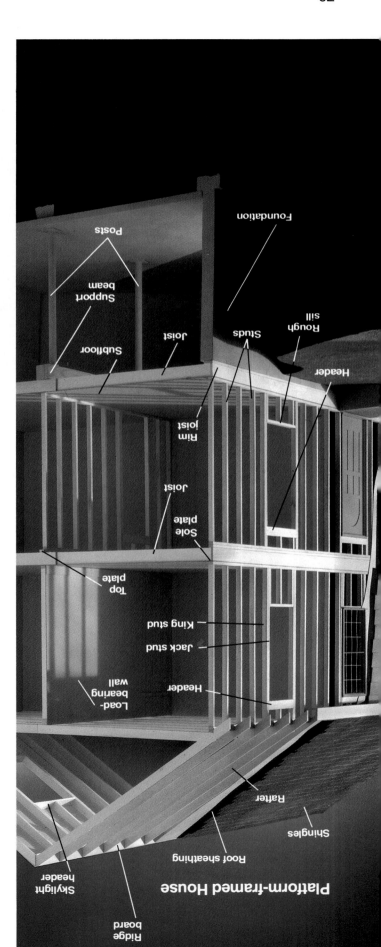

Platform-framed House

Foundation · Posts · Support beam · Subfloor · Joist · Studs · Rough sill · Header · Rim joist · Joist · Sole plate · Top plate · King stud · Jack stud · Header · Load-bearing wall · Rafter · Shingles · Roof sheathing · Skylight header · Ridge board

## Project Planning
# The Anatomy of Your House

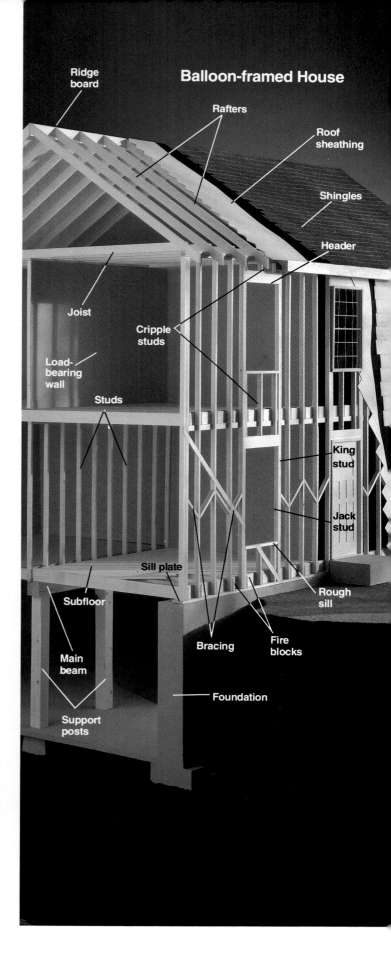

Planning a do-it-yourself remodeling project requires that you understand a few basics of home construction and building terminology. For general reference, use the models shown on these pages while planning your project.

If you plan to modify exterior walls, you must determine if your house was built using platform- or balloon-style framing. The framing style of your home determines what kind of temporary supports you will need to install while the work is in progress. If you have trouble determining what type of framing was used in your home, refer to original blueprints, if you have them, or consult a building contractor or licensed home inspector.

### Anatomy of a Balloon-framed House

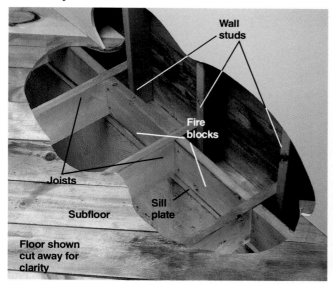

**Balloon framing** (photos, right and above) is identified by wall studs that run uninterrupted from the roof to a sill plate on the foundation, without the sole plates and top plates found in platform-framed walls (page opposite). Balloon framing was used in houses built before 1930, and is still used in some new home styles, especially those with high vaulted ceilings.

## Floor & Ceiling Anatomy

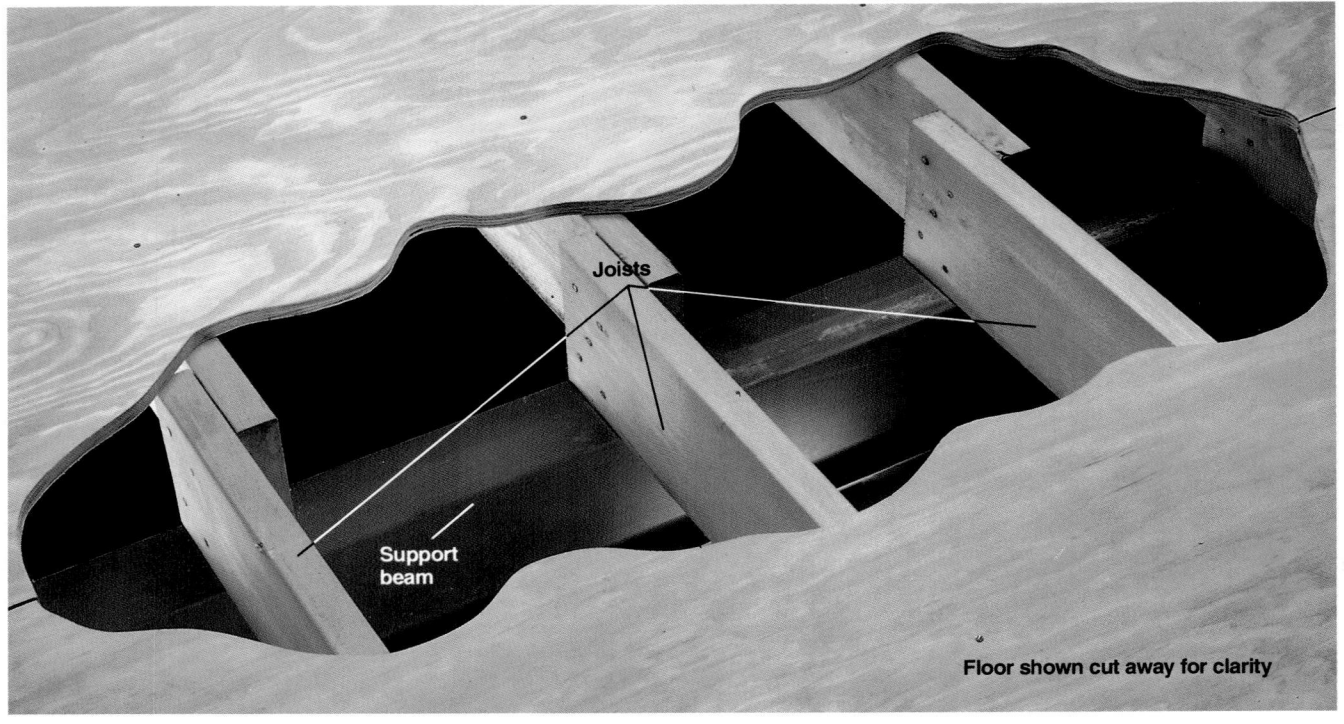

**Floor shown cut away for clarity**

**Joists** carry the structural load of floors and ceilings. The ends of the joists are held up by support beams, foundations, or load-bearing walls. Rooms used as living areas must be supported by floor joists that are at least 2 × 8 in size. Floors with smaller joists can be reinforced with "sister" joists (photos, below).

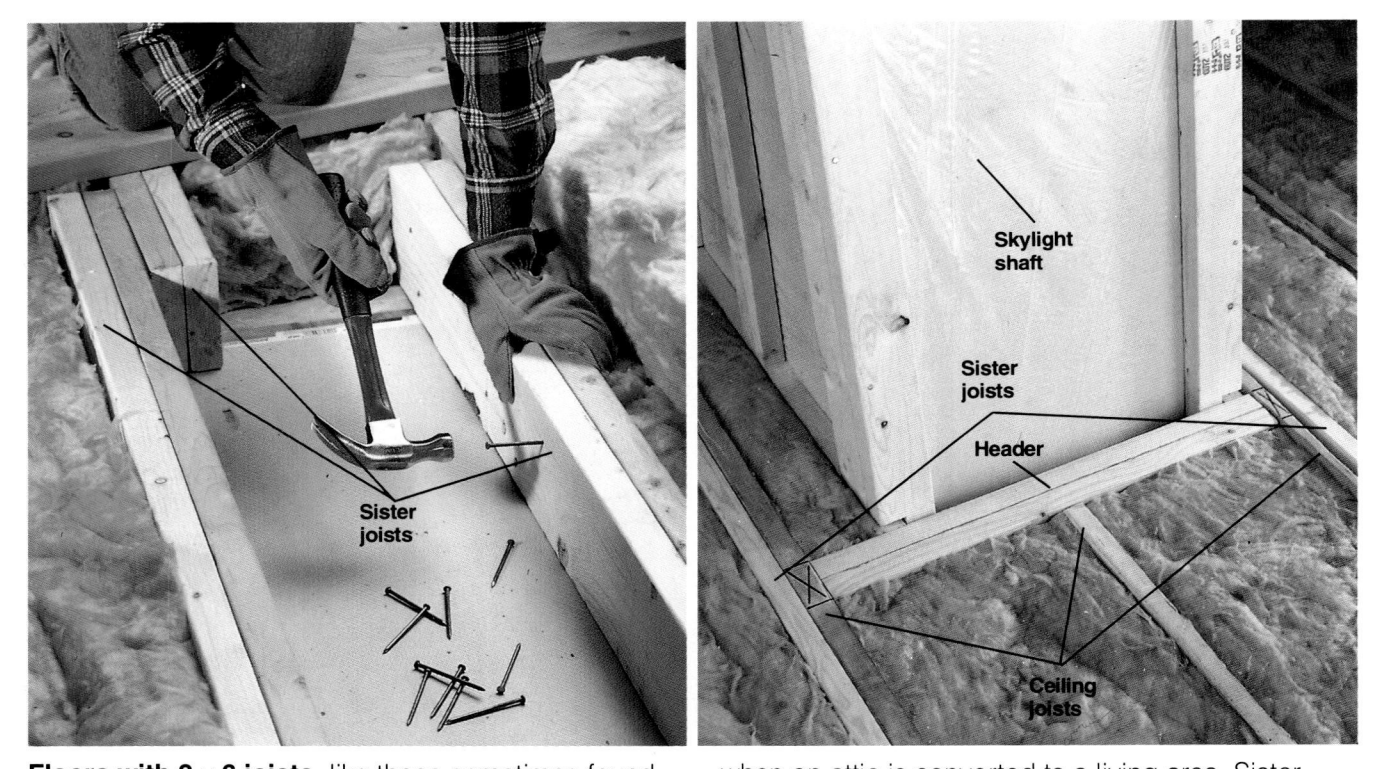

**Floors with 2 × 6 joists**, like those sometimes found in attics, cannot support living areas unless "sister" joists are attached alongside each original joist to strengthen it (above, left). This often is necessary when an attic is converted to a living area. Sister joists also are used to help support a header when ceiling joists must be cut, such as when framing a skylight shaft (above, right; and page 178).

## Roof Anatomy

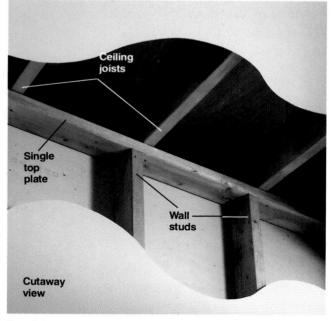

**Rafters** made from 2 × 4s or 2 × 6s spaced every 16" or 24" are used to support roofs in most houses built before 1950. If necessary, rafters can be cut to make room for a large skylight. Check in your attic to determine if your roof is framed with rafters or roof trusses (right).

**Trusses** are prefabricated "webs" made from 2" dimension lumber. They are found in many houses built after 1950. Never cut through or alter roof trusses. If you want to install a skylight in a house with roof trusses, buy skylights that fit in the space between the trusses.

## Wall Anatomy

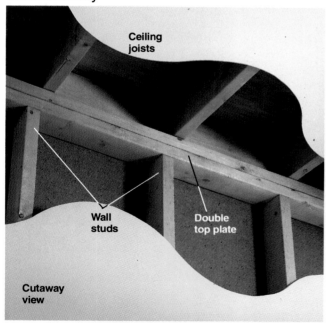

**Load-bearing walls** carry the structural weight of your home. In platform-framed houses, load-bearing walls can be identified by double top plates made from two layers of framing lumber. Load-bearing walls include all exterior walls, and any interior walls that are aligned above support beams (page 78).

**Partition walls** are interior walls that are not load-bearing. Partition walls have a single top plate. They can be perpendicular to the floor and ceiling joists but will not be aligned above support beams. Any interior wall that is parallel to floor and ceiling joists is a partition wall.

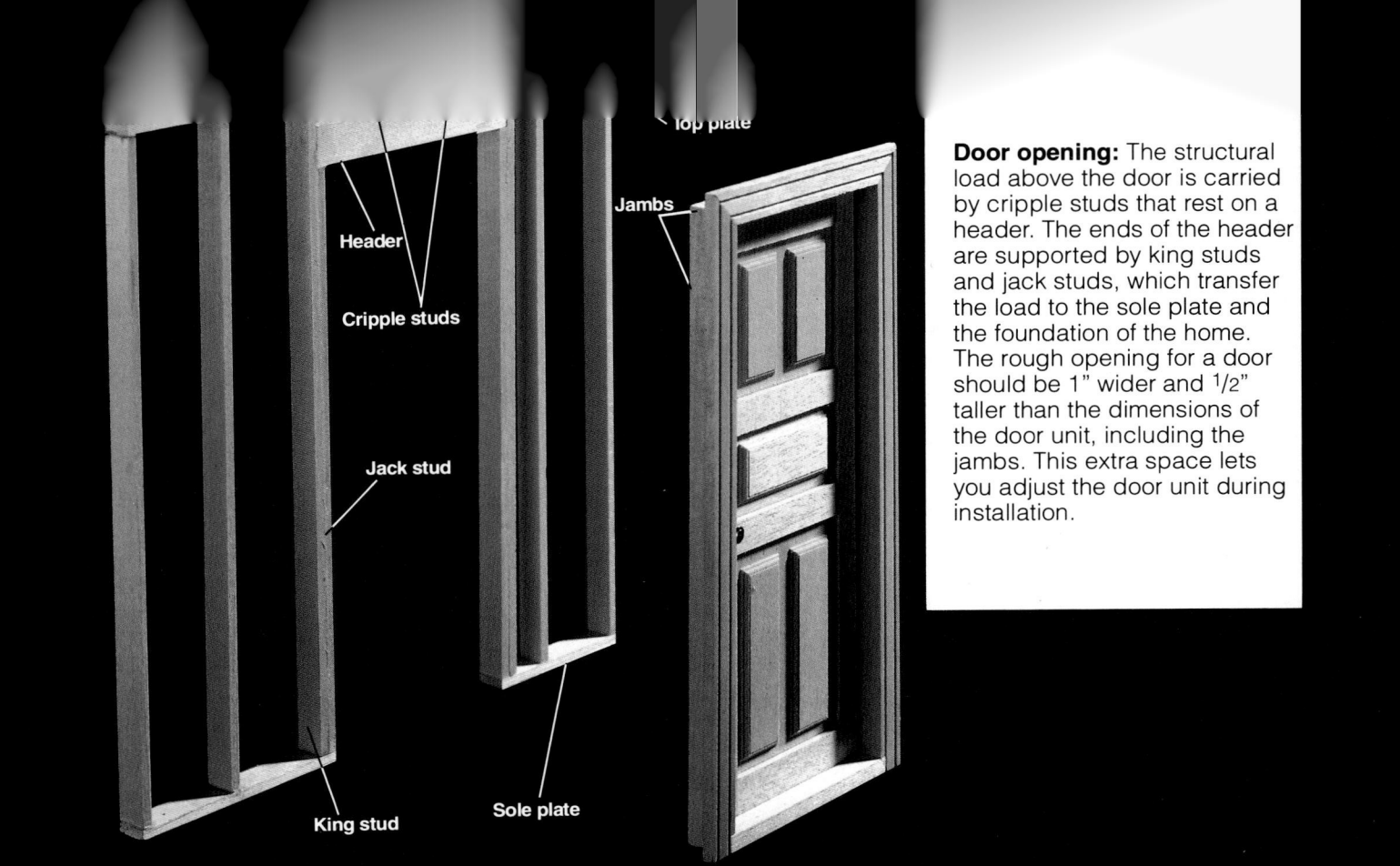

**Door opening:** The structural load above the door is carried by cripple studs that rest on a header. The ends of the header are supported by king studs and jack studs, which transfer the load to the sole plate and the foundation of the home. The rough opening for a door should be 1" wider and 1/2" taller than the dimensions of the door unit, including the jambs. This extra space lets you adjust the door unit during installation.

## Anatomy of Window & Door Openings

Many remodeling projects, like installing new doors or windows, require that you cut one or more studs in a load-bearing wall to create an opening. When planning your project, remember that the wall openings will require a permanent support beam, called a header, to carry the structural load directly above the removed studs.

The required size for the header is set by the Building Code, and varies according to the width of the rough opening. For a window or door opening, a header can be built from two pieces of 2" dimension lumber sandwiched around 3/8" plywood (chart, right). When a large portion of a load-bearing wall (or the entire wall) is removed, a laminated beam product can be used to make the new header (page 125).

If you will be cutting more than one wall stud, make temporary supports to carry the structural load until the header is installed (pages 120 to 123).

### Recommended Header Sizes

| Rough Opening Width | Recommended Header Construction |
|---|---|
| Up to 3 ft. | 3/8" plywood between two 2 x 4s |
| 3 ft. to 5 ft. | 3/8" plywood between two 2 x 6s |
| 5 ft. to 7 ft. | 3/8" plywood between two 2 x 8s |
| 7 ft. to 8 ft. | 3/8" plywood between two 2 x 10s |

**Recommended header sizes** shown above are suitable for projects where a full story and roof are located above the rough opening. This chart is intended for rough estimating purposes only. For actual requirements, contact an architect or your local building inspector. For spans greater than 8 ft., see page 125.

**Window opening:** The structural load above the window is carried by cripple studs resting on a header. The ends of the header are supported by king studs and jack studs, which transfer the load to the sole plate and the foundation of the home. The rough sill, which helps anchor the window unit but carries no structural weight, is supported by cripple studs. To provide room for adjustments during installation, the rough opening for a window should be 1" wider and 1/2" taller than the window unit, including the jambs.

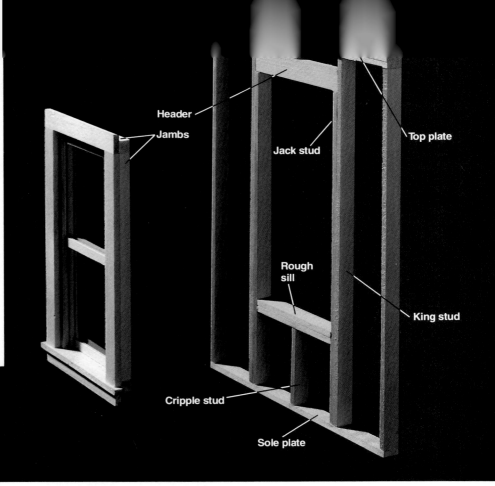

Header

Jambs

Jack stud

Top plate

Rough sill

King stud

Cripple stud

Sole plate

## Framing Options for Window & Door Openings (new lumber shown in yellow)

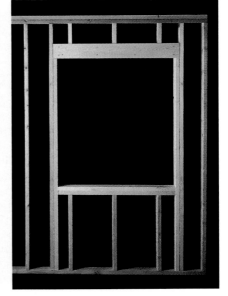

**Use an existing opening** to avoid new framing work. This is a good option in homes with masonry exteriors, which are difficult to alter. Order a replacement unit that is 1" narrower and 1/2" shorter than the rough opening.

**Enlarge an existing opening** to simplify the framing work. In many cases you can use an existing king stud and jack stud to form one side of the enlarged opening.

**Frame a new opening** when installing a window or door where none existed, or when replacing a smaller unit with one that is much larger.

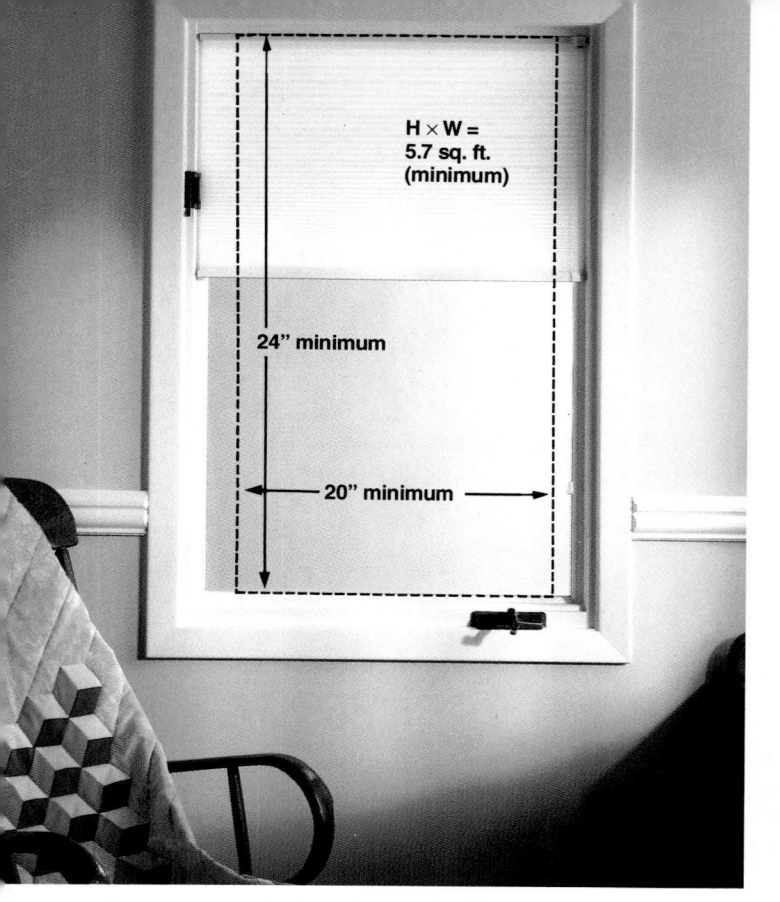

H × W =
5.7 sq. ft.
(minimum)

24" minimum

20" minimum

**An egress window** is required in rooms used for sleeping if there is no other escape route. A window used as an egress should provide an unobstructed opening of 5.7 sq. ft. Height can be no less than 24" and width can be no less than 20". Casement windows offer a large clear opening, making them a good choice for egress installations.

6 ft. 8"
miminum

32" minimum

**One entry door** in a home must have a clear opening at least 32" wide and 6 ft. 8" high. Smaller doors are allowed for secondary entries.

Project Planning

# Code Requirements

To ensure safe houses and protect property values, your community requires that all remodeling projects conform to a standard Building Code. Specific codes and standards vary from community to community, but most are based on a model code known as the national Uniform Building Code (UBC). The requirements shown on these pages are from this Code. The UBC contains minimum construction safety standards, and is revised every three years. Copies of the UBC are available at most libraries and bookstores.

Your local building inspector is the best source of information about local Building Codes. Visit or call your inspector early during your planning to find out which parts of the project are subject to local Code, and what you must do to comply. Remember that local Codes vary, and they always

take precedence over the UBC standards. For projects that require changes to the framing members in your home, you always need to get a formal building permit and have your work approved by an official building inspector.

If the inspector feels that strict compliance with the Code would cause an unreasonable restriction to the free use of your property, he may grant you a conditional exemption, called a variance.

If your remodeling project involves changes to the heating, air conditioning, electrical, or plumbing systems, there will be additional code requirements to follow. Most communities require separate work permits and inspections when these systems are altered.

## Common Code Requirements for Remodeling Projects

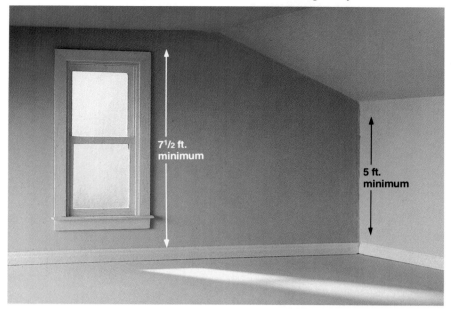

| Room Type | Minimum Size |
|---|---|
| Bedroom | 80 sq. ft. |
| Living room | 150 sq. ft. |
| Family room | 110 sq. ft. |
| Office | 64 sq. ft. |
| Kitchen | 50 sq. ft. |
| Bathroom (full) | 35 sq. ft. |
| Other rooms | 70 sq. ft. |
| Hallway | 3 ft. wide |

**Ceiling height** for rooms used as living areas must be at least $7^1/_2$ ft. In rooms with sloped ceilings, at least half the floor space must meet minimum ceiling height requirements, and all walls must be at least 5 ft. high. In kitchens, halls, and bathrooms, ceilings must be be least 7 ft. high.

**Room size recommendations** depend on the use of the space, and vary from community to community. Use the chart above as a general reference, but always contact your local building inspector for complete details.

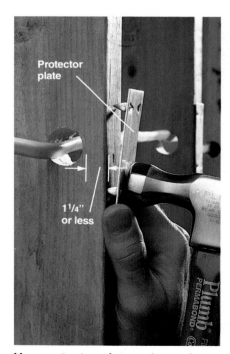

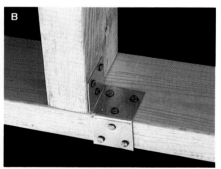

**Use protector plates** where wires or pipes pass through framing members and are less than $1^1/_4$" from the face. The plates prevent wallboard screws or nails from puncturing wires or pipes.

**Metal framing connectors** may be required in some communities, especially in areas prone to high winds or earthquakes. Metal joist hangers (A), stud ties (B), connector straps (C), and post-and-beam saddles (D) all provide extra reinforcement to structural joints. Wood joints made with metal connectors are stronger than toenailed joints.

# Planning Door & Window Installations

**Most windows and doors** are prehung units designed for easy installation. They are available in a vast range of styles and finishes. The units are preassembled, and trim moldings are either preattached or packed with the unit. Metal hardware is included with all window units, and with some doors. Top-quality windows and doors usually must be special ordered, and require two to four weeks for delivery.

Doors and windows link your home to the outside world and are the most important design elements in any remodeling project. Adding new windows makes your home brighter and makes living spaces feel larger. Replacing a shabby entry door can make your home more inviting to guests and more secure against intruders.

When planning your remodeling project, remember that the choice and placement of doors and windows will affect your life-style. For example, installing a large patio door is a good way to join indoor and outdoor living areas, but it also changes the traffic patterns through your house and affects your personal privacy.

In addition to style, consider the size and placement of windows and doors as you plan the project. Most homeowners install new windows to provide a better view, but remember that a well-positioned window also can reduce heating and cooling bills by serving as a passive solar collector in the cooler months and by improving ventilation in the summer.

**Choose new doors and windows** that match the style and shape of your home. For traditional home styles, strive for balance when planning windows and doors. In the colonial-style home shown on the left, carefully chosen window units match the scale and proportions of the structure, creating a pleasing symmetry. In the home on the right, mismatched windows conflict with the traditional look of the home.

# Tips for Planning Door & Window Installations

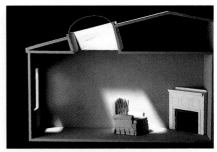

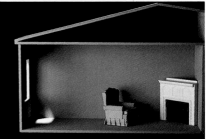

**Traffic patterns** through the home are determined by the placement of doors. Rooms with many doors seem smaller because traffic patterns consume much of the available space (top). When planning room layout, reserve plenty of space for doors to swing freely.

**Divided window panes** in windows and patio doors lend a traditional appearance to a home, and help create interesting lighting patterns in a room. Snap-in grills (shown), available for most windows and doors, are an inexpensive way to achieve this effect.

**Consider the effect of sunlight** when planning window positions. For example, when installing a skylight, choose a location and build a shaft to direct sunlight where you want it.

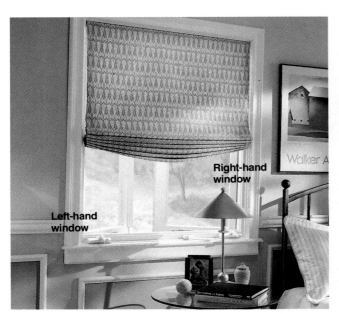

**Right-hand vs. left-hand:** Doors and casement windows are available in both right-hand or left-hand models, and this swing direction must be specified when ordering the units. When opened away from the operator, right-hand units swing to the right, left-hand units to the left. Double window units often have one right-hand and one left-hand unit. If you are installing a single window, choose a model that will catch prevailing breezes when it is opened.

**Window combinations** can be custom-ordered from the manufacturer. Unusual shapes, like the casement window with attached round top shown here, work well in contemporary-style homes, and also can help create a visual accent in a traditional-style home.

# Window Styles

**Casement** windows pivot on hinges mounted on the side. They are available in many sizes, and in multi-window units that combine as many as five separate windows. Casement windows have a contemporary look, and offer an unobstructed view and good ventilation. They work well as egress windows (page 84).

**Double-hung** windows slide up and down, and have a traditional appearance. New double-hung windows have a spring-mounted operating mechanism, instead of the troublesome sash weights found on older windows.

**Awning windows** pivot on hinges mounted at the top. Awning windows work well in combination with other windows, and because they provide ventilation without letting moisture in, they are a good choice in damp climates.

**Sliding windows** are inexpensive and require little maintenance, but do not provide as much open ventilation as casement windows, since only half of the window can be open at one time.

**Skylights** introduce extra light into rooms that have limited wall space. Skylights serve as solar collectors on sunny days, and those that also can be opened improve ventilation in the home.

**Bay windows** make a house feel larger without expensive structural changes. They are available in dozens of sizes and styles.

# Door Styles

**Interior panel** doors have an elegant, traditional look. They are very durable and provide good soundproofing.

**Interior hollow-core** prehung doors have a contemporary look, and are available in many stock sizes. Hollow-core doors are lightweight and inexpensive.

**Decorative storm doors** can improve the security, energy efficiency, and appearance of your entry. A storm door prolongs the life of an expensive entry door by protecting it from the elements.

**Entry doors with sidelights** brighten a dark entry hall, and give an inviting look to your home. In better models, sidelights contain tempered, double-pane glass for better security and energy efficiency.

**Sliding patio doors** offer good visibility and lighting. Because they slide on tracks and require no floor space for operation, sliding doors are a good choice for cramped spaces where swinging doors do not fit.

**French patio doors** have an elegant appearance. Weathertight models are used to join indoor and outdoor living areas, while indoor models are used to link two rooms. Because they open on hinges, your room design must allow space for the doors to swing.

# Tips for Choosing Doors & Windows

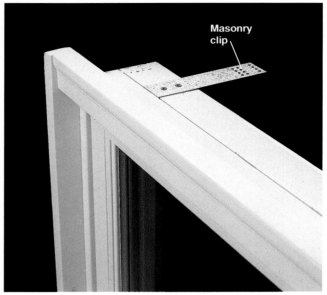

**Wood-frames** (left) are a good choice for windows and patio doors used in remodeling projects. Their preattached exterior brick moldings blend well with the look of existing windows. **Clad-frame** windows and doors (right) feature an aluminum or vinyl shell. They are used most frequently in new construction, and are attached with nailing flanges (page 189) that fit underneath the siding material.

**Polymer coatings** are optional on some wood-frame windows and doors. Polymer-coated windows and doors are available in a variety of colors, and do not need painting. To avoid using casing nails, which would pierce the weatherproof coating, you can anchor polymer-coated units with masonry clips that are screwed to the jambs and to the interior framing members (page 167).

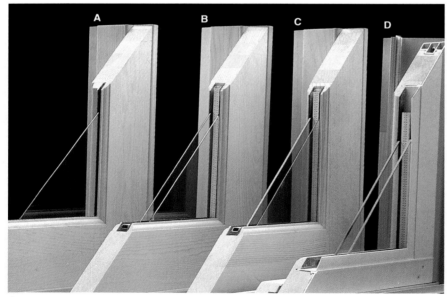

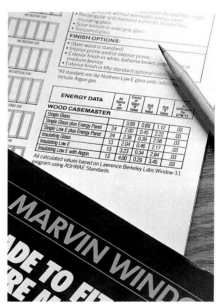

**Several types of glass** are available from window and door manufacturers. Single-pane glass (A) is suitable only in very mild climates. Double-pane (B) have a sealed air space between the layers of glass to reduce heat loss. They are available in several variations with improved insulating ability, including "low-E" glass with an invisible coating of metal on one surface, and gas-filled windows containing an inert gas, like argon. In southern climates, double-glazed tinted glass (C) reduces heat buildup. Tempered glass (D) has extra strength for use in patio doors and large picture windows.

**R-values** of windows and doors, listed in manufacturers' catalogs, indicate the energy efficiency of the unit. Higher R-values indicate better insulating properties. Top-quality windows can have an R-value as high as 4.0. Exterior doors with R-values above 10 are considered energy-efficient.

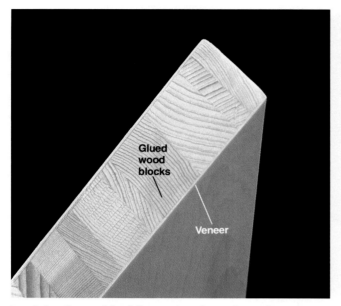

**Look for "core-block"** construction when choosing exterior wooden doors. Core-block doors are made from layers of glued or laminated wood blocks covered with a veneer. Because the direction of the wood grain alternates, core-block doors are less likely to warp than solid-core doors.

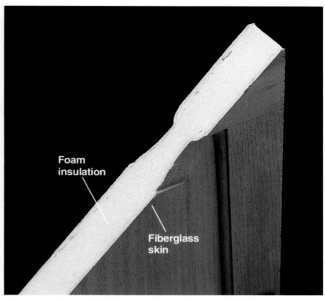

**Fiberglass doors** are expensive, but they are sturdy, have excellent insulating values, and require little maintenance. The fiberglass surface is designed to have the texture of wood and can be stained or painted different colors.

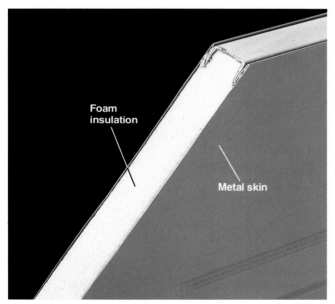

**Steel entry doors** are well insulated and have tight-fitting magnetic weather seals. Steel doors are less expensive than wooden doors and require little maintenance.

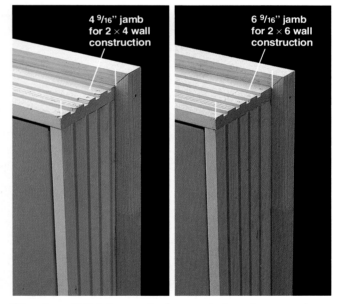

**Check wall thickness** before ordering doors and windows. Manufacturers will customize the frame jambs to match whatever wall construction you have. Find your wall thickness by measuring the jamb width on an existing door or window.

**Inexpensive computer software** designed for the home remodeler can help create a floor plan for your project. Many public libraries have computers and software available for use, and some building centers provide computer-assisted design services to their customers.

Project Planning

# Drawing Plans & Getting a Building Permit

How to Draw Plans

Any remodeling project that includes additions or changes to the home structure requires a building permit from your local building inspector. Before beginning any project, always contact your inspector to find out if you need a permit. If your project includes changes to mechanical systems, like the wiring or plumbing, you will need additional permits for this work.

To obtain a building permit, you must have a floor plan, elevation drawing, and a materials list to show to the inspector. You also must pay a small permit fee. The amount of the fee depends on the estimated cost of your project.

When the inspector issues the work permit, you also will receive a schedule for the required on-site inspections. For most projects, the inspector will visit your site after the framing work is done, but before the walls are finished.

**1** Use existing blueprints of your home, if available, to trace original floor plans and elevation drawings onto white paper. Copy the measurement scale of the original blueprints onto the traced drawings. Make photocopies of the traced drawings, then use the photocopies to experiment with remodeling ideas. Test your ideas in the project area (top photo, page opposite).

## How to Test Remodeling Ideas

couch

**Plot possible locations** for new windows and doors with masking tape. Always mark the full swinging arc of hinged doors. Use newspaper or cardboard to make full-size cutouts of furniture, and use them to experiment with different room layouts. Designers recommend that your floor plan allow ample room around furniture: 22" around a bed; 36" around couches, chairs, and tables; 40" in front of dressers, chests, and closets. Walk through the room along different paths to judge how the room elements will interact. Remember to allow a 40"-wide path for foot traffic across a room. Once you have found a pleasing layout, make final floor plan and elevation drawings (below).

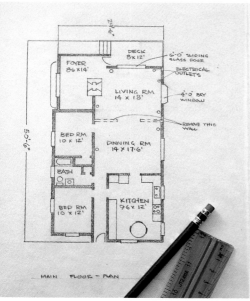

**2** Make a detailed floor plan showing the layout of the area that will be remodeled, including accurate measurements. Show the location of new and existing doors and windows, wiring, and plumbing fixtures.

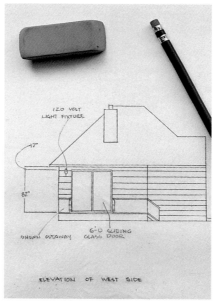

**3** Make elevation drawings showing the side view layout of windows and doors, as viewed from both inside and outside the home. Indicate the size of windows and doors, ceiling heights, and the location of wiring and plumbing fixtures.

**4** Create a complete list showing the materials you intend to use. The list will help the inspector determine if the materials meet accepted standards for strength and fire resistance, and will help you estimate the cost of the project.

## Project Planning
# Tools & Materials

In addition to basic carpentry items, your remodeling project probably will require some of the specialty tools and materials shown in these photos. Whenever you are using a new tool, practice your skills on scrap materials.

Before starting, you should be familiar with common hand tools, power tools, and lumber products used in basic carpentry work. These tools and materials are listed in the chart below.

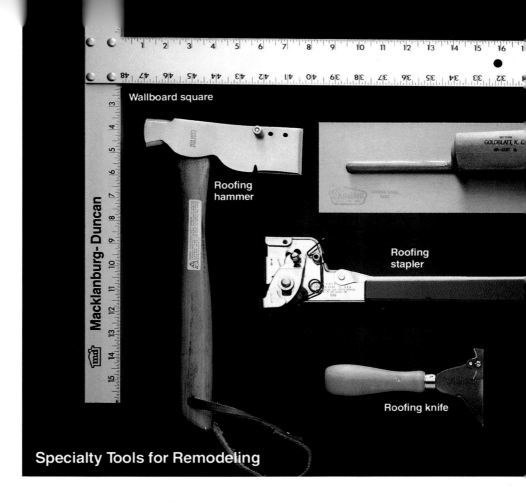

**Specialty Tools for Remodeling**

## Basic Tools & Materials

**Hand tools:**
- Carpenter's level
- Caulk gun
- Chalk line
- Channel-type pliers
- Combination square
- Coping saw
- Hammer
- Framing square
- Handsaw
- Metal snips
- Pencils/pens
- Plumb bob
- Pry bars
- Ratchet wrench
- Screwdrivers
- Stapler
- Tape measure
- Utility knife
- Wallboard taping knives
- Wheelbarrow
- Wood chisel
- Work belt
- Workmate® bench

**Power tools:**
- Circular saw
- Cordless screwdrivers
- Drill & bits
- Miter saw

**Materials:**
- 2" framing lumber
- Common nails
- Drop cloths
- Fiberglass insulation
- Masking tape
- Neon circuit tester
- Plywood
- Shingles
- Siding
- Trim moldings
- Wallboard
- Wallboard compound
- Wallboard tape
- Wood shims
- Wood screws

## Materials for Remodeling

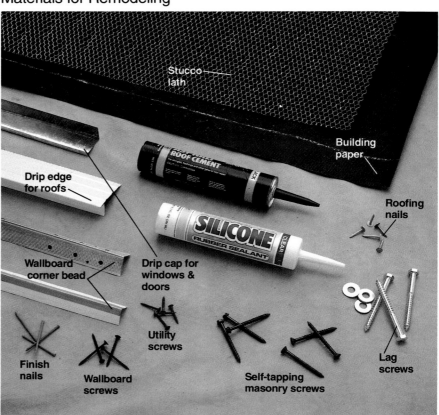

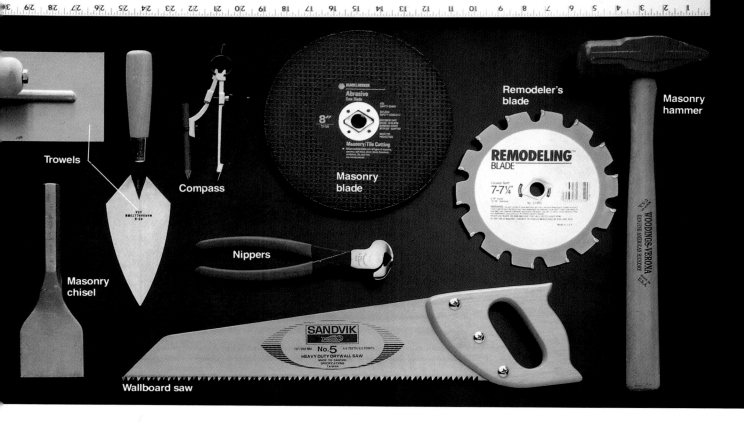

Trowels

Compass

Masonry blade

Remodeler's blade

Masonry hammer

Masonry chisel

Nippers

**REMODELING BLADE**
7-7¼

**SANDVIK No.5** HEAVY DUTY DRYWALL SAW

Wallboard saw

## Safety Equipment

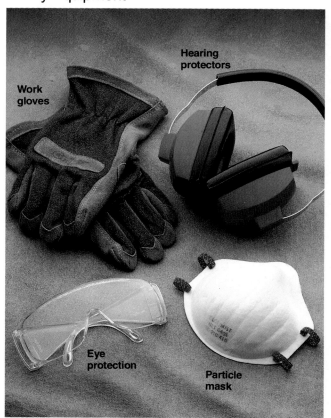

Work gloves

Hearing protectors

Eye protection

Particle mask

## Tools You Can Rent

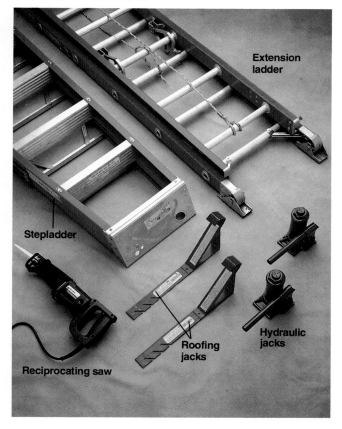

Extension ladder

Stepladder

Reciprocating saw

Roofing jacks

Hydraulic jacks

**After**

**Before**

# Remodeling Projects

# A Remodeling Project Step-by-Step

On the following few pages (98 to 101), you will find a step-by-step overview of a major home remodeling project. Individual projects differ greatly, but most jobs can be organized into these basic steps.

A common mistake made by homeowners is underestimating the project costs and work time. Shop carefully to secure the best prices on materials, and be realistic when estimating the time it will take to complete the job.

Many homeowners budget both their money and time by dividing a large project into separate stages that can be done over a period of months or even years. For example, you might choose to remove an interior wall and install a bay window one summer, then add a skylight and patio door later. If you work in stages, first create a master plan to ensure that each step fits into your overall design.

**A Planning Checklist:** Before you begin hands-on work, make sure you can answer YES to the following questions:

❑ Do you have a working floor plan and elevation drawings for your project?

❑ Have you made a complete materials list and estimated the job costs?

❑ Do you have the required work permits, and are they displayed properly?

❑ Have you ordered all materials you will need, including window and door units?

❑ Have you scheduled your time realistically and arranged for helpers, if needed?

❑ Have you made provisions for removing demolition materials?

❑ Have you arranged for upgrades to the wiring and plumbing systems?

❑ Do you have the necessary tools and rental equipment?

**1** Prepare the work area (pages 103 to 105). Remove trim moldings, and shut off power and plumbing to the wall areas that will be altered. Remove coverplates from the switches, receptacles, and heating ducts in the project area. Protect the floors with drop cloths, and cover doors leading to other areas of the house with plastic to confine dust to the remodeling areas.

**2** Remove interior surfaces (pages 106 to 109). Mark rough openings for the new doors and windows, then remove the interior wall surfaces. Make sure to remove enough wall surface to provide easy access for installing new framing members. After removing wall surfaces, remove old door and window units (pages 110 to 111). Clear away all trash before continuing with your project.

**3** Make temporary supports (pages 120 to 123) if your project requires you to cut more than one stud in a load-bearing wall. Temporary supports help brace the upper structure of your home until the framing work is done. Load-bearing walls include all exterior walls, and most interior walls that run perpendicular to floor joists. Interior walls running parallel to joists are non-load-bearing (partition) walls, and do not require temporary supports.

Temporary support

(continued next page)

**4** Remove and build walls (pages 126 to 133). If you are removing an interior non-load-bearing wall, simply remove the wall surfaces and cut away the studs. However, if you are removing a load-bearing wall, you must make temporary supports and replace the wall with a sturdy permanent header and posts to support the weight previously carried by the removed wall.

Non-load-bearing wall

**5** Frame the openings for the doors (pages 136 to 141) and windows (pages 160 to 163). After the framing work is complete, remove the exterior surfaces (pages 112 to 117) and install the door and window units.

**6** Install doors (pages 142 to 155) and windows (pages 164 to 187). Complete the exterior finishing work as soon as possible to protect the wall cavities against moisture.

**7** Complete the project (pages 188 to 203). First patch and paint the exterior siding and attach any required exterior moldings. When completing the interior work, install the wallboard first, then panel, paint, or attach wallcovering. Finally, patch the floors, and install wood trim moldings.

# Remodeling Basics

Most remodeling projects share the same basic preparation techniques and follow a similar sequence. Organizing your project into stages helps you work efficiently and lets you break large projects into a series of weekend jobs.

During the demolition phase, try to salvage or recycle materials wherever possible. Window and door units, molding, carpeting, electrical and plumbing fixtures that are in good shape can be used elsewhere or sold to salvage yards. Most raw metals are accepted at recycling centers. Wallboard and insulation seldom are worth salvaging.

If your project requires a permit from the local building inspector, do not begin work until the inspector has approved your plans and issued the permit. Display the permit sticker on a window or outer wall so it is visible from the street. If your project requires plumbing or electrical work, additional permits are needed.

Information in this section:

- Preparing the work area (pages 103 to 105)

- Removing interior surfaces (pages 106 to 109)

- Removing old doors and windows (pages 110 to 111)

- Removing exterior surfaces (pages 112 to 119)

- Making temporary supports when cutting studs (pages 120 to 123)

## Remodeling Basics
# Preparing the Work Area

Good preparation of the work area shortens work time, simplifies cleanup, and protects the rest of your house from dirt and damage.

A job site cluttered with old nails, boards, and other materials poses a safety hazard, so take the time to clear away the trash whenever materials begin to pile up. For large jobs, rent a dumpster to hold the demolition debris.

Many remodeling jobs require that you shut off and reroute electrical wiring, plumbing pipes, and other utility lines that run through the walls. If you are not comfortable doing this work yourself, hire a professional.

**Everything You Need:**

Tools: screwdrivers, broom, trash containers, neon circuit tester, electronic stud finder, flat pry bar, channel-type pliers.

Materials: drop cloths, masking tape, building paper, plywood.

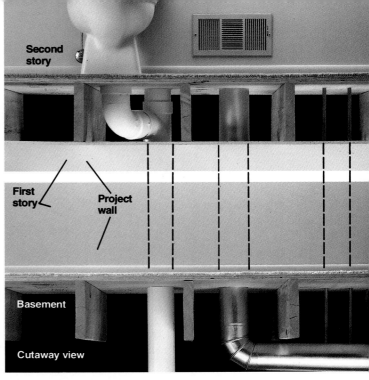

**Check for hidden plumbing lines**, ductwork, and gas pipes before you cut into a wall. To determine the location of the pipes and ducts, examine the areas directly below and above the project wall. In most cases, pipes, utility lines, and ductwork run through the wall vertically between floors. Original blueprints for your house, if available, usually show the location of the utility lines.

## Preparation Tips

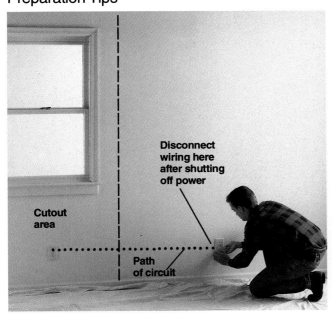

**Disconnect electrical wiring** before you cut into walls. Trace the wiring back to a fixture outside the cutout area, then shut off the power and disconnect the wires leading into the cutout area. Turn the power back on and test for current before cutting into the walls.

**Shovel debris** through a convenient window into a wheelbarrow to speed up demolition work. Use sheets of plywood to cover shrubs and flower gardens next to open windows and doors. Cover adjoining lawn areas with sheets of plastic or canvas to simplify cleanup.

103

## How to Prepare the Project Area

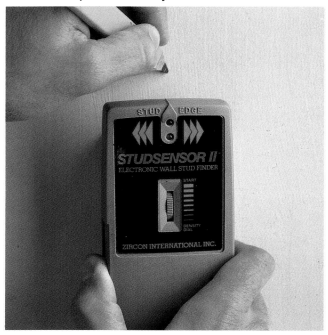

**1** Locate framing members in wall and ceiling areas where you will be working, using an electronic stud finder.

**2** Verify the locations of framing members by driving finishing nails through the wall. Mark the studs every 2 ft. from floor to ceiling.

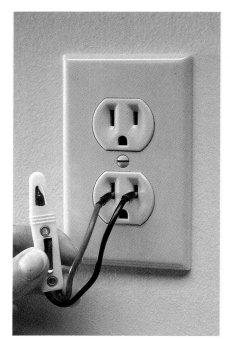

**3** Shut off or disconnect the power to electrical fixtures in the wall and ceiling areas where you will be working. Check for power at each fixture, using a neon circuit tester.

**4** Shut off the water supply at the main shutoff valve if you are working on wall areas that contain water supply pipes.

**5** Remove coverplates from electrical fixtures inside the wall area that will be removed. Tape the mounting screws to the coverplates, and store them in a safe location.

**6** Tape dropcloths over doors and heating/air-conditioning ducts to keep demolition dust from circulating through the house. Cover the floors with cardboard and drop cloths to shield them from dust and damage.

**7** Provide ventilation by placing fans in opened windows in the project area. If you have shut off the power, run heavy-duty extension cords from other parts of the house to provide electricity.

**8** Loosen trim moldings by prying them up with a flat pry bar. Use a wood block to prevent the pry bar from damaging the wall. When the entire length of molding is loose, separate it from the wall. Be careful when removing trim moldings that will be reused or salvaged: old moldings are brittle and break easily. Label any pieces that will be reused.

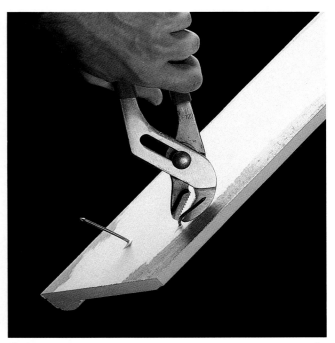

**9** Remove the nails after you remove each piece of trim molding. To avoid splintering, use a channel-type pliers or nail puller to pull the nails through from the back side of the trim.

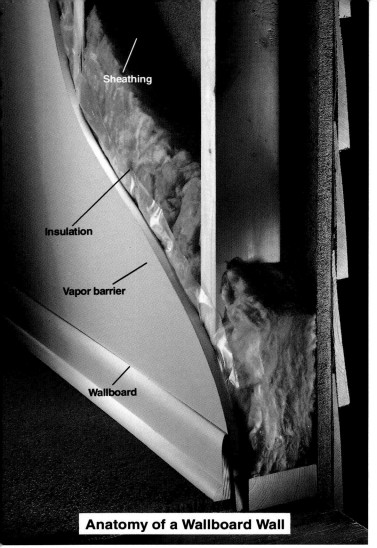

**Sheathing**

**Insulation**

**Vapor barrier**

**Wallboard**

**Anatomy of a Wallboard Wall**

# Removing Interior Surfaces

You must remove interior wall surfaces before you can do the framing work for most remodeling projects. Remove enough surface so there is plenty of room to install the new framing members. When installing a window or door, remove the wall surface from floor to ceiling and all the way to the first wall studs beyond either side of the planned rough opening.

If you have wood paneling, remove it in full sheets if you intend to reuse it. It may be difficult to find new paneling to match the style of your old paneling.

## Removing Wallboard

Demolishing a section of wallboard is a messy job, but it is not difficult. If your wallboard was attached with construction adhesive, use a rasp or old chisel to remove the dried adhesive and create a flat surface on the framing members.

**Everything You Need:**

Tools: tape measure, pencil, stud finder, chalk line, circular saw with remodeler's blade, utility knife, pry bar, eye protection, hammer.

## How to Mark Interior Surfaces for Removal

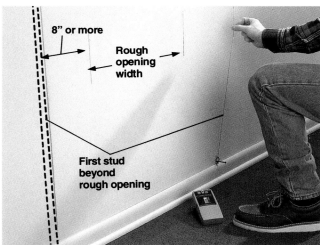

8" or more

Rough opening width

First stud beyond rough opening

**Mark the width of the rough opening** on the wall, then locate the first stud beyond either side of the planned rough opening. **If the rough opening is more than 8" from the next stud,** use a chalk line to mark a cutting line on the inside edge of the stud. An extra nailing stud will be attached to provide a surface for anchoring wallboard (page 192).

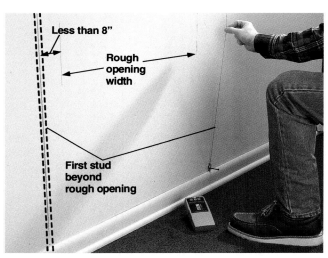

Less than 8"

Rough opening width

First stud beyond rough opening

**Variation:** If rough opening is less than 8" from the next stud, you will not have room to attach an extra nailing stud. Use a chalk line to mark the cutting line down the center of the wall stud. The exposed portion of the stud will provide a surface for attaching new wallboard when finishing the room.

## How to Remove Wallboard

**1** Remove the baseboards and other trim, and prepare the work area (pages 103 to 105). Make a 3/4"-deep cut from floor to ceiling along both cutting lines, using a circular saw. Use a utility knife to finish the cuts at the top and bottom, and to cut through the taped horizontal seam where the wall meets the ceiling surface.

**2** Insert the end of a pry bar into the cut near a corner of the opening. Pull the pry bar until the wallboard breaks, then tear away the broken pieces. Take care to avoid damaging wallboard outside the project area.

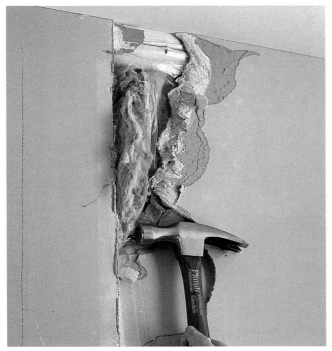

**3** Continue removing wallboard by striking the surface with the side of a hammer, then pulling it away from the wall with the pry bar or your hands.

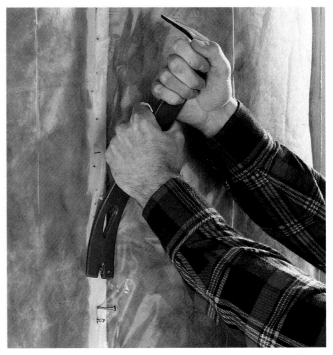

**4** Remove nails, screws, and any remaining wallboard from the framing members, using a pry bar. Remove any vapor barrier and insulation.

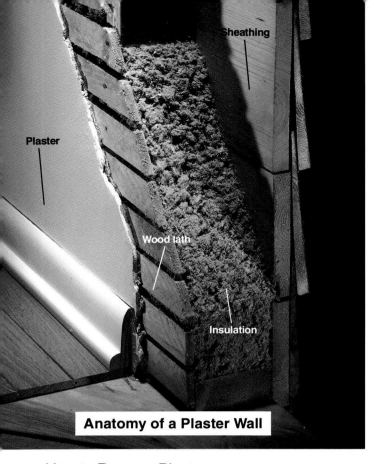

**Anatomy of a Plaster Wall**

## Removing Plaster

Plaster removal is a dusty job, so always wear eye protection and a particle mask during demolition, and use sheets of plastic to protect furniture and to block open doorways. Plaster walls are very brittle, so work carefully to avoid cracking the plaster in areas that will not be removed.

If the material being removed is most of the wall surface, consider removing the whole interior surface of the wall. Replacing the entire wall with wallboard is easier and produces better results than trying to patch around the project area.

**Everything You Need:**

Tools: straightedge, pencil, chalk line, utility knife, eye protection, particle mask, work gloves, hammer, pry bar, reciprocating saw or jig saw, metal snips.

Materials: masking tape, scrap piece of 2 × 4.

## How to Remove Plaster

**1** Mark the wall area to be removed by following the directions on page 106. Apply a double layer of masking tape along the outside edge of each cutting line.

**2** Score each line several times with a utility knife, using a straightedge as a guide. Scored lines should be at least 1/8" deep.

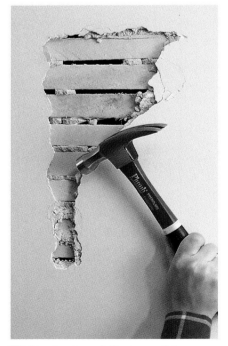

**3** Beginning at the top of the wall in the center of the planned opening, break up the plaster by striking the wall lightly with the side of a hammer. Clear away all plaster from floor to ceiling to within 3" of the lines.

**4** Break the plaster along the edges by holding a scrap piece of 2 × 4 on edge just inside the scored line, and rapping it with a hammer. Use a pry bar to remove the remaining plaster.

**5** Shut off power and examine the wall for wiring and plumbing. Cut through the lath along the edges of the plaster, using a reciprocating saw or jig saw.

**Metal lath**

**Variation:** If the wall has metal lath laid over the wood lath, use a metal snips to clip the edges of the metal lath. Press the jagged edges of the lath flat against the stud. The cut edges of metal lath are very sharp, so be sure to wear work gloves.

**6** Remove the lath from the studs, using a pry bar. Pry away any remaining nails, and remove any vapor barrier and insulation.

Masking tape used to keep glass from shattering.

## Project Basics
# Removing Old Doors & Windows

If your remodeling project requires removing old doors and windows, do not start this work until all preparation work is finished and the interior wall surfaces and trim have been removed. You will want to close up the wall openings as soon as possible, so make sure you have all the tools, framing lumber, and new window and door units you will need before starting the final stages of demolition. Be prepared to finish the work as quickly as possible.

Doors and windows are removed using the same basic procedures. In many cases, the old units can be salvaged for resale or later use, so use care when removing them.

### Everything You Need:

Tools: utility knife, flat pry bar, screwdriver, hammer, reciprocating saw.

Materials: plywood sheets.

**If wall openings cannot be filled** immediately, protect your home by covering the openings with scrap pieces of plywood screwed to the framing members. Plastic sheeting stapled to the outside of the openings will prevent moisture damage.

## How to Remove Old Windows & Doors

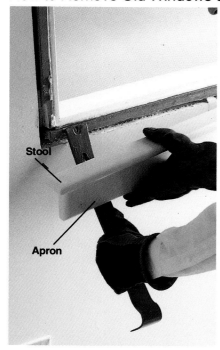

**1** Pry off the window aprons and stools, using a pry bar.

**2** For double-hung windows with sash weights, remove the weights by cutting the cords and pulling the weights from pockets.

**3** Cut through the nails holding the window and door frames to the framing members, using a reciprocating saw.

**4** Pry the outside brick moldings free from the framing members, using a pry bar.

**5** Pull the unit from the rough opening, using a pry bar.

**Variation:** For windows and doors attached with nailing fins, cut or pry loose the siding material or brick moldings, then remove the mounting nails holding the unit to the sheathing.

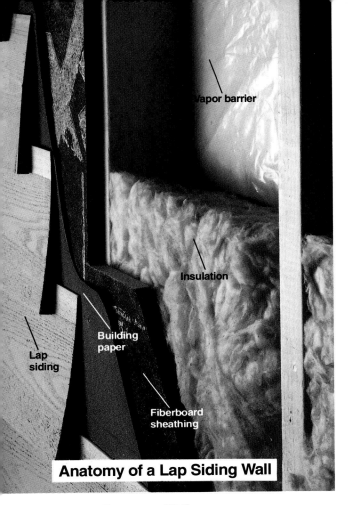

**Anatomy of a Lap Siding Wall**

Labels: Vapor barrier, Insulation, Building paper, Lap siding, Fiberboard sheathing

# Removing Exterior Surfaces

Do not remove exterior surfaces until the interior surfaces have been removed and the opening is framed. To protect wall cavities against moisture, install windows or doors as soon as you remove the exterior surfaces.

Working with a brick facade is difficult. You can do the interior framing work yourself, but hire a professional to remove and patch the brickwork.

## Removing Siding

Exterior lap siding comes in many types. All are removed using the same basic method, but some materials require specialty saw blades (page 94).

**Everything You Need:**

Tools: drill with 3/16" × 8" bit, hammer, tape measure, chalk line, circular saw with remodeler's blade, reciprocating saw, eye protection.

Materials: 8d casing nails, straight 1 × 4.

## How to Remove Siding

**1** From inside, drill through the wall at the corners of the framed opening. Push casing nails through the holes to mark their location. For round-top windows, drill several holes around the curved outline (page 164).

**2** Measure the distance between the nails on the outside of the wall to make sure the dimensions are accurate. Mark the cutting lines with a chalk line stretched between the nails. Push the nails back through the wall.

**3** Nail a straight 1 × 4 flush against inside edge of right cutting line. Drive nail heads slightly under wood surface with a nail set to prevent scratches to the saw foot. Set circular saw to maximum blade depth.

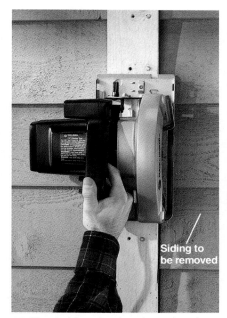

**4** Rest the saw on the 1 × 4, and cut along the marked line, using the edge of the board as a guide. Stop the cuts about 1" short of the corners to keep from damaging the framing members.

**5** Reposition the 1 × 4, and make the remaining straight cuts. Drive nails within 1½" of the edge of the board, because the siding under this area will be removed to make room for door or window brick moldings.

**Variation:** For round-top windows, make curved cuts using a reciprocating saw or jig saw. Move the saw slowly to ensure smooth, straight cuts. To draw an outline for round-top windows, use a cardboard template (page 163).

**6** Complete the cuts at the corner with a reciprocating saw or jig saw.

**7** Remove the cut wall section. If you are working with metal siding, wear work gloves. If you wish, remove the siding pieces from the sheathing and save them for future use.

**Anatomy of a Stucco Wall**

Labels: Metal lath, Insulation, Building paper, Sheathing, Stucco layers

## Removing Stucco

Stucco is a very hard wall material requiring special cutting tools designed for masonry. Wear safety equipment when doing the cutting.

Repaired areas are difficult to blend into existing stucco, so take care to make accurate, smooth cuts.

### Everything You Need:

Tools: drill with $3/16" \times 8"$ twist and masonry bits, tape measure, chalk line, compass, masonry chisel, masonry hammer, eye and hearing protection, circular saw and blades (masonry-cutting and remodeler's), masonry chisels, pry bar.

Materials: 8d casing nails.

## How to Remove Stucco

**1** From inside, drill through the wall at the corners of the framed opening. Use a twist bit to drill through the sheathing, then change to a masonry bit to finish the holes. Push casing nails through the holes to mark their locations.

**2** On the outside wall, measure distances between the nails to make sure the rough opening dimensions are accurate. Mark cutting lines between the nails, using a chalk line.

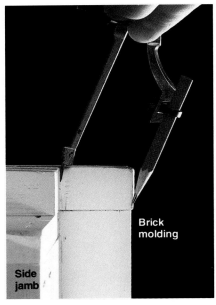

**3** Spread the legs of a compass to match the distance between the side jambs and the edge of the brick molding on the window or door.

Labels: Brick molding, Side jamb

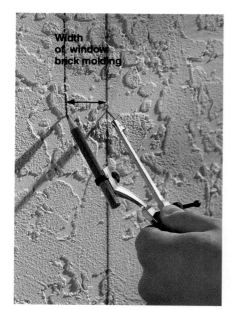

**4** Scribe a cutting line on the stucco by moving the compass along the outline, with the compass point held on the marked line. This added margin will allow the window brick molding to fit tight against the wall sheathing.

**5** Score the stucco surface around the outside edge of the scribed line, using a masonry chisel and masonry hammer. The scored grooves should be at least 1/8" deep to serve as a guide for the circular saw blade.

**6** Make straight cuts using a circular saw and masonry-cutting blade. Make several passes with the saw, gradually deepening cuts until blade just cuts through the metal lath, causing sparks to fly. Stop cuts just before the corners to avoid damaging the stucco past the cutting line, then complete the cuts with a masonry chisel.

**Variation:** For round-top windows, mark the outline on the stucco, using a cardboard template (page 163), then drill a series of holes around the outline, using a masonry bit. Complete the cut with a masonry chisel.

**7** Break up the stucco with a masonry hammer or sledgehammer, exposing the underlying metal lath. Use metal snips to cut through the lath around the opening. Use a pry bar to pull away the lath and attached stucco.

**8** Outline the rough opening on the sheathing, using a straightedge as a guide. Cut the rough opening along the inside edge of the framing members, using a circular saw or reciprocating saw (steps 4 and 5, page 113). Remove the cut section of sheathing.

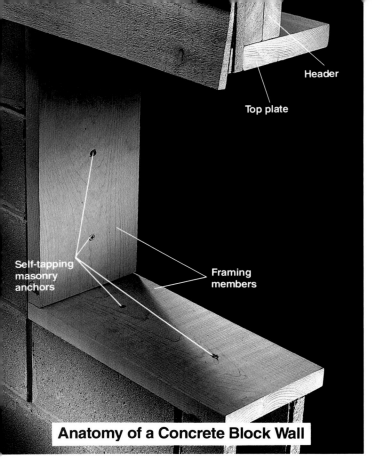

Header

Top plate

Self-tapping masonry anchors

Framing members

**Anatomy of a Concrete Block Wall**

## Removing Concrete Block

Making a new opening in a concrete wall is complicated and can cause damage to your house structure, so leave this work to a professional. However, you can extend an existing opening downward, so long as you leave the load-bearing header intact.

For example, if you have an exposed basement, you can remove an existing picture window and extend the opening in order to install a patio door leading to the back yard. Or, you can extend a small existing window opening to provide an egress window — a Building Code requirement for any sleeping room (page 84).

### Everything You Need:

Tools: level, pencil, circular saw with masonry blade, masonry chisel, masonry hammer, eye protection, work gloves, hearing protectors, caulk gun, trowel, drill with 3/16" masonry bit.

Materials: premixed dry concrete, construction adhesive, 2" pressure-treated lumber, self-tapping masonry anchors.

## How to Remove Concrete Block

**1** Remove old window unit and frame, then mark the rough opening on both the interior and exterior sides of the wall, using a level as a guide.

**2** Score the cutting lines, using a masonry chisel and masonry hammer, wearing eye protection and work gloves.

**3** Cut along the scored lines with a circular saw and masonry blade. Make many passes with the saw, gradually deepening the cut until the saw blade is at maximum depth.

116

**4** Break both the inside and outside mortar lines on all sides of the center block in the top row of blocks being removed. Use a masonry chisel and hammer.

**5** Strike the face of the center block with a masonry hammer until the block either dislodges or breaks into pieces.

**6** Chip out large pieces with a masonry chisel. Break mortar around remaining blocks, then chip them out with the masonry chisel and hammer.

## How to Frame a Rough Opening in Concrete Block

**1** When all blocks are removed, create a smooth surface by filling the hollow areas in the cut blocks with scrap pieces of concrete block, then troweling fresh concrete over the surfaces. Make sure surfaces are flat, then let concrete dry overnight.

**2** Install 2" pressure-treated lumber to frame the opening, using construction adhesive. If the interior wall is finished, size the framing members so they are flush with any existing studs or furring strips.

**3** Anchor framing members by drilling pilot holes with a 3/16" masonry bit, then driving self-tapping masonry anchors into the blocks, spaced every 10".

117

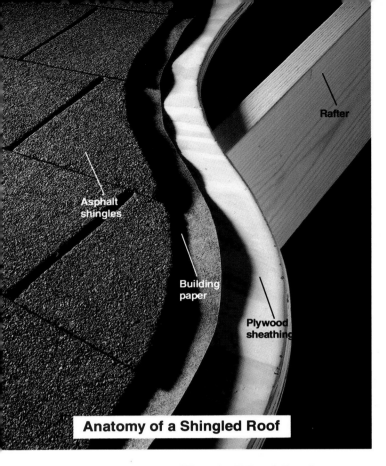

**Asphalt shingles**

**Rafter**

**Building paper**

**Plywood sheathing**

**Anatomy of a Shingled Roof**

## Removing a Shingled Roof Section

When installing a skylight, you will need to remove a section of roof. Asphalt or fiberglass shingles are easy to remove; but slate, tile, or wood-shingle roofs should be left to a professional.

Use extreme caution whenever you are working on a roof. Never work on a roof alone, and always wear long pants and rubber-soled shoes. Use metal roofing jacks and 2 × 10s to provide a foot rest below the work area (page opposite). If possible, start your roofing project on a calm, clear day when the temperature is between 50° and 70°F. Cold shingles are slippery from condensation, and warm shingles are easily damaged.

### Everything You Need:

Tools: ladder, hammer, chalk line, tape measure, roofing jacks, circular saw with old remodeler's blade.

Materials: 8d casing nails, 2 × 4, straight 1 × 4, roofing cement.

## How to Remove a Shingled Roof Section

**1** After framing the rough opening from the inside (pages 180 to 181), mark the rough opening by driving 8d casing nails through the interior roof sheathing at the corners of the frame.

**2** Nail a 2 × 4 diagonally across the framed opening to keep the roof section from falling through when it is cut loose.

**Work area**

**Roofing jack below work area**

**Roofing jack at roof edge**

**3** Attach a pair of roofing jacks just above the roof edge, and attach another pair just below the work area. Lay 2"- thick planks across each pair of jacks.

**4** Measure between the nails to make sure the rough opening dimensions are accurate. Snap chalk lines on the shingles between the nails to mark the rough opening. Drive nails back through roof.

**5** Use casing nails to attach a straight 1 × 4 flush along the inside edge of one cutting line. Use a nail set to drive the heads below the wood surface so they do not scratch the saw foot.

**6** Cut through the shingles and sheathing along the marked line, using a circular saw and remodeler's blade set to maximum depth. (Use an old saw blade, because mineral particles in shingles will ruin a new blade.) Rest the saw foot on the 1 × 4 to protect it from scratches, and use the edge of the board as a guide. Reposition the 1 × 4 and cut along the remaining lines. **Do not stand or lean on the cutout area.**

**7** After the cut section drops down onto the diagonal 2 × 4 brace, carefully lift it out of the hole. Remove the diagonal brace and continue with the skylight installation (pages 178 to 187). When the job is done, remove the roofing jacks, and fill the nail holes with roofing cement.

**Temporary supports for a platform-framed house** must support the ceiling joists, since the ceiling platform carries the load of the upstairs structure. Platform framing can be identified by the sole plate to which the wall studs are nailed.

**Temporary supports for a balloon-framed house** support the wall studs, which carry the upstairs load. The temporary support header, called a whaler, is anchored to the wall studs above the planned rough opening, and is supported by wall studs and bracing adjacent to the rough opening. Balloon framing can be identified by long wall studs that pass uncut through the floor to a sill plate resting on the foundation.

# Making Temporary Supports

If your project requires you to remove more than one stud in a load-bearing wall, temporary supports will be needed while you do the framing. To identify a load-bearing wall, see page 81. The techniques for making temporary supports vary, depending on whether your house uses platform framing or balloon framing (see photos, left; and pages 78 to 79).

Platform framing is found in most homes built after 1930. To make temporary supports, use hydraulic jacks (page opposite) or a temporary stud wall (page 122). The stud wall method is the better choice if the supports must remain in place for more than one day.

If the ceiling and floor joists run parallel to the wall you are working on, use the method shown at the bottom of page 122.

Balloon framing is found in many homes built before 1930. To make temporary supports for balloon framing, use the method shown on page 123.

Some remodeling jobs require two temporary supports. For example, when making a large opening in an interior load-bearing wall, you must install supports on both sides of the wall (page 126).

**Everything You Need:**

Tools: tape measure, circular saw, hammer, ratchet, drill and spade bit, hydraulic jacks.

Materials: 2 × 4 lumber, 3" lag screws, 2" utility screws, 10d nails, cloths.

120

# How to Support Platform Framing with Hydraulic Jacks when Joists Are Perpendicular to Wall

**1** Measure width of planned rough opening, and add 4 ft. so temporary support will reach well past rough opening. Cut three 2 × 4s to that length. Nail two of the 2 × 4s together with 10d nails to make a top plate for temporary support. The remaining 2 × 4 will be the sole plate for the temporary support. Place the temporary sole plate on the floor 3 ft. from the wall, centering it on the planned rough opening.

**2** Set hydraulic jacks on the temporary sole plate, 2 ft. in from the ends. (Use three jacks if opening will be more than 8 ft. wide.) For each jack, build a post by nailing together a pair of 2 × 4s. Posts should be about 4" shorter than the distance between the ceiling and the top of the jacks. Attach the posts to the top plate, 2 ft. from the ends, using countersunk lag screws.

Direction of joists

**3** Cover the top of the plate with a thick layer of cloth to protect the ceiling from cracking, then lift the support structure onto the hydraulic jacks.

**4** Adjust the support structure so the posts are exactly plumb, then raise the hydraulic jacks until the top plate just begins to lift the ceiling. Do not lift too far, or you may damage the floor and ceiling.

## Alternate: How to Support Platform Framing with a Temporary Stud Wall (Joists Perpendicular to Wall)

**1** Build a 2 × 4 stud wall that is 4 ft. wider than the planned wall opening and 1³/4" shorter than the distance from floor to ceiling.

**2** Raise the stud wall up and position it 3 ft. from the wall, centered on the planned rough opening.

**3** Slide a 2 × 4 top plate between temporary wall and ceiling. Check to make sure wall is plumb, then drive shims under the top plate at 12" intervals until the wall is wedged tightly in place.

## How to Support Platform Framing when Joists Are Parallel to Wall

**1** Follow directions on page 121, except: Build two 4-ft.-long cross braces, using pairs of 2 × 4s nailed together. Attach the cross braces to the double top plate, 1 ft. from the ends, using countersunk lag screws.

**2** Place a 2 × 4 sole plate directly over a floor joist, then set hydraulic jacks on the sole plate. For each jack, build a post 8" shorter than the jack-to-ceiling distance. Nail posts to top plate, 2 ft. from ends. Cover braces with cloth, and set support structure on jacks.

**3** Adjust the support structure so the posts are exactly plumb, then pump the hydraulic jacks until the cross braces just begin to lift the ceiling. Do not lift too far, or you may damage the floor or ceiling.

# How to Support Balloon Framing

**1** Remove the wall surfaces around the rough opening from floor to ceiling (pages 106 to 109). Make a temporary support header (called a whaler) by cutting a 2 × 8 long enough to extend at least 20" past each side of the planned rough opening. Center the whaler against the wall studs, flush with the ceiling. Tack the whaler in place with 2" utility screws.

**2** Cut two lengths of 2 × 4 to fit snugly between the bottom of the whaler and the floor. Slide 2 × 4s into place at the ends of the whaler, then attach them with nailing plates and 10d nails.

**3** Drill two 3/16" holes through the whaler and into each stud it spans. Secure the whaler with 3/8" × 4" lag screws.

**4** Drive shims between the bottom of each 2 × 4 and the floor to help secure the support structure.

123

**After**

Header made from two pieces of MicroLam®

Post

Post

Spacing blocks

Spacing blocks

Nailing strip

**Before**

Load-bearing wall

**When removing a wall,** first tear off the wall surface, exposing the framing members. Do not cut wall studs until you know if you are working with a load-bearing wall, or a non-load-bearing (partition) wall (page 81). If the wall is load-bearing, you will need to install temporary supports (pages 120 to 123) while cutting out the studs. When removing a load-bearing wall, you must replace it with a permanent header and posts strong enough to carry the structural weight once borne by the wall. The posts will be hidden inside the adjacent walls after the wallboard is patched. The header will be visible, but covering it with wallboard will help it blend in with the ceiling. NOTE: Load-bearing walls more than 12 ft. long should be removed only by a professional.

# Removing & Building Walls

Removing an existing wall or building a new wall are easy ways to create more usable space without the expense of building an addition. By removing a wall, you can turn two small rooms into a large space perfect for family living. By adding new walls in a larger area, you can create a private space to use as a quiet study or as a new bedroom for a growing family.

The techniques for removing a wall vary greatly, depending on the location and structural function of the wall (see pages 79 to 81). Partition walls are relatively easy to work with, while load-bearing walls require special planning.

In addition to defining living areas and supporting the house structure, walls also hold the essential mechanical systems that run through your home. You will need to consider how your project affects electrical wiring, plumbing pipes, gas pipes, and heating and air-conditioning ductwork. Unless you are confident of your own skills, it is a good idea to have a professional make changes to these systems.

Included in this section:

- Removing a wall (pages 126 to 127)
- Installing a permanent header (pages 128 to 129)
- Building a partition wall (pages 130 to 133)

## Materials for Building a Header

Beam made from 2 × 12s and plywood: 8-ft. maximum recommended span

Double 9¹/₂" MicroLam® beam: 10-ft. maximum recommended span. MicroLam framing members are made from thin layers of wood laminate glued together.

Double 11³/₈" MicroLam® beam: 11-ft maximum recommended span

12" GlueLam® beam: 12-ft. maximum recommended span. GlueLam beams are made from layers of dimension lumber laminated together. GlueLam beans can be stained and left exposed for an attractive appearance.

**Manufactured support members** are stronger and more durable than 2" dimension lumber, so they work well for building a header to replace a load-bearing wall. *Always consult your building inspector or a professional builder* when choosing materials and sizes for a support header.

125

# Removing a Wall

When removing a wall, you must determine if you are working with a load-bearing wall, or a non-load-bearing (partition) wall. (See page 81.) When removing a load-bearing wall, you will need to make temporary supports and install a header.

To maintain some separation between joined rooms, you may choose to remove just a section of the wall.

## Everything You Need:

Tools: tape measure, pencil, drill and bits, reciprocating saw, pry bar, hammer.

Materials (for installing a header): 2" dimension lumber, MicroLam® framing members, 10d nails.

## How to Remove a Wall

**1** Prepare the project site, remove the surfaces from the wall being removed, then remove or reroute any wiring, plumbing lines, or ductwork. (See pages 103 to 109.)

**2** Remove the surface of the adjoining walls to expose the permanent studs.

**3** Determine if the wall being removed is load-bearing or non-load-bearing (page 81). If the wall is load-bearing, install temporary supports on each side of the wall being removed (pages 120 to 123).

**4** Remove studs by cutting them through the middle and prying them away from the sole plate and top plate.

**5** Remove the end stud on each end of the wall. If wall being removed is load-bearing, also remove any nailing studs or blocking in the adjoining walls directly behind the removed wall.

**6** Make two cuts through the top plate, at least 3" apart, using a reciprocating saw or handsaw. Remove the cut section with a pry bar.

**7** Remove the remaining sections of the top plate, using a pry bar.

**8** Remove a 3"-wide section of sole plate, using a reciprocating saw. Pry out entire sole plate using a pry bar. If removed wall was load-bearing, install a permanent header (page 128).

## Tips for Removing a Section of Wall

**When removing wall surfaces**, expose the wall back to the first permanent studs at each side of the opening.

**Leave a small portion of exposed sole plate** to serve as the base for posts. In a load-bearing wall (A), leave 3" of sole plate to hold the double 2 × 4 post that will support the permanent header. In a non-load-bearing wall (B), leave 1 1/2" of exposed sole plate to hold one extra wall stud. Top plates should be removed over the entire width of the opening.

## How to Install a Permanent Header when Removing a Load-bearing Wall

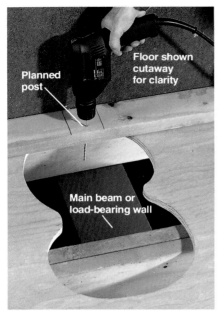

**1** Mark the location of the planned support posts on the sole plate. Drill through the sole plate where support posts will rest to make sure there is a joist directly underneath. If not, install blocking under the post locations (step 2).

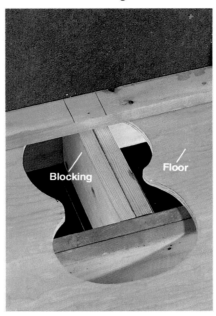

**2** If necessary, cut and install double 2" blocking between joists. (You may need to cut into a finished ceiling to gain access to this space.) Blocking should be same size lumber as joists. Attach blocks to joists with 10d nails.

**3** Build a support header to span the width of the removed wall, including the width of the support posts. See page 125 for header recommendations: in this project, the header is built with two lengths of MicroLam® joined with 10d nails.

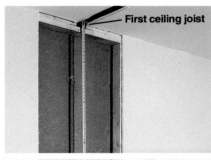

**4** Lay the ends of the header on the sole plates. Find the length for each support post by measuring between the top of the header and the bottom of the first ceiling joist in from the wall.

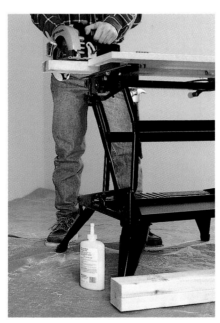

**5** Make support posts by cutting pairs of 2 × 4s to length and joining them side by side with wood glue and 10d nails.

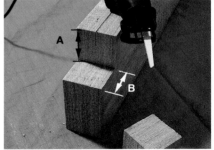

**6** Measure the thickness (A) and width (B) of the top plate at each end, then notch the top corners of the header to fit around the top plates, using a reciprocating saw.

**7** Lift the header against the ceiling joists, then set the posts under the ends of the header. If the header will not fit due to sagging ceiling joists, then raise the joists by jacking up or shimming the temporary supports.

**8** Toenail the posts to the header with 10d nails.

**9** Check each post for plumb with a carpenter's level, and adjust it if necessary by tapping the bottom with a hammer. When post is plumb, mark a reference line on the sole plate, and toenail the bottom of each post to the sole plate.

**10** Cut 2 × 4 nailing strips and attach them to each side of the post and header with 10d nails. Nailing strips provide a surface for attaching new wallboard.

**11** Cut and toenail spacing blocks to fit into the gaps between the permanent studs and the nailing strips. Patch and finish the wall and beam as directed on pages 192 to 195.

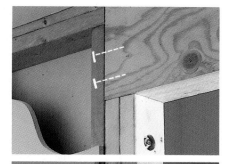

Wall surface and studs shown cutaway for clarity

**When removing a section** of a wall, attach the posts to the wall studs with countersunk lag screws (bottom). Endnail the wall studs to the header with 10d nails (top).

# Building a Partition Wall

Partition walls divide spaces into rooms, but do not carry any significant structural weight. Because partition walls are not load-bearing, the framing techniques are simple. However, take care to make sure the new wall you build is plumb, straight, and perpendicular to the adjoining walls.

Interior partition walls usually are built with 2 × 4 lumber, but in some situations it is better to frame with 2 × 6 lumber (photo, left). Before finishing the walls with wallboard (pages 192 to 195), have the building inspector review your work. The inspector also may check to see that any required plumbing and wiring changes are complete.

**Use 2 × 6 lumber** to frame a new wall that must hold large plumbing pipes. Where wall plates must be cut to fit pipes, use metal straps to join the framing members (inset). For improved soundproofing, you can also fill walls with fiberglass insulation.

> ### Everything You Need:
>
> Tools: drill and twist bit, chalk line, tape measure, combination square, pencil, framing square, ladder, plumb bob, hammer.
>
> Materials: framing lumber, 10d nails.

## Variations for Fastening New Walls to Joists

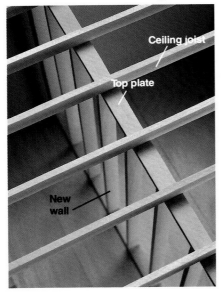

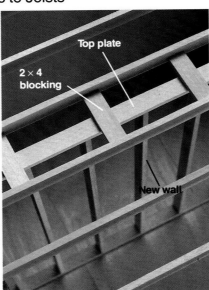

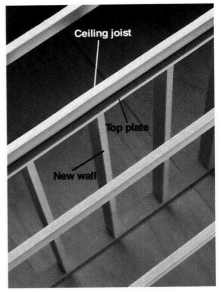

**New wall perpendicular to joists:** Attach the top plate and sole plate directly to the ceiling and floor joists with 10d nails.

**New wall parallel to joists, but not aligned:** Install 2 × 4 blocking between the joists every 2 ft., using 10d nails. Bottom of blocking should be flush with the edges of joists. Anchor plates with 10d nails driven into the blocking.

**New wall aligned with parallel joists:** Attach top plate to ceiling joist and sole plate to the floor, using 10d nails.

## How to Build a Partition Wall

**1** Mark the location of the new wall on the ceiling, then snap two chalk lines to outline the position of the new top plate. Locate the first ceiling joist or cross block by drilling into the ceiling between the lines, then measure to find the remaining joists.

**2** Make the top and bottom wall plates by cutting two 2 × 4s to wall length. Lay the plates side by side, and use a combination square to outline the stud locations at 16" intervals.

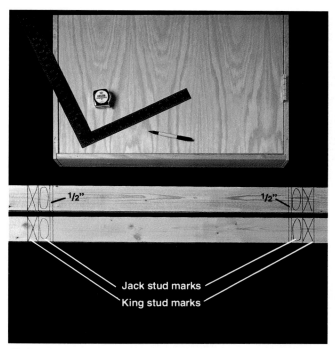

Jack stud marks
King stud marks

**3** Mark the position of the door framing members on the top plate and sole plate, using Xs for king studs and Os for jack studs. The rough opening measured between the insides of jack studs should be about 1" wider than the actual width of the door to allow for adjustments during installation.

**4** Position the top plate against the ceiling between the chalk lines, and use two 10d nails to tack it in place with the stud marks facing down. Use a framing square to make sure the plate is perpendicular to the adjoining walls, then anchor the plate to the joists with 10d nails.

(continued next page)

**5** Determine position of sole plate by hanging a plumb bob from edge of the top plate near an adjoining wall so the plumb bob tip nearly touches the floor. When the plumb bob is motionless, mark its position on the floor. Repeat at the opposite end of top plate, then snap a chalk line between the marks to show the location of the sole plate edge.

**6** Cut away the portion of the sole plate where the door framing will fit, then position the remaining pieces against the sole plate outline on the floor. On wood floors, anchor the sole plate pieces with 10d nails driven into the floor joists.

**On concrete floors**, attach the sole plate with a stud driver, available at rental centers. A stud driver fires a small gunpowder charge to drive a masonry nail through the framing member and into the concrete. Wear hearing protectors when using a stud driver.

**7** Find the length of the first stud by measuring the distance between the sole plate and the top plate at the first stud mark. Add 1/8" to ensure a snug fit, and cut the stud to length.

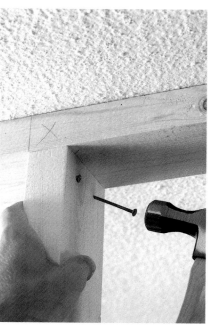

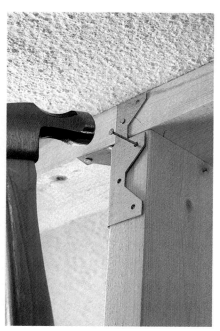

**8** Position the stud between the top plate and sole plate so the stud markings are covered.

**9** Attach the stud by toenailing through the sides of the studs and into the top plate and sole plate. Measure, cut, and install all remaining studs one at a time.

**Option:** Attach the studs to sole plate and top plate with metal connectors and 4d nails.

**10** Frame the rough opening for the door (see pages 136 to 137).

**11** Install 2 × 4 blocking between studs, 4 ft. from the floor. Arrange to have the wiring and any other utility work completed, then have your project inspected. Install wallboard and trim the wall as shown on pages 192 to 195 and 200 to 201.

New
wallboard

2 × 4 framing

Old
wallboard

Sound Stop
board

# Soundproofing Walls & Ceilings

The easiest way to soundproof is by using special materials and methods during construction, when framing is accessible. Your existing walls can also be soundproofed by adding materials like Sound Stop® board, or a layer of additional wallboard attached to resilient steel channels. These methods cushion the wall against noise transmission.

Walls and ceilings are rated for sound transmission by a system called Sound Transmission Class (STC). The higher the STC rating, the quieter the house. For example, if a wall is rated at 30 to 35 STC, loud speech can be understood through the wall. At 42 STC, loud speech is reduced to a murmur. At 50 STC, loud speech cannot be heard.

Standard construction methods result in a 32 STC rating, while soundproofed walls and ceilings can carry a rating of up to 48 STC.

**Before You Start:**
**Tools & Materials for new walls:** 2 × 6 top and sole plates, fiberglass batt insulation.
**Tools & Materials for existing walls:** Sound Stop® board, resilient steel channels, ⅝-inch-thick wallboard.

Tip: When building new walls, caulk along the floor and ceiling joints to reduce sound transmission.

## Standard & Soundproofed Floor & Ceiling Construction

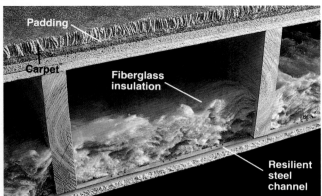

**Standard construction,** with plywood over wooden subfloor and ½-inch-thick wallboard on ceiling, carries a sound transmission rating of 32 STC.

**Soundproofed construction** uses carpeting and padding on floor, fiberglass batt insulation, resilient steel channel nailed to joists, and ⅝-inch wallboard on ceiling. Rating for this system is 48 STC.

## How to Soundproof New Walls

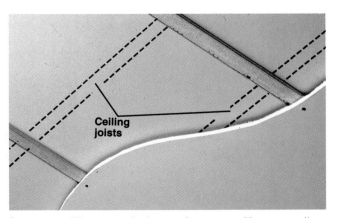

**1** Build walls with 2 × 6 top and sole plates. Position 2 × 4 studs every 12", staggering them against alternate edges of plates.

**2** Weave 3½-inch unfaced fiberglass batt insulation between 2 × 4 studs throughout wall. When covered with ½-inch-thick wallboard, this wall has rating of 48 STC.

## How to Soundproof Existing Walls & Ceilings

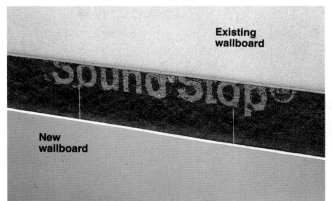

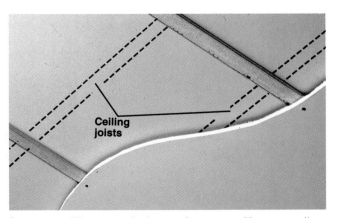

**Nail ½-inch Sound Stop®** board over existing surface with 1½-inch wallboard nails. Glue ½-inch-thick wallboard over Sound Stop with construction adhesive. Sound rating is 46 STC.

**Screw resilient steel channels** over ceiling or wall, spaced 24" on-center, perpendicular to existing framing. Attach ⅝-inch-thick wallboard to channels with 1-inch wallboard screws. Sound rating is 44 STC.

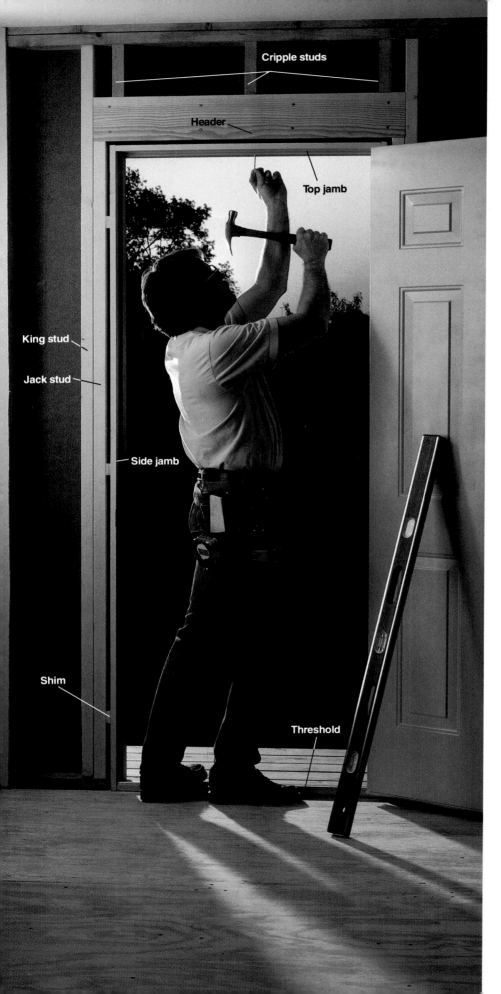

Cripple studs

Header

Top jamb

King stud

Jack stud

Side jamb

Shim

Threshold

# Framing & Installing Doors

Your local home center carries many interior and exterior doors in stock sizes. For custom sizes, have the home center special-order the doors from the manufacturer. Special orders generally take three or four weeks for delivery.

For easy installation, buy "prehung" interior and exterior doors, which are already mounted in their jambs. Although unmounted doors are widely available, installing them is a complicated job that is best left to a professional.

When replacing an existing door, choosing a new unit the same size as the old door makes your work easier, because you can use framing members already in place.

This section shows:

- Framing a door opening (pages 137 to 141)

- Installing an interior door (pages 142 to 143)

- Installing an entry door (pages 144 to 147)

- Installing a storm door (pages 148 to 149)

- Installing a patio door (pages 150 to 154)

The following pages show installation techniques for wood-frame houses with lap siding. If your home exterior is stucco or masonry, see pages 114 to 117 for more information on working with these materials.

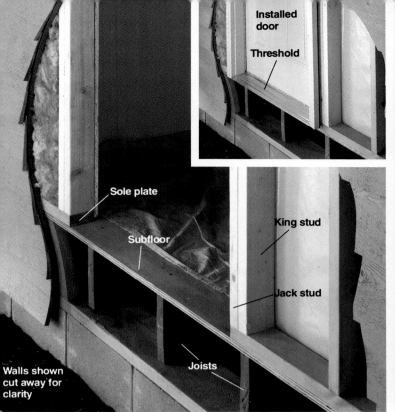

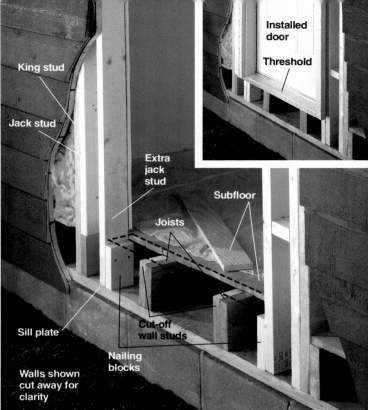

**New door opening in a platform-framed house** has studs that rest on a sole plate running across the top of the subfloor. The sole plate between the jack studs is cut away so the threshold for the new door can rest directly on the subfloor.

**New door opening in a balloon-framed house** has studs extending past the subfloor to rest on the sill plate. Jack studs rest either on the sill plate or on top of the joists. To provide a surface for the door threshold, install nailing blocks, and extend the subfloor out to the ends of the joists, using plywood.

Framing & Installing Doors

# Framing a Door Opening

The rough opening for a new door should be framed after the interior preparation work is done (pages 102 to 117), but before the exterior wall surfaces are removed. The methods for framing the opening will vary, depending on whether your house is built with platform framing or balloon framing. (See photos, above; and pages 78 to 79.)

**Always build temporary supports** to hold up the ceiling if your project requires that you cut or remove more than one stud in a load-bearing wall (pages 120 to 123).

| **Everything You Need:** |
| --- |
| Tools: tape measure, pencil, level, plumb bob, reciprocating saw, circular saw, handsaw, hammer, pry bar, nippers. |
| Materials: 2" dimension lumber, 3/8" plywood, 10d nails. |

**When framing a door opening in a new wall,** install the door framing members at the same time you install the wall studs (pages 130 to 133). Cut and install cripple studs to reach between the top of the header and the top plate. Cripples should be spaced at the same interval as the wall studs, and anchored with 10d nails.

## How to Frame a Door Opening

**1** Prepare the project site and remove the interior wall surfaces (pages 103 to 109).

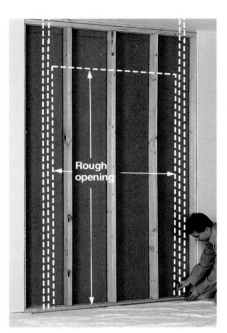

**2** Measure and mark the rough opening width on the sole plate. Mark the locations of the jack studs and king studs on the sole plate. (Where practical, use existing studs as king studs.)

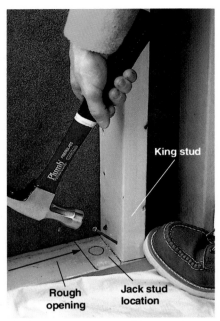

**3** Measure and cut king studs to fit between the sole plate and top plate. Position the king studs and toenail them to the sole plate with 10d nails.

**4** Check the king studs with a level to make sure they are plumb, then toenail them to the top plate with 10d nails.

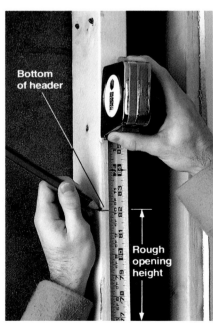

**5** Measuring from the floor, mark the rough opening height on one king stud. For most doors, the recommended rough opening is 1/2" greater than the height of the door jamb. This line marks the bottom of the door header.

**6** Measure and mark where the top of the header will fit against a king stud. Header size depends on the distance between the king studs (page 82). Use a level to extend the lines across the intermediate studs to the opposite king stud.

138

**7** Cut two jack studs to reach from the top of the sole plate to the rough opening marks on the king studs. Nail the jack studs to the king studs with 10d nails driven every 12". **Make temporary supports** (pages 120 to 123) if wall is load-bearing and you are removing more than one stud.

**8** Use a circular saw set to maximum blade depth to cut through the old studs that will be removed. The remaining stud sections will be used as cripple studs for the door frame. Do not cut king studs. Make additional cuts 3" below the first cuts, then finish the cuts with a handsaw.

**9** Knock out the 3" stud sections, then tear out the rest of the studs with a pry bar. Clip away any exposed nails, using a nippers.

**10** Build a header to fit between the king studs on top of the jack studs. Use two pieces of 2" dimension lumber sandwiched around 3/8" plywood (page 162). Attach the header to the jack studs, king studs, and cripple studs, using 10d nails.

**11** Use a reciprocating saw to cut through the sole plate next to each jack stud, then remove the sole plate with a pry bar. Cut off any exposed nails or anchors, using a nippers.

# How to Frame a Door Opening in a Balloon-framed House

**1** Prepare the project site and remove the interior wall surfaces (pages 103 to 109). Select two existing studs to use as king studs. The distance between selected studs must be at least 3" wider than the planned rough opening. Measuring from the floor, mark the rough opening height on a king stud.

**2** Measure and mark where the top of the header will fit against the king stud. Header size depends on the distance between the king studs (page 82). Use a level to extend the line across the studs to the opposite king stud.

**3** Use a reciprocating saw to cut open the subfloor between the studs, then remove any fire blocking in the stud cavities. This allows access to the sill plate when installing the jack studs. If you will be removing more than one wall stud, **make temporary supports** (pages 120 to 123).

**4** Use a circular saw to cut studs along the lines marking the top of header. Do not cut king studs. Make two additional cuts on each cut stud, 3" below the first cut and 6" above the floor. Finish cuts with a handsaw, then knock out 3" sections with a hammer. Remove the studs with a pry bar (page 139).

**5** Cut two jack studs to reach from the top of the sill plate to the rough opening mark on the king studs. Nail the jack studs to the king studs with 10d nails driven every 12".

**6** Build a header to fit between the king studs on top of the jack studs, using two pieces of 2" dimension lumber sandwiched around 3/8" plywood (page 162). Attach the header to the jack studs, king studs, and cripple studs, using 10d nails.

**7** Measure and mark the rough opening width on the header. Use a plumb bob to mark the rough opening on the sill plate (inset).

**8** Cut and install additional jack studs, as necessary, to frame the sides of the rough opening. Toenail the jack studs to the top plate and the sill plate, using 10d nails. NOTE: You may have to go to the basement to do this.

**9** Install horizontal 2 × 4 blocking, where necessary, between the studs on each side of the rough opening, using 10d nails. Blocking should be installed at the lock-set location and at the hinge locations on the new door.

**10** Remove the exterior wall surface as directed on pages 112 to 117.

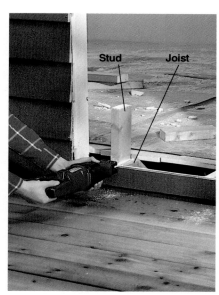

**11** Cut off the ends of the exposed studs flush with the tops of the floor joists, using a reciprocating saw or handsaw.

**12** Install 2 × 4 nailing blocks next to the jack studs and joists, flush with the tops of the floor joists (See NOTE in Step 8). Reinstall any fire-blocking that was removed. Patch the subfloor area between the jack studs with plywood to form a flat, level surface for the door threshold.

Top jamb

Side jamb

Case molding

# Installing an Interior Door

Install prehung interior doors after the framing work is completed and the wallboard has been installed (see pages 192 to 195). If the rough opening for the door has been framed accurately, installing the door takes about an hour.

Most standard prehung doors are sized to fit walls with 2 x 4 construction. If you have thicker walls, you can special-order a door to match, or you can add jamb extensions to a standard-size door (photo, below).

**Everything You Need:**

Tools: level, hammer, handsaw.

Materials: wood shims, 8d casing nails.

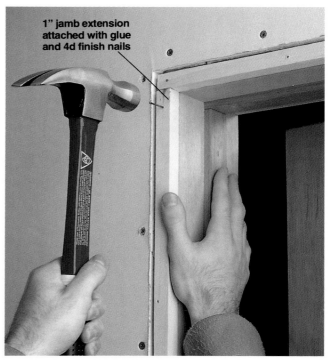

1" jamb extension attached with glue and 4d finish nails

**Standard prehung doors** have 4 9/16"-wide jambs, and are designed for 2 x 4 wall construction with 1/2" wallboard. If your walls are thicker, you will need to attach jamb extensions to the edge of the door frame. For example, if your walls are built with 2 x 6 studs, extend the jambs by attaching 3/4"-wide wood strips to the jamb edges.

## How to Install a Prehung Interior Door

**1** Slide the door unit into the framed opening so the edges of the jambs are flush with the wall surface and the hinge side jamb is plumb.

**2** Insert pairs of wood shims driven from opposite directions into the space between the framing members and the hinge side jamb, spaced every 12". Check the hinge-side jamb to make sure it is still plumb and does not bow.

**3** Anchor the hinge-side jamb with 8d casing nails driven through the jamb and shims and into the jack stud.

**4** Insert pairs of shims in the space between the framing members and the latch-side jamb and top jamb, spaced every 12". With the door closed, adjust the shims so the gap between door edge and jamb is 1/8" wide. Drive casing nails through the jambs and shims and into the framing members.

**5** Cut off the shims flush with the wall surface, using a handsaw. Hold the saw vertically to prevent damage to the door jamb or wall. Finish the door and install the lockset as directed by the manufacturer. See pages 192 to 195 and 200 to 201 to finish the walls and trim the door.

# Installing an Entry Door

Prehung entry doors come in many styles, but all are installed using the same basic methods. Because entry doors are very heavy—some large units weigh several hundred pounds—make sure you have help before beginning installation.

To speed your work, do the indoor surface removal and framing work in advance. Before installing the door, make sure you have purchased all necessary locksets and hardware. After installation, protect your door against the weather by painting or staining it immediately, and by adding a storm door (pages 148 to 149) as soon as possible.

## Everything You Need:

Tools: metal snips, hammer, level, pencil, circular saw, wood chisel, nail set, caulk gun.

Materials: building paper, drip edge, wood shims, fiberglass insulation, 10d casing nails, silicone caulk.

## How to Install an Entry Door

**1** Remove the door unit from its packing. Do not remove the retaining brackets that hold the door closed. Remove the exterior surface material inside the framed opening as directed on pages 112 to 117.

**2** Test-fit the door unit, centering it in the rough opening. Check to make sure door is plumb. If necessary, shim under the lower side jamb until the door is plumb and level.

Brick molding

**3** Trace outline of brick molding on siding. NOTE: If you have vinyl or metal siding, enlarge the outline to make room for the extra trim moldings required by these sidings. Remove the door unit after finishing the outline.

**4** Cut the siding along the outline, just down to the sheathing, using a circular saw. Stop just short of the corners to prevent damage to the siding that will remain.

**5** Finish the cuts at the corners with a sharp wood chisel.

**6** Cut 8"-wide strips of building paper and slide them between the siding and sheathing at the top and sides of the opening, to shield framing members from moisture. Bend paper around the framing members and staple it in place.

Drip edge

**7** To provide an added moisture barrier, cut a piece of drip edge to fit the width of the rough opening, then slide between the siding and the building paper at the top of the opening. Do not nail the drip edge.

**8** Apply several thick beads of silicone caulk to the subfloor at the bottom of the door opening. Also apply silicone caulk over the building paper on the front edges of the jack studs and header.

(continued next page)

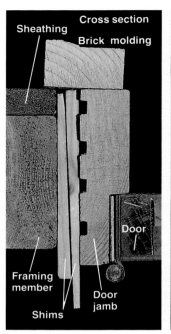

**9** Center the door unit in the rough opening, and push the brick molding tight against the sheathing. Have a helper hold the door unit in place until it is nailed in place.

**10** From inside, place pairs of hardwood wedge shims together to form flat shims (inset), and insert shims into the gaps between the door jambs and framing members. Insert shims at the lockset and hinge locations, and every 12" thereafter.

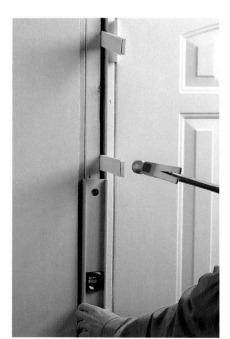

**11** Make sure the door unit is plumb. Adjust the shims, if necessary, until the door is plumb and level. Fill the gaps between the jambs and the framing members with loosely packed fiberglass insulation.

**12** From outside, drive 10d casing nails through the door jambs and into the framing members at each shim location. Use a nail set to drive the nail heads below the surface of the wood.

**13** Remove the retaining brackets installed by the manufacturer, then open and close the door to make sure it works properly.

**14** Remove two of the screws on the top hinge and replace them with long anchor screws (usually included with the unit). These anchor screws will penetrate into the framing members to strengthen the installation.

**15** Anchor brick molding to the framing members with 10d galvanized casing nails driven every 12". Use a nail set to drive the nail heads below the surface of the wood.

**16** Adjust the door threshold to create a tight seal, following manufacturer's recommendations.

**17** Cut off the shims flush with the framing members, using a handsaw.

**18** Apply silicone caulk around the entire door unit. Fill nail holes with caulk. Finish the door and install the lockset as directed by the manufacturer. See pages 192 to 195 and 200 to 201 to finish the walls and trim the interior of the door.

# Installing a Storm Door

Install a storm door to improve the appearance and weather-resistance of an old entry door, or to protect a newly installed door against weathering. In all climates, adding a storm door can extend the life of an entry door by years.

When buying a storm door, look for models that have a solid inner core and seamless outer shell construction. Carefully note the dimensions of your door opening, measuring from the inside edges of the entry door's brick molding. Choose a storm door that opens from the same side as your entry door.

**Everything You Need:**

Tools: tape measure, pencil, plumb bob, hacksaw, hammer, drill and bits, screwdrivers.

Materials: storm door unit, wood spacer strips, 4d casing nails.

**Adjustable sweeps** help make storm doors weathertight. Before installing the door, attach the sweep to the bottom of the door. After the door is mounted, adjust the height of the sweep so it brushes the top of the sill lightly when the door is closed.

## How To Cut a Storm Door Frame to Fit a Door Opening

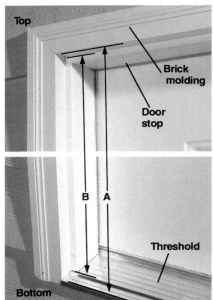

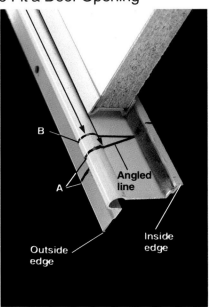

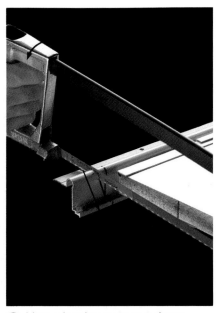

**1** Because entry door thresholds are slanted, the bottom of the storm door frame needs to be cut to match the threshold angle. First, measure from the threshold to the top of the door opening along the corner of the brick molding (A), and along the front edge of entry door stop (B).

**2** Subtract 1/8" from measurements A and B to allow for small adjustments when the door is installed. Measuring from the top of the storm door frame, mark adjusted points A and B on the corner bead. Draw a line from point A to outside edge of frame and from point B to inside edge. Draw an angled line from point A on corner bead to point B on the inside edge.

**3** Use a hacksaw to cut down through the bottom of the storm door frame, following the angled line. Make sure to hold the hacksaw at the same slant as the angled line to ensure that the the cut will be smooth and straight.

## How to Fit & Install a Storm Door

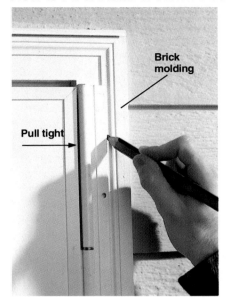

**1** Position the storm door in the opening and pull the frame tight against the brick molding on the hinge side of the storm door, then draw a reference line onto the brick molding, following the edge of the storm door frame.

**2** Push the storm door tight against the brick molding on the latch side, then measure the gap between the reference line and the hinge side of the door frame. If the distance is greater than 3/8", then spacer strips must be installed to ensure the door will fit snugly.

**3** To install spacers, remove the door then nail thin strips of wood to the inside of the brick molding at storm door hinge locations. The thickness of the wood strips should be 1/8" less than the gap measured in step 5.

**4** Replace the storm door and push it tightly against the brick molding on the hinge side. Drill pilot holes through the hinge side frame of the storm door and into the brick molding, then attach the frame with mounting screws spaced every 12".

**5** Remove any spacer clips holding the frame to the storm door. With the storm door closed, drill pilot holes and attach the latch side frame to the brick molding. Use a coin to keep an even gap between the storm door and the storm door frame.

**6** Center the top piece of the storm door frame on top of the frame sides. Drill pilot holes and screw the top piece to the brick molding. Adjust the bottom sweep, then attach locks and latch hardware as directed by the manufacturer.

## Framing & Installing Doors
# Installing a Patio Door

For easy installation, buy a patio door with the door panels already mounted in preassembled frames. Avoid patio doors sold with frame kits that require complicated assembly.

Because patio doors have very long bottom sills and top jambs, they are susceptible to bowing and warping. To avoid these problems, be very careful to install the patio door so it is level and plumb, and to anchor the unit securely to framing members. Yearly caulking and touch-up painting helps prevent moisture from warping the jambs.

### Everything You Need:

Tools: pencil, hammer, circular saw, wood chisel, stapler, caulk gun, pry bar, level, cordless screwdriver, handsaw, drill and bits.

Materials: shims, drip edge, building paper, silicone caulk, 10d casing nails, 3" wood screw, sill nosing.

### Patio Door Accessory

**Screen doors,** if not included with the unit, can be ordered from most patio door manufacturers. Screen doors have spring-mounted rollers that fit into a narrow track on the outside of the patio door threshold.

## Installation Tips

**Heavy glass panels may be removed** if you must install the door without help. Reinstall the panels after the frame has been placed in the rough opening and nailed at opposite corners. To remove and install the panels, remove the stop rail, found on the top jamb of the door unit.

**Adjust the bottom rollers** after installation is complete. Remove the coverplate on the adjusting screw, found on the inside edge of the bottom rail. Turn the screw in small increments until the door rolls smoothly along the track without binding when it is opened and closed.

## Tips for Installing French-style Patio Doors

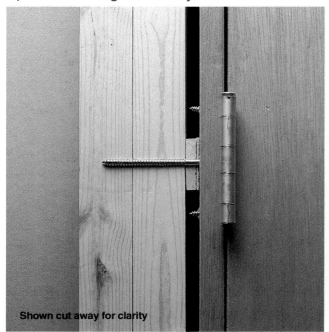

Shown cut away for clarity

**Provide extra support for door hinges** by replacing the center mounting screw on each hinge with a 3" wood screw. These long screws extend through the side jambs and deep into the framing members.

**Keep a uniform 1/8" gap** between the door and the side jambs and top jamb to ensure that the door will swing freely without binding. Check this gap frequently as you shim around the door unit.

## How to Install a Patio Door

**1** Prepare the work area and remove the interior wall surfaces (pages 103 to 109), then frame the rough opening for the patio door (pages 136 to 141). Remove the exterior surfaces inside the framed opening (pages 112 to 115).

**2** Test-fit the door unit, centering it in the rough opening. Check to make sure door is plumb. If necessary, shim under the lower side jamb until the door is plumb and level. Have a helper hold the door in place while it is unattached.

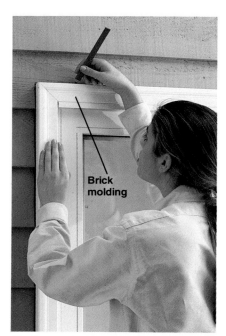

**3** Trace the outline of the brick molding onto the siding, then remove the door unit. NOTE: If you have vinyl or metal siding, enlarge the outline to make room for the extra trim moldings required by these sidings.

Brick molding

**4** Cut the siding along the out-line, just down to the sheath-ing, using a circular saw. Stop just short of the corners to pre-vent damage to the siding that will remain. Finish the cuts at the corners with a sharp wood chisel.

**5** To provide an added moisture barrier, cut a piece of drip edge to fit the width of the rough opening, then slide it between the siding and the existing building paper at the top of the opening. Do not nail the drip edge.

Drip edge

**6** Cut 8"-wide strips of building paper and slide them between the siding and the sheathing. Bend the paper around the framing members and staple it in place.

**7** Apply several thick beads of silicone caulk to the subfloor at the bottom of the door opening.

**8** Apply silicone caulk around the front edge of the framing members, where the siding meets the building paper.

**9** Center the patio door unit in the rough opening so the brick molding is tight against the sheathing. Have a helper hold the door unit from outside until it is shimmed and nailed in place.

**10** Check the door threshold to make sure it is level. If necessary, shim under the lower side jamb until the patio door unit is level.

(continued next page)

**11** If there are gaps between the threshold and subfloor, insert shims coated with caulk into the gaps, spaced every 6". Shims should be snug, but not so tight that they cause the threshold to bow. Clear off excess caulk immediately.

**12** Place pairs of hardwood wedge shims together to form flat shims. Insert the shims into the gaps between the side jambs and the jack studs, spaced every 12". For sliding doors, shim behind the strike plate for the door latch.

**13** Insert shims into the gap between the top jamb and the header, spaced every 12".

**14** From outside, drive 10d casing nails, spaced every 12", through the brick molding and into the framing members. Use a nail set to drive the nail heads below the surface of the wood.

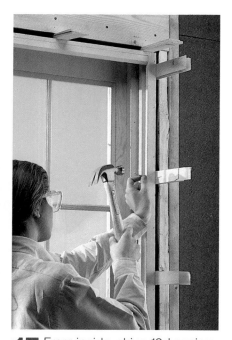

**15** From inside, drive 10d casing nails through the door jambs and into the framing members at each shim location. Use a nail set to drive the nail heads below the surface of the wood.

**16** Remove one of the screws on the stop block found in the center of the threshold. Replace the screw with a 3" wood screw driven into the subfloor as an anchor.

**17** Cut off the shims flush with the face of the framing members, using a handsaw. Fill gaps around the door jambs and beneath the threshold with loosely packed fiberglass insulation.

Sill nosing

**18** Reinforce and seal the edge of the threshold by installing sill nosing under the threshold and against the wall. Drill pilot holes and attach the sill nosing with 10d casing nails.

**19** Make sure the drip edge is tight against the top brick molding, then apply silicone caulk along the top of the drip edge and along the outside edge of the side brick moldings. Fill all exterior nail holes with silicone caulk.

**20** Caulk completely around the sill nosing, using your finger to press the caulk into cracks. As soon as the caulk is dry, paint the sill nosing. Finish the door and install the lockset as directed by the manufacturer. See pages 192 to 195 and 200 to 201 to finish the walls and trim the interior of the door.

# Cutting Off an Interior Door

Prehung interior doors are sized to allow a ¾-inch gap between the bottom of the door and the floor. This gap lets the door swing without binding on the carpet or floorcovering. If thicker carpeting or a larger threshold is installed, a small portion of the door may need to be cut off with a circular saw.

Wider cuts may be needed if a door is altered to fit a special installation, like in a child's room or an undersized storage closet.

Hollow-core interior doors have a solid wood frame, with centers that are hollow. If the entire bottom frame member is cut away when shortening the door, it can be reinserted to close the hollow door cavity.

**Before You Start:**
Tools & Materials: tape measure, hammer, screwdriver, utility knife, sawhorses, circular saw and straightedge, chisel, carpenter's glue, clamps.

Tip: Measure carefully when marking a door for cutting. Measure from the top of the carpeting, not from the floor.

## How to Cut Off an Interior Door

**1** With door in place, measure ⅜'' up from top of floorcovering and mark door. Remove door from the hinges by removing the hinge pins.

156

**2** Mark cutting line. Cut through door veneer with sharp utility knife to prevent it from chipping when the door is sawed.

**3** Lay door on sawhorses. Clamp a straightedge to the door as a cutting guide.

**4** Saw off bottom of the door. The hollow core of the door may be exposed.

**5** To replace a cut-off frame in the bottom of the door, chisel the veneer from both sides of the re-moved portion.

**6** Apply wood glue to cut-off frame. Insert frame into opening, and clamp. Wipe away excess glue and let dry overnight.

# Installing a Security Lock

How to Install a Security Lock

Security locks have long bolts that extend into the door jamb. They are also called deadbolts. The bolt of a security lock is moved in and out by a keyed mechanism.

Security locks help stop possible break-ins. Often home insurance rates can be lowered with the installation of security locks on exterior doors.

### Before You Start:

Tools & Materials: tape measure, security lock (deadbolt), lockset drill kit (including hole saw and spade bit), drill, chisel.

Tip: A double-cylinder deadbolt lock has a key on both sides, and is the best choice for doors that have windows. Knob-type deadbolts can be opened by reaching through broken glass.

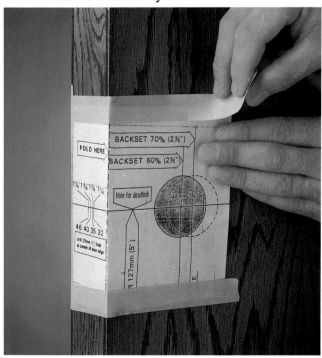

**1** Measure to find lock location. Tape cardboard template, supplied with lockset, onto door. Use a nail or awl to mark centerpoints of cylinder and latch-bolt holes on door.

158

**2** Bore cylinder hole with a hole saw and drill. To avoid splintering door, drill through one side until hole saw pilot (mandrel) just comes out other side. Remove hole saw, then complete hole from opposite side of door.

**3** Use a spade bit and drill to bore latchbolt hole from edge of door into the cylinder hole. Make sure to keep drill perpendicular to door edge while drilling.

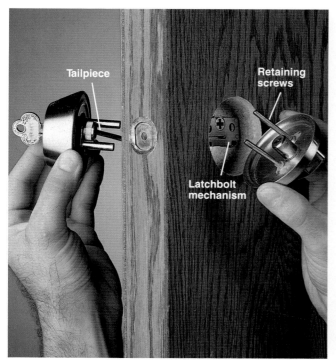

**4** Insert latchbolt into edge hole. Insert lock tailpiece and connecting screws through the latchbolt mechanism, and screw the cylinders together. Close door to find point where latchbolt meets door jamb.

**5** Cut a mortise for strike plate with a chisel (pages 42 to 43). Bore latchbolt hole in center of mortise with spade bit. Install strike plate, using retaining screws provided with lockset.

Header

Angled stud

Jambs

Shims

Double rough sill

Cripple studs

Insulation

Jack stud

King stud

# Framing & Installing Windows

Most good windows must be custom-ordered several weeks in advance. To save time, do the interior framing work before the window unit arrives. But never open the outside wall surface until you have the window and accessories, and are ready to install them.

Follow the manufacturer's specifications for rough opening size when framing for a window. The listed opening usually is 1" wider and 1/2" higher than the actual dimension of the window unit.

This section shows:
- Framing a window opening (pages 161 to 163)
- Installing a window (pages 164 to 167)
- Installing a bay window (pages 168 to 177)
- Framing & installing a skylight (pages 178 to 187)

The following pages show techniques for wood-frame houses with siding. If your home's exterior is stucco or masonry, see pages 114 to 117 for more information. If your house has balloon framing (page 79), use the method shown on page 140 (steps 1 to 6) to install a header.

If you have masonry walls, or if you are installing polymer-coated windows, you may want to attach your window using masonry clips instead of nails (page 167).

## Everything You Need:

Tools: tape measure, pencil, combination square, hammer, level, circular saw, handsaw, pry bar, nippers, drill and bits, reciprocating saw, stapler, nail set, caulk gun.

Materials: 10d nails, 2" dimension lumber, 3/8" plywood, shims, building paper, drip edge, casing nails (16d, 8d), fiberglass insulation, silicone caulk.

# How to Frame a Window Opening

**1** Prepare the project site and remove the interior wall surfaces (pages 103 to 109). Measure and mark rough opening width on sole plate. Mark the locations of the jack studs and king studs on sole plate. Where practical, use existing studs as king studs.

**2** Measure and cut king studs, as needed, to fit between the sole plate and top plate. Position the king studs and toenail them to the sole plate with 10d nails.

**3** Check the king studs with a level to make sure they are plumb, then toenail them to the top plate with 10d nails.

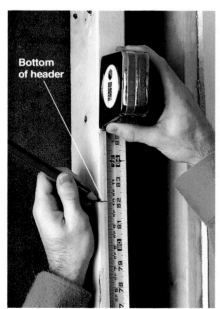

Bottom of header

**4** Measuring from the floor, mark the rough opening height on one of the king studs. For most windows, the recommended rough opening is 1/2" taller than the height of the window frame. This line marks the bottom of the window header.

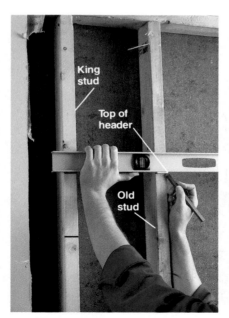

King stud

Top of header

Old stud

**5** Measure and mark where the top of the window header will fit against the king stud. The header size depends on the distance between the king studs (page 82). Use a carpenter's level to extend the lines across the old studs to the opposite king stud.

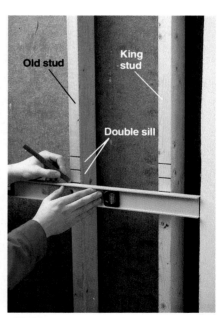

Old stud

King stud

Double sill

**6** Measure down from header line and outline the double rough sill on the king stud. Use a carpenter's level to extend the lines across the old studs to the opposite king stud. **Make temporary supports** (pages 120 to 123) if you will be removing more than one stud.

(continued next page)

# How to Frame a Window Opening (continued)

**7** Use a circular saw set to maximum blade depth to cut through the old studs along the lines marking the bottom of the rough sill, and along the lines marking the top of the header. Do not cut the king studs. On each stud, make an additional cut about 3" above the first cut. Finish the cuts with a handsaw.

**8** Knock out the 3" stud sections, then tear out the old studs inside the rough opening, using a pry bar. Clip away any exposed nails, using a nippers. The remaining sections of the cut studs will serve as cripple studs for the window.

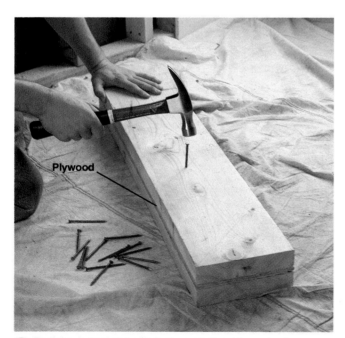

**9** Build a header to fit between the king studs on top of the jack studs, using two pieces of 2" dimension lumber sandwiched around 3/8" plywood.

**10** Cut two jack studs to reach from the top of the sole plate to the bottom header lines on the king studs. Nail the jack studs to the king studs with 10d nails driven every 12". NOTE: On a balloon-frame house the jack studs will reach to the sill plate, or only to the subfloor, if you are working on the second story (page 137).

162

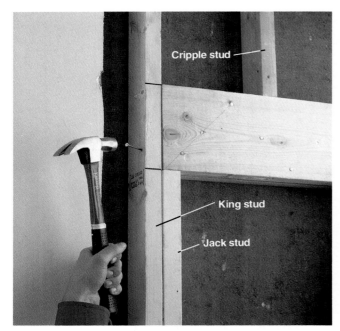

**11** Position the header on the jack studs, using a hammer if necessary. Attach the header to the king studs, jack studs, and cripple studs, using 10d nails.

**12** Build the rough sill to reach between the jack studs by nailing a pair of 2 × 4s together. Position the rough sill on the cripple studs, and nail it to the jack studs and cripple studs with 10d nails.

## Variations for Round-top Windows

**Create a template** to help you mark the rough opening on the sheathing. Scribe the outline of the curved frame on cardboard, allowing an extra 1/2" for adjustments within the rough opening. A 1/4" × 1 1/4" metal washer makes a good spacer for scribing the outline. Cut out the template along the scribed line.

**Tape the template to the sheathing,** with the top flush against the header. Use the template as a guide for attaching diagonal framing members across the top corners of the framed opening. The diagonal members should just touch the template. Outline the template on the sheathing as a guide for cutting the rough opening (page 112).

## How to Install a Window

**1** Remove the exterior wall surface as directed on pages 112 to 117, then test-fit the window, centering it in the rough opening. Support the window with wood blocks and shims placed under the bottom jamb. Check to make sure the window is plumb and level, and adjust the shims, if necessary.

**2** Trace the outline of the brick molding on the siding. NOTE: If you have vinyl or metal siding, enlarge the outline to make room for the extra J-channel moldings required by these sidings (page 189). Remove the window after finishing the outline.

**3** Cut the siding along the outline just down to the sheathing. For a round-top window, use a recipro-cating saw held at a shallow angle. For straight cuts, you can use a circular saw adjusted so blade depth equals the thickness of the siding, then use a sharp chisel to complete the cuts at the corners (page 145).

**4** Cut 8"-wide strips of building paper and slide them between the siding and sheathing around the entire window opening. Bend the paper around the framing members and staple it in place.

**5** Cut a length of drip edge to fit over the top of the window, then slide it between the siding and building paper. For round-top windows, use flexible vinyl drip edge; for rectangular windows, use rigid metal drip edge (inset).

**6** Insert the window in the opening, and push the brick molding tight against the sheathing.

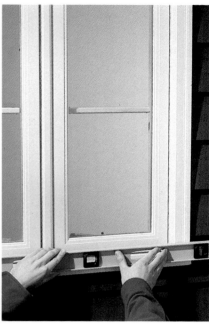

**7** Check to make sure the window is level.

**8** If the window is perfectly level, nail both bottom corners of the brick molding with 10d casing nails. If window is not perfectly level, nail only at the higher of the two bottom corners.

**9** If necessary, have a helper adjust the shim under the low corner of the window from the inside, until the window is level.

**10** From outside, drive 10d casing nails through the brick molding and into the framing members near the remaining corners of the window.

(continued next page)

**11** Place pairs of shims together to form flat shims. From inside, insert shims into the gaps between the jambs and framing members, spaced every 12". On round-top windows, also shim between the angled braces and curved jamb.

**12** Adjust the shims so they are snug, but not so tight that they cause the jambs to bow. On multiple-unit windows, make sure the shims under the mull posts are tight.

**13** Use a straightedge to check the side jambs to make sure they do not bow. Adjust the shims, if necessary, until the jambs are flat. Open and close the window to make sure it works properly.

**14** At each shim location, drill a pilot hole, then drive an 8d casing nail through the jamb and shims and into the framing member, being careful not to damage the window. Drive the nail heads below the wood surface with a nail set.

**15** Fill the gaps between the window jambs and the framing members with loosely packed fiberglass insulation. Wear work gloves when handling insulation.

Brick molding

**16** Trim the shims flush with the framing members, using a handsaw.

**17** From outside, drive 10d galvanized casing nails, spaced every 12", through the brick moldings and into the framing members. Drive all nail heads below the wood surface with a nail set.

**18** Apply silicone caulk around the entire window unit. Fill nail holes with caulk. See pages 118 to 123 to finish the walls and trim the interior of the window.

## Installation Variation: Masonry Clips

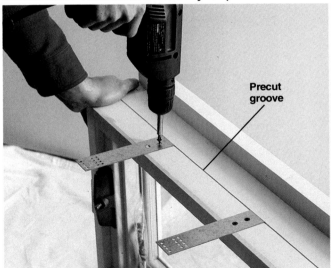

Precut groove

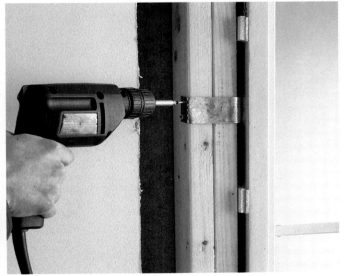

**Use metal masonry clips** when the brick molding on a window cannot be nailed because it rests against a masonry or brick surface. The masonry clips hook into precut grooves in the window jambs (above, left), and are attached to the jambs with utility screws. After the window unit is positioned in the rough opening, the masonry clips are bent around the framing members and anchored with

utility screws (above, right). NOTE: masonry clips also can be used in ordinary lap siding installations if you want to avoid making nail holes in the smooth surface of the brick moldings. For example, windows that are precoated with polymer-based paint can be installed with masonry clips so that the brick moldings are not punctured with nails.

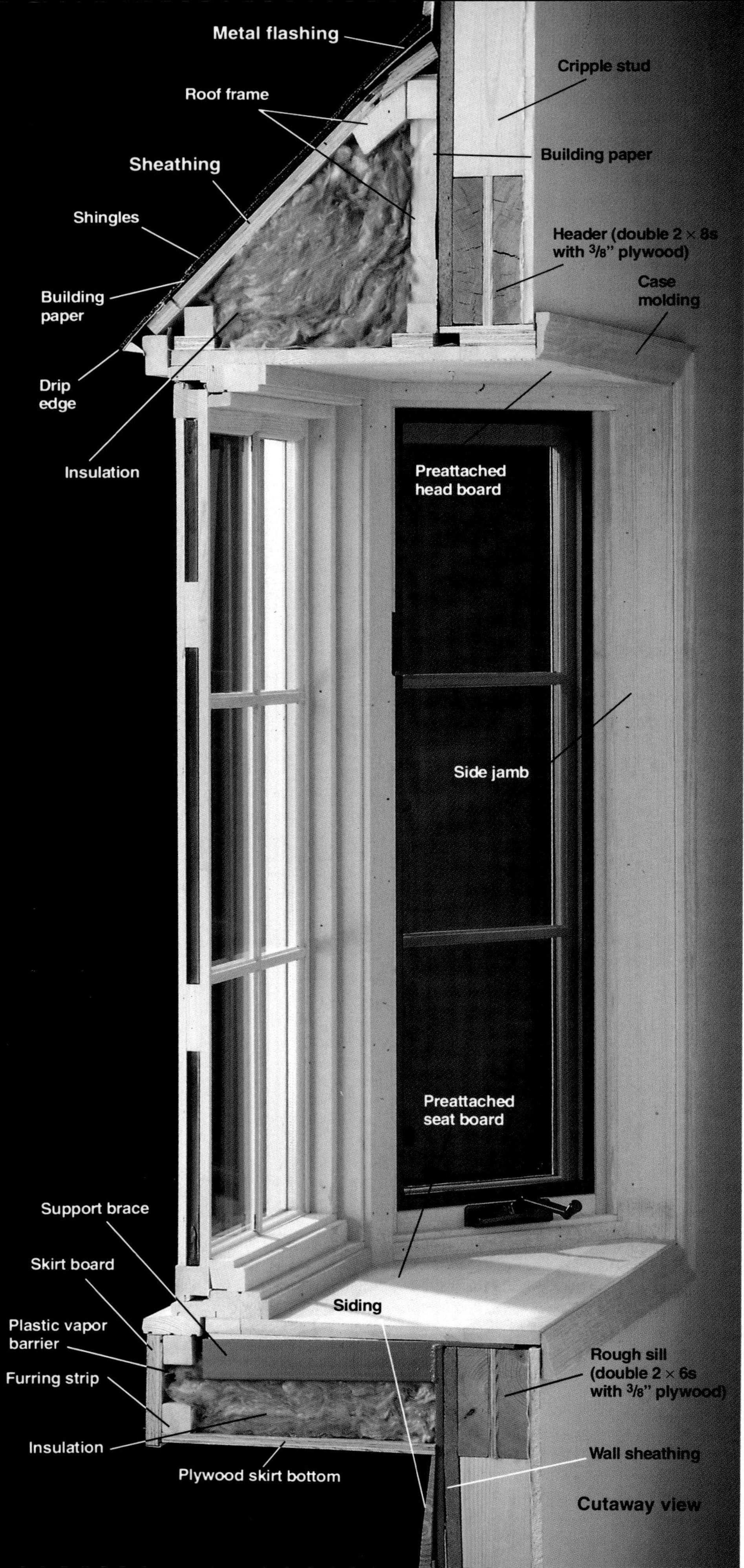

Metal flashing

Roof frame

Sheathing

Shingles

Building
paper

Drip
edge

Insulation

Cripple stud

Building paper

Header (double 2 × 8s
with 3/8" plywood)

Case
molding

Preattached
head board

Side jamb

Preattached
seat board

Support brace

Skirt board

Plastic vapor
barrier

Furring strip

Insulation

Plywood skirt bottom

Siding

Rough sill
(double 2 × 6s
with 3/8" plywood)

Wall sheathing

Cutaway view

# Installing a Bay Window

Modern bay windows are pre-assembled for easy installation, but you should still plan on several days to complete the work. Bay windows are large and heavy, and installing them requires special techniques. Have at least one helper to assist you, and try to schedule the work when the chance of rain is small. Use prebuilt bay window accessories (page opposite) to speed your work.

A large bay window can weigh several hundred pounds, so it must be anchored securely to framing members in the wall, and supported by braces attached to framing members below the window. Some window manufacturers include cable-support hardware that can be used instead of metal support braces.

## Everything You Need:

Tools: circular saw, caulk gun, hammer, screw gun, framing square, tape measure, level, screwdriver, chisel, stapler, metal snips, roofing knife, T-bevel, utility knife.

Materials: bay window, pre-built roof skirt, metal support brackets, galvanized utility screws (2", 2 1/2", 3"), building paper, sheet plastic, fiberglass insulation, 2 × 2 lumber, 5 1/2" skirt board, 3/4" exterior-grade plywood, shingles, roofing cement, wood shims, galvanized casing nails (16d, 8d), silicone caulk.

## Prebuilt Accessories for Bay Windows

**For easy installation,** use prebuilt accessories when installing a bay window. Roof frames (A) come complete with sheathing (B), metal top flashing (C) and step flashing (D) and can be special-ordered at home centers that sell bay windows. You will need to specify the exact size of your window unit, and the angle (pitch) you want for the roof. You can cover the roof inexpensively with building paper and shingles, or order a copper or aluminum shell from your home center. Metal support braces (E) and skirt boards (F) can be ordered at your home center if they are not included with the window unit. Use two braces for bay windows up to 5 ft. wide, and three braces for larger windows. Skirt boards are clad with aluminum or vinyl, and can be cut to fit with a circular saw or power miter saw.

## Framing a Bay Window

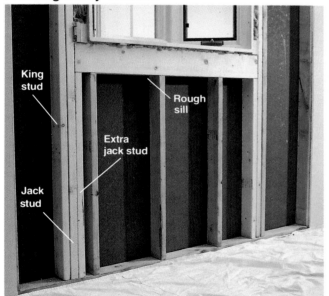

**Bay window framing** resembles that for a standard window, except that it requires an extra-strong rough sill built from a pair of 2 × 6s sandwiched around a layer of 3/8" plywood (page 162). Because the sill carries considerable weight, extra jack studs are installed under each end of the sill. See pages 160 to 163 for basic window framing techniques.

## Roof Framing Variation

**Build an enclosure** above the bay window if the roof soffit overhangs the window. Build a 2 × 2 frame (top) to match the angles of the bay window, and attach the frame securely to the wall and overhanging soffit. Install a vapor barrier and insulation (page 173), then finish the enclosure so it matches the house siding (bottom).

169

# How to Install a Bay Window

**1** Prepare project site and remove interior wall surfaces (pages 103 to 109), then frame rough opening (pages 161 to 163). Remove exterior wall surface as directed on pages 112 to 117. Mark a section of siding directly below rough opening for removal. Width of marked area should equal that of window unit, and height should equal that of skirt board.

**2** Set the blade on a circular saw just deep enough to cut through the siding, then cut along the outline. Stop just short of the corners to avoid damaging the siding outside the outline. Use a sharp chisel to complete the corner cuts (page 145). Remove the cut siding inside the outline.

**3** Position the support braces along the rough sill within the widest part of the bay window and above the cripple stud locations. Add cripple studs to match support brace locations if necessary. Draw outlines of the braces on the top of the sill. Use a chisel or circular saw to notch the sill to a depth equal to the thickness of the support braces.

**4** Slide the support braces down between the siding and the sheathing. You may need to pry the siding material away from the sheathing slightly to make room for the braces. NOTE: On stucco, you will need to chisel notches in masonry wall surface to fit the support braces.

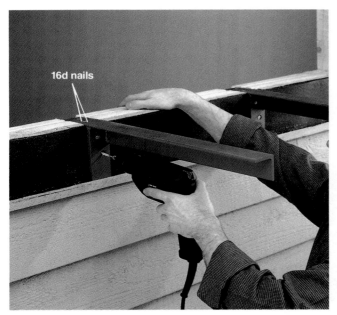

**5** Attach the braces to the rough sill with galvanized 16d nails. Drive 3" utility screws through the front of the braces and into the rough sill to prevent twisting.

**6** Lift the bay window onto the support braces and slide it into the rough opening  Center the window in the opening.

**7** Check the window unit to make sure it is level. If necessary, drive shims under the low side to level the window. Temporarily brace the outside bottom edge of the window with 2 × 4s to keep it from moving on the braces.

**8** Set the roof frame on top of the window, with sheathing loosely tacked in place. Trace the outline of the window and roof unit onto the siding. Leave a gap of about 1/2" around the roof unit to allow room for the flashing and shingles.

**9** Mark and cut wood blocks to bridge the gap between side jambs and studs, if gap is more than 1" wide. (Smaller gaps require no blocks.) Leave a small space for inserting wood shims. Remove the window, then attach blocks every 12" along the studs.

(continued next page)

**10** Cut the siding just down to the sheathing along the outline, using a circular saw. Stop just short of corners, then use a wood chisel to complete the corner cuts. Remove cut siding. Pry remaining siding slightly away from the sheathing around the roof outline to allow for easy installation of the metal flashing. Cover the exposed sheathing with 8"-wide strips of building paper (see step 4, page 164).

**11** Set the bay window unit back on the braces and slide it back into the rough opening until the brick moldings are tight against the sheathing. Insert wood shims between the outside end of the metal braces and the seat board (inset). Check the window to make sure it is level, and adjust the shims if necessary.

**12** Anchor the window by driving 16d galvanized casing nails through the outside brick molding and into the framing members. Space the nails every 12", and use a nail set to drive the nail heads below the surface of the wood.

**13** Drive wood shims into the spaces between the side jambs and the blocking or jack studs, and between the headboard and header. Space the shims every 12". Fill the spaces around the window with loosely packed fiberglass insulation. At each shim location, drive 16d casing nails through the jambs and shims and into the framing members. Cut off the shims flush with the framing members, using a handsaw. Use a nail set to drive the nail heads below the surface of the wood.

**14** Staple sheet plastic over the top of the window unit to serve as a vapor barrier. Trim the edges of the plastic around the top of the window with a utility knife.

**15** Remove the sheathing pieces from the roof frame, then position the frame on top of the window unit. Attach the roof frame to the window and to the wall at stud locations, using 3" utility screws.

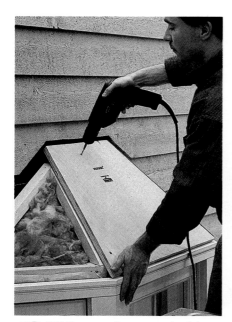

**16** Fill the empty space inside the roof frame with loosely packed fiberglass insulation. Screw the sheathing back onto the roof frame.

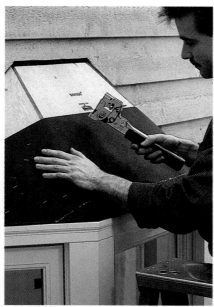

**17** Staple asphalt building paper over the roof sheathing. Make sure each piece overlaps the one below by at least 5".

**18** Cut drip edges with metal snips, then attach them around the edge of the roof sheathing, using roofing nails.

(continued next page)

**19** Cut and fit a piece of step flashing on each side of the roof unit. Adjust the flashing so it overhangs the drip edge by 1/4". Flashings help guard against moisture damage.

**20** Trim the end of the flashing to the same angle as the drip edge. Nail flashing to the sheathing with roofing nails.

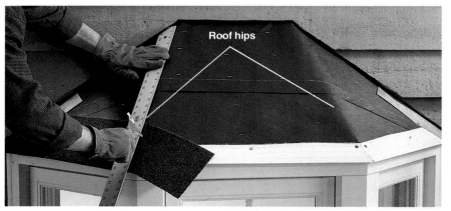

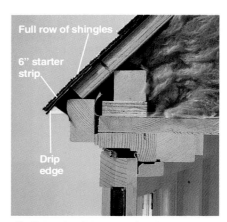

**21** Cut a 6"-wide strip of shingles for the starter row. Use roofing nails to attach the starter row so it overhangs the drip edge by about 1/2" (photo, right). Cut the shingles along the roof hips with a straightedge and roofing knife.

**22** Nail a full row of shingles over the starter row. Bottom edges should be flush with bottom of the starter row, and notches should not be aligned.

**23** Install another piece of step flashing on each side of the roof, overlapping the first piece of flashing by about 5".

**24** Cut and install another row of full shingles. Bottom edges should overlap the tops of the notches on previous row by 1/2". Attach the shingles with roofing nails driven just above the notches.

**25** Continue installing alternate rows of step flashing and shingles to top of roof. Bend the last pieces of step flashing to fit over the roof hips.

**26** When roof sheathing is covered with shingles, install top flashing. Cut and bend the ends over the roof hips, and attach with roofing nails. Attach remaining rows of shingles over the top flashing.

**27** Find the height of final rows of shingles by measuring from the top of the roof to a point 1/2" below the top of the notches on the last installed shingle. Trim shingles to this measurement.

**28** Attach the final row of shingles with a thick bead of roofing cement, not nails. Press firmly to ensure a good bond.

**29** Make ridge caps by cutting shingles into 1-ft. sections. Use a roofing knife to trim off the top corners of each piece, so ridge caps will be narrower at the top than at the bottom.

**30** Install the ridge caps over the roof hips, beginning at the bottom of the roof. Trim the bottom ridge caps to match the edges of the roof. Keep the same amount of overlap with each layer.

(continued next page)

**31** At the top of the roof hips, use a roofing knife to cut the shingles to fit flush with the wall. Attach the shingles with roofing cement. Do not nail.

**32** Staple sheet plastic over the bottom of the window to serve as a vapor barrier. Trim plastic around the bottom of the window with a utility knife.

**33** Cut and attach a 2 × 2 skirt frame around the bottom of the bay window, using 3" galvanized utility screws. The skirt frame should be set back about 1" from the edges of the window.

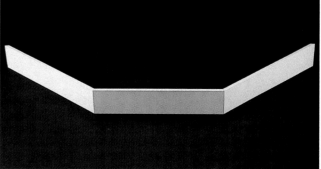

**34** Cut skirt boards to match the shape of the bay window bottom, mitering the ends to ensure a tight fit. Test-fit the skirt board pieces to make sure they match the bay window bottom.

**35** Cut a 2 × 2 furring strip for each skirt board. Miter the ends to the same angles as the skirt boards. Attach the furring strips to the back of the skirt boards, 1" from the bottom edges, using 2" galvanized utility screws.

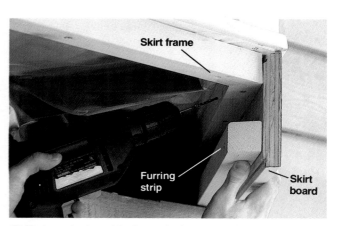

**36** Attach the skirt board pieces to the skirt frame. Drill 1/8" pilot holes every 6" through the back of the skirt frame and into the skirt boards, then attach the skirt boards with 2" galvanized utility screws.

**37** Measure the space inside the skirt boards, using a T-bevel to duplicate the angles. Cut a skirt bottom from 3/4" exterior-grade plywood to fit this space.

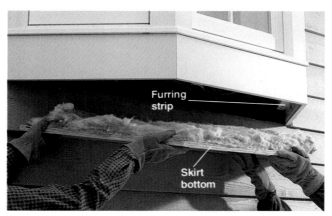

**38** Lay fiberglass insulation on the skirt bottom. Position the skirt bottom against the furring strips and attach it by driving 2" galvanized utility screws every 6" through the bottom and into the furring strips.

**39** Install any additional trim pieces specified by your window manufacturer (inset), using casing nails. Seal roof edges with roofing cement, and seal around the rest of the window with silicone caulk. Complete the inside finish work (pages 192 to 195 and 200 to 201).

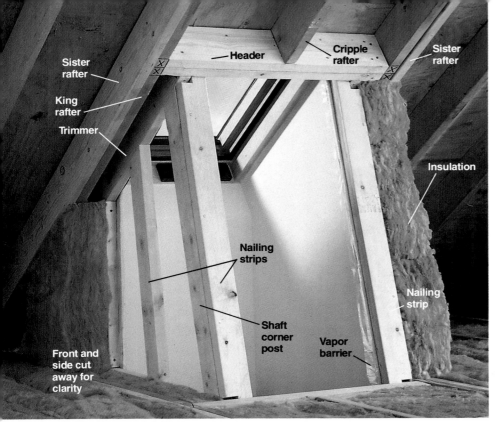

Sister rafter

King rafter

Trimmer

Header

Cripple rafter

Sister rafter

Insulation

Nailing strips

Nailing strip

Shaft corner post

Vapor barrier

Front and side cut away for clarity

**A typical skylight installation** requires a framed opening in the roof to hold the skylight, another opening in the ceiling, and a framed shaft that joins the two openings. In a home with rafter construction, one or two rafters may be cut to make room for a large skylight, as long as the openings are reinforced with double headers and "sister" framing members. The shaft is made with 2 × 4 lumber and wallboard, and includes a vapor barrier and fiberglass insulation.

Nailing flange

Step flashing

**Weatherproof your skylight** with metal flashing on all sides. Even if your window has a "self-flashing" mounting flange, it is a good idea to install additional flashings. Flashing kits, available from skylight manufacturers, include step flashings (shown above), a sill flashing to fit the bottom of the window, and a head flashing to fit the top. Sheet-metal shops can fabricate flashings according to your measurements.

# Installing a Skylight

A skylight (sometimes called a roof window) is an ideal way to provide additional light and ventilation in areas where standard windows are not practical.

Many homeowners have resisted installing skylights because older models were prone to leakage. But today's skylights, with metal-clad frames and pre-attached flashings, are extremely reliable. When installed correctly, good skylights have the same life-expectancy as windows.

If your roof is supported with trusses (page 81), choose a narrow skylight that fits between the trusses. Roof trusses should never be cut. If your roof is supported with rafters, you can safely cut and remove one or two rafters to frame the skylight opening.

Many people install skylights in direct sunlight, but in warmer climates, it is better to install them on the north side of the roof or in shaded areas.

This section includes:

- Installing a skylight (pages 180 to 183)
- Building a skylight shaft (pages 184 to 187)

**Everything You Need:**

Tools: tape measure, level, pencil, combination square, reciprocating saw, flat pry bar, miter saw, hammer, ladders, roofing jacks, stapler, roofing knife, caulk gun, metal snips, plumb bob.

Materials: 2" dimension lumber, 10d nails, building paper, roofing cement, skylight flashings, roofing nails, insulation, twine, sheet plastic.

## Skylight Shaft Options

**Straight shafts** are easy to build, and work well if you prefer soft, diffuse natural lighting. The sides of the light shaft run straight down to the framed ceiling opening.

**Angled shafts** are longer at the base, allowing a greater amount of direct sunlight into a room. An angled shaft also is more effective for directing light toward a particular area of a room.

## Installation Variations

Trusses

**No light shaft is required** for skylights in finished attics where the ceiling surface is attached directly to rafters. Install the window low enough on the roof to provide a view of the surrounding landscape.

**Install several small skylights,** instead of one large one, if your home is framed with roof trusses instead of rafters (page 81). Each skylight must fit in the space between the roof trusses. Trusses are critical to the structural strength of the roof, and should never be cut or altered.

## How to Install a Skylight

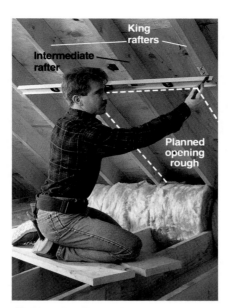

**1** Prepare the project area by removing any insulation between the joists or rafters. (In a finished attic, you will need to expose the rafters by removing the interior surfaces (pages 106 to 109).

**2** Use the first rafter on each side of the planned rough opening to serve as king rafters. Measure and mark where the double header and double sill will fit against one of the king rafters. Use a carpenter's level to extend the marks across the intermediate rafter to the opposite king rafter.

**3** Brace each intermediate rafter by nailing two 2 × 4s between the rafter and the joist below. Braces should be positioned just above the header marks and just below the sill marks.

**4** Reinforce each king rafter by attaching a full-length "sister" rafter against the outside edge, using 10d nails. Use a combination square to mark the section of intermediate rafter that will be removed. To accommodate the double header and sill, the removed section of rafter should be 6" longer than the listed rough opening height of the skylight.

**5** Remove the intermediate rafter by cutting along the marked lines, using a reciprocating saw. Make an additional cut about 3" inside the first cut, then knock out the small rafter section. Pry out the remaining section of cut rafter with a pry bar.

**6** Build a double header and double sill to reach between the king rafters, using 2" dimension lumber that is the same size as the rafters.

**Cripple rafter**

**7** Install the header and sill, anchoring them to the king rafters and cripple rafters with 10d nails. The ends of the header and sill should be aligned with the marked lines on the king rafters.

**8** Measure and mark the rough opening width on the header and sill. For some skylight sizes, this measurement will equal the distance between the king rafters. If the measurement is less than the distance between king rafters, trimmers need to be installed.

**Trimmers**

**9** Cut and install trimmers to complete the skylight frame. Inside edges of trimmers should just touch the rough opening width marks on the header and sill. Avoid installing trimmers by using rafters and joists to frame the opening whenever possible.

**10** Remove the 2 × 4 braces supporting the cripple rafters, then mark the rough opening, and cut and remove the roof section as directed on pages 118 to 119.

**11** Remove shingles around the rough opening with a flat pry bar, exposing at least 9" of building paper or sheathing on all sides of the roof opening. Remove entire shingles only; do not cut them.

(continued next page)

**12** Cut 1-ft.-wide strips of building paper and slide them between the shingles and existing building paper or sheathing. Bend the paper around the framing members and staple it in place.

**13** Spread a 5"-wide layer of roofing cement around the rough opening. Insert the skylight in the rough opening so the nailing flange rests tightly against the building paper.

**14** Nail through the nailing flange and into the framing members with 2" galvanized roofing nails spaced every 6". (NOTE: If your skylight uses L-shaped brackets instead of a nailing flange, follow the manufacturer's instructions.)

**15** Patch in shingles up to the bottom edge of the skylight. Attach the shingles with roofing nails driven just below the adhesive strip. (If necessary, cut the shingles with a roofing knife to make them fit against the bottom of the skylight.)

**16** Spread roofing cement on the bottom edge of the sill flashing, then fit the flashing around the bottom of the skylight unit. Attach the flashing by driving 3/4" galvanized nails through the vertical side flanges near the top of the flashing and into the skylight jambs.

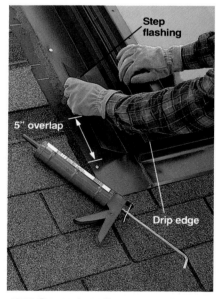

**17** Spread roofing cement on the bottom of a piece of step flashing, then slide the flashing under the drip edge on one side of the skylight. Step flashing should overlap the sill (bottom) flashing by 5". Press the step flashing down to bond it. Repeat at the opposite side of the skylight.

**18** Patch in next row of shingles on each side of the skylight, following the existing shingle pattern. Drive a roofing nail through each shingle and the step flashing, into the sheathing. Drive additional nails just above the notches in the shingles.

**19** Continue applying alternate layers of step flashing and shingles, using roofing cement and roofing nails. Each flashing should overlap the preceding flashing by 5".

**20** At the top of the skylight, cut and bend the last step flashing on each side, so the vertical flange wraps around the corner of the skylight. Patch in the next row of shingles.

**21** Spread roofing cement on the bottom of the head flashing to bond it to the roof. Position the flashing against the top of the skylight so the vertical flange fits under the skylight drip edge, and the horizontal flange fits under the shingles above the skylight.

**22** Fill in the remaining shingles, cutting them to fit, if necessary. Attach the shingles with roofing nails driven just above the notches.

**23** Apply a complete bead of roofing cement along the joint between the shingles and skylight. Remove roofing jacks and fill nail holes with roofing cement.

183

## How to Build a Skylight Shaft

**1** Remove any insulation in the area where the ceiling opening will be located. If there is electrical wiring running through the project area, shut off the power and reroute the circuit before continuing (pages 103 to 104).

**2** Using a plumb bob as a guide, mark reference points on the ceiling surface, directly below the inside corners of the skylight frame. If you are installing a straight shaft, these points will mark the corners of the ceiling opening.

**3** If the skylight shaft will be angled, measure from the plumb marks and mark the corners of the ceiling opening. Drive finish nails through the ceiling surface to mark the points.

**4** From the room below, mark lines between the finish nails, then remove the ceiling surface (pages 106 to 109).

**5** Use one joist on each side of the ceiling opening to serve as king joists. Measure and mark where the double header and double sill will fit against the king joists, and where the outside edge of the header and sill will cross any intermediate joists.

**6** If you will be removing a section of an intermediate joist, reinforce the king joists by nailing full-length "sister" joists to the outside edge of the king joists, using 10d nails.

**7** Use a combination square to extend cutting lines down the sides of the intermediate joist, then cut out the joist section with a reciprocating saw. Pry the joist loose, being careful not to damage ceiling surface.

**8** Build a double header and double sill to span the distance between the king joists, using 2" dimension lumber the same size as the joists.

(continued next page)

**9** Install the double header and double sill, anchoring them to the king joists and cripple joists with 10d nails. The inside edges of the header and sill should be aligned with the edge of the ceiling cutout.

**10** Complete the ceiling opening by cutting and attaching trimmers, if required, along the sides of the ceiling cutout between the header and sill. End-nail the trimmers to the header and sill with 10d nails.

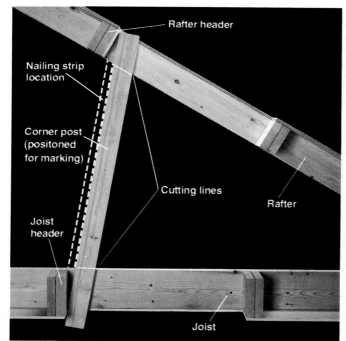

**11** Install 2 × 4 corner posts for the skylight shaft. To measure posts, begin with a 2 × 4 that is long enough to reach from the top to the bottom of the shaft. Hold the 2 × 4 against the inside of the framed openings, so it is flush with the top of the rafter header and the bottom of the joist header

(left). Mark cutting lines where the 2 × 4 meets the top of the joist or trimmer, and the bottom of the rafter or trimmer (right). Cut along the lines, then toenail the posts to the top and bottom of the frame with 10d nails.

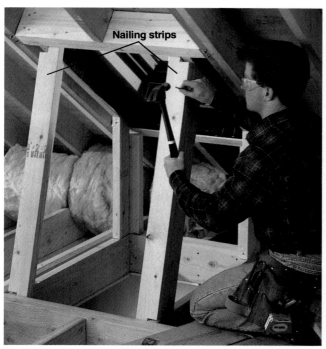

**12** Attach a 2 × 4 nailing strip to the outside edge of each corner post to provide a surface for attaching wallboard. Ends of nailing strips should be notched to fit around the trimmers, but a perfect fit is not necessary.

**13** Install additional 2 × 4 nailing strips between posts if the distances between corners posts is more than 24". The top ends of the nailing strips should be mitered to fit against the rafter trimmers.

**14** Wrap the skylight shaft with fiberglass insulation. Secure the insulation by wrapping twine or duct tape around the shaft and insulation.

**15** From inside the shaft, staple a plastic vapor barrier over the insulation.

**16** Finish the inside of the shaft using metal corner beads and wallboard (pages 192 to 195). TIP: To reflect light, paint shaft interior with light semi-gloss paint.

# Completing the Project

When finishing a remodeling project, strive to make the new work blend in with the rest of your home. A good remodeling project looks like an original part of the home design, not like an afterthought. Wherever possible, use materials and installation techniques that match those found elsewhere in the home.

Because exteriors are exposed to the rain and sun, protect these surfaces by doing the outdoor finishing work first. Patched siding and new trim should be caulked and painted as soon as possible to seal them against the weather.

If your project required one or more work permits, have the building inspector review and

approve your work before you close up walls and complete the interior finish work.

Complete all interior work on the walls, including painting or wallcovering, before you attach the trim moldings. If your floors must be patched, do not install baseboard until the patching work is done.

This section shows:

- Finishing the exterior, including exterior moldings (page 189), patching wood lap siding (page 190), and patching stucco (page 191)

- Finishing walls and ceilings (pages 192 to 195)

- Installing trim moldings (pages 200 to 201)

- Patching flooring (pages 202 to 203)

## Completing the Project
# Finishing the Exterior

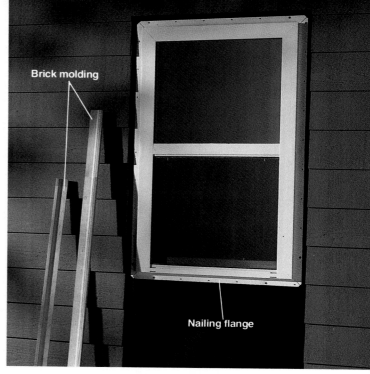

For many remodeling projects, the only exterior completion work required is painting and caulking. Some projects, however, require more work. For example, if you have replaced an old door or window with a smaller unit, you will need to patch the exposed wall area to match the surrounding siding. Windows and doors with clad frames require exterior moldings (photo, right).

To patch lap siding, bring a sample of the original siding to your home center and match it as closely as you can. If the match is not perfect, use siding from a hidden area of your house or garage to patch the project area.

To patch stucco walls (page 191), practice first on scrap materials, because duplicating stucco textures takes some skill.

**Windows and doors with clad frames** have nailing flanges that must be covered with wood or metal moldings, purchased separately. This window was installed in an old door opening, which required patching beneath the window with sheathing, building paper, and siding (see next page).

### How to Install Exterior Moldings

**1** Cut each molding piece to length, mitering the ends at 45˚. Position the molding over the window jamb and against the siding. Drill pilot holes through the molding and sheathing, and into the framing members.

**2** Attach the moldings with 8d casing nails. Drive the nails below the wood surface with a nail set. Use silicone caulk to seal around the moldings and to fill nail holes. Paint the moldings as soon as the caulk is dry.

## How to Patch Wood Lap Siding

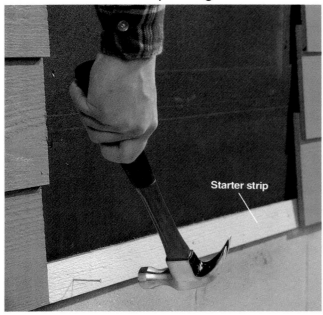

**1** Cover the patch area with sheathing and building paper, if not already present. If the bottom row of siding is missing, nail a 1 × 2 starter strip along the bottom of the patch area, using 6d siding nails. Leave a 1/4" gap at each joint in the starter strip to allow for expansion.

**2** Use a pry bar to remove lengths of lap siding on both sides of the patch area, creating a staggered pattern. When new siding is installed, the end joints will be offset for a less conspicuous appearance.

**3** Cut the bottom piece of lap siding to span the entire opening, and lay it over the starter strip. Allow a 1/4" expansion gap between board ends. Attach siding with pairs of 6d siding nails driven at each stud location.

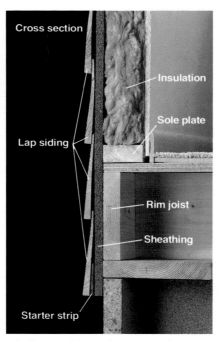

Cross section

Insulation

Sole plate

Lap siding

Rim joist

Sheathing

Starter strip

**4** Cut and install succeeding rows of siding, nailing only near the top of the siding at stud locations. Work upward from the bottom to create the proper overlap.

**5** Fill joints between siding pieces with silicone caulk. Repaint the entire wall surface as soon as the caulk dries to protect the new siding against the weather.

## How to Patch Stucco

**For small jobs,** use premixed stucco, available at building centers. For best results, apply the stucco in two or three layers, letting each layer dry completely between applications. Premixed stucco also can be used on larger areas, but it is more expensive than mixing your own ingredients.

**1** Cut self-furring metal lath and attach to the sheathing with roofing nails. Pieces of lath should overlap by 2". NOTE: If the patch area goes to the base of the stucco wall, attach metal "stop bead" at the bottom of the opening to prevent the stucco material from leaking out.

**2** Mix first stucco coat by combining 3 parts sand, 2 parts portland cement, 1 part masonry cement, and water. Mixture should be just moist enough to hold its shape when squeezed (inset).

**3** Use a trowel to apply the first stucco coat in 3/8"-thick layer, directly onto the metal lath. Scratch horizontal grooves into the wet surface of the stucco. Let the stucco set for two days, dampening it every few hours with fine spray to help it cure evenly.

**4** Mix and apply a second stucco coat in a smooth layer, so the patch area is within 1/4" of wall surface. Let second coat set for two days, dampening it every few hours. Mix a stucco finish coat made of 1 part lime, 3 parts sand, 6 parts white cement, and water.

**5** Dampen the wall, then apply the finish coat to match the old stucco. Practice helps. The finish coat above was dabbed on with a whisk broom, then flattened with a trowel. Keep the finish coat damp for a week, and let it dry for several more days if you plan to paint it.

**New wallboard**  **Old plaster wall**

**Use a pointed tool** to score old plaster wall surface near patching seams to improve bonding when patching with wallboard and wallboard compound. If the plaster and lath is thicker than the wallboard, you will need to install furring strips on the studs before attaching the wallboard.

# Finishing Walls & Ceilings

Use wallboard both to finish new walls and to patch existing wall and ceiling areas exposed during the remodeling project. Wallboard is an ideal base for paint, wallcovering, or paneling.

Openings in smooth plaster walls usually can be patched with wallboard, but if you need to match a textured plaster surface, it is best to hire a plasterer to do the work.

Wallboard is available in 4 × 8 or 4 × 10 sheets, and in 3/8", 1/2", and 5/8" thicknesses. For new walls, 1/2"-thick wallboard is standard.

### Everything You Need:

Tools: wallboard hammer, tape measure, wallboard lifter, utility knife, straightedge, T-square, sawhorses, wallboard saw, cordless jigsaw, wallboard knives, wallboard wet sander.

Materials: wallboard, wallboard nails or screws, wallboard compound, wallboard tape, sandpaper, steel corner bead (inside and outside).

## How to Install Wallboard

**1** Measure the thickness of the wall surface at the edge of the patch area. Buy new wallboard to match. On plaster walls, include thickness of lath when measuring.

**2** Trim any uneven surface edges around the patch area, and make sure framing members have a smooth nailing surface.

**3** Where necessary, provide a nailing surface around the edges of the patch area by attaching 2 × 4 nailing strips to the existing framing members.

**4** Insulate exterior walls and roof areas by stapling fiberglass insulation to the framing members. The paper backing should face into the house. Staple a plastic vapor barrier over the insulation.

**5** Mark the location of the framing members and nailing strips on the floor and ceiling. This will allow you to attach wallboard without relying on a stud finder.

**6** Measure the exposed area to find the dimensions for wallboard panels. Joints should fall over studs or nailing strips, but should not be aligned with corners of windows or doors. Leave a gap of no more than 1/4" between wallboard and jambs.

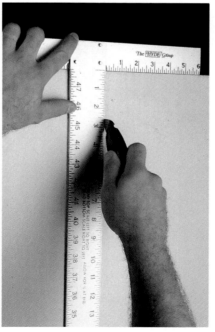

**7** Set the wallboard panel on sawhorses with the smooth side facing up. Mark the panel for cutting according to your measurements.

**8** To make straight cuts, score the face paper with a utility knife, using a wallboard T-square as a guide, then deepen the cuts.

**9** Complete straight cuts by bending the panel away from the scored line until it breaks. Cut through the back paper with a utility knife to separate the pieces.

(continued next page)

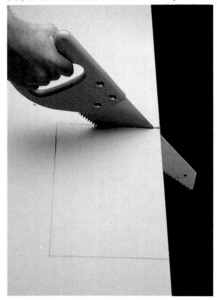

**10** To cut notches, use a wallboard saw to make the parallel cuts. Score the remaining line with a utility knife, then snap the notched piece backward and cut through the back paper.

**11** To make cutouts for receptacles, round-top windows, or other unusual shapes, rub chalk on the outer edges of the object. Press the wallboard against the wall, as in step 12, transferring the chalk to the back of the panel. Remove the panel and cut just outside chalk lines with a jig saw.

**12** Position the wallboard panel tightly against the framing members. For large panels, use a wallboard lifter or wood shims to raise the wallboard so it fits snugly against the ceiling.

**13** Anchor wallboard panels by driving wallboard screws, spaced every 10", into the framing members. Screw heads should be just below the wallboard surface.

**14** At outside corners, cut metal corner bead to length, and attach with wallboard nails, spaced every 8". Apply a double layer of wallboard compound to each side of the corner, using a 6" wallboard knife.

**15** At inside corners, apply a thin layer of wallboard compound to each side, using a wallboard knife. Cut inside corner bead (inset) to length, then press it into the corners. Scrape away excess compound.

**16** At joints, use a 6" wallboard knife to apply a single layer of wallboard compound to seams and screw heads.

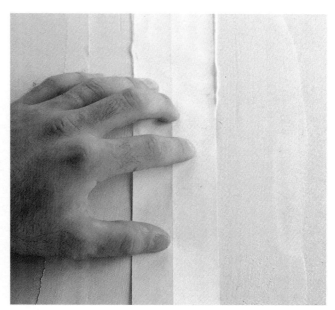

**17** Cut a strip of wallboard tape and press it into the wallboard compound at each joint. Smooth the joint with 6" wallboard knife. Cover remaining screw heads with a layer of wallboard compound.

**18** Let wallboard compound dry completely, then apply another thin layer to joints, corners, and screw heads, using a 12" wallboard knife. Let compound dry completely.

**19** When wallboard compound is dry, use a wallboard wet sander to sand joints smooth. Sander should be damp but not dripping, and should be rinsed frequently.

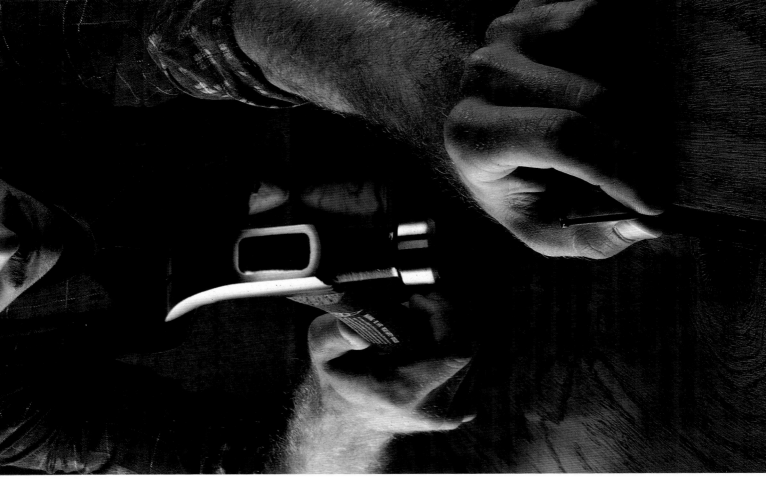

# Installing Paneling

Paneling is a versatile wall-surfacing material that comes in a wide range of styles, colors, and prices. Wood paneling is a rich-looking alternative to paint or wallcovering, and is also used as an inexpensive cover-up for damaged plaster walls. It comes in 4 × 8-foot sheets, and is usually 3/16 or 1/4 inch thick. Paneling is available in both prefinished and unfinished sheets.

Paneling is durable and easy to clean, and is often used as wainscoting in a dining room or family room.

**Before You Start:**
Tools & Materials: pry bar, stud finder, tape measure, plumb bob, paneling sheets, circular saw, straightedge, hammer, 4d finish nails, carpenter's level, compass, jig saw, wood stain, caulk gun, panel adhesive, powdered chalk.

Tip: Room corners are often irregular. To fit paneling in corners that are not perfectly square, scribe the corner profile onto the first sheet of paneling with a compass. When marked profile is cut, paneling fits perfectly.

### How to Cut & Fit Paneling

**1** Remove all trim and molding from baseboards, windows, doors and ceilings. Use wood block under the pry bar to protect walls from damage.

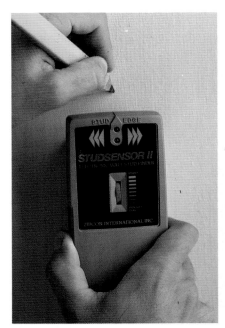

**2** Use an electronic stud finder to locate studs. Start in corner farthest from entry, and find stud that is closest to, but less than, 48" from corner. Find and mark studs every 48" from first marked stud.

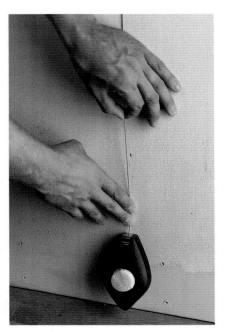

**3** Snap a chalk line on wall to make plumb lines through stud marks. Paneling seams will fall along these lines.

Straightedge

**4** Lay first paneling sheet face-side-down. Measure distance from corner to first plumb mark and add 1" to allow for scribing. Use a circular saw and clamped straight-edge to cut paneling to this measurement.

**5** Position first sheet of paneling against wall so that cut edge is 1" away from corner, and opposite finished edge is plumb. Temporarily tack top of paneling to wall.

**6** Spread legs of compass to 1¼". With point against wall corner and pencil against face of paneling, run compass down full height of wall. Corner irregularities are scribed on face of paneling. Remove paneling from wall.

**7** Lay paneling face-side up, and cut along scribed line with jig saw. To prevent splintering, use a fine-tooth wood-cutting blade. Scribed edge fits perfectly against wall corner.

## How to Install Paneling

**1** Apply stain to wall at plumb line so the wall will not show through slight gaps at joints. Select a stain that matches color of paneling edges, which may be darker than paneling surface.

**2** Use a caulk gun to apply 1-inch-long beads of panel adhesive to the wall at 6-inch intervals. Keep beads about 1'' back from plumb lines, to prevent adhesive from seeping out through joints. For new construction, apply adhesive directly to studs.

**3** Attach paneling to top of wall, using 4d finishing nails driven every 16''. Press paneling against adhesive, then pull away from wall. Press paneling back against wall when adhesive is tacky, about 2 minutes.

**4** Hang remaining paneling so that there is a slight space at the joints. This space allows paneling to expand in damp weather. Use a dime as a spacing gauge.

# How to Cut Openings in Paneling

**1** Measure window and door openings, and mark outlines of openings on back side of paneling.

**2** Coat edges of electrical and telephone outlets and heating vents with chalk or lipstick.

**3** Press back-side of paneling against wall. Marks on outlets and vents are transferred to paneling.

**4** Lay paneling face-side-down. Drill pilot holes at one corner of each outline. Use a jig saw and fine-tooth woodcutting blade to make cutouts.

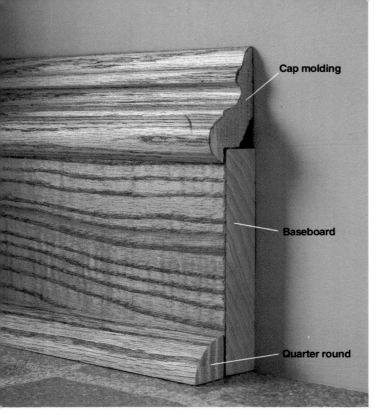

**Ornamental trim styles** can be created by combining two or more types of standard trim. Molding styles that are no longer produced can be duplicated with this method.

# Installing Trim Moldings

When finishing the trim work on a remodeling project, use moldings that match the style found elsewhere in your home. Home centers sell moldings in many styles, but may not stock the unusual moldings found in older homes.

Many salvage yards carry molding styles no longer manufactured. Or, if you saved trim moldings during your demolition work, use these materials when trimming the new project. Some elaborate molding can be duplicated by combining several different moldings (photo, left).

Wood trim moldings are expensive, so it is a good idea to practice your cutting and fitting techniques on scrap materials.

## Everything You Need:

Tools: tape measure, pencil, coping saw, straightedge, miter saw, drill & bits, hammer.

Materials: moldings, finish nails, wood putty.

## How To Install Baseboard Molding

**1** Outline the profile of the baseboard onto the back of a baseboard section, using a scrap piece of baseboard as a template. Cut along the outline with a coping saw.

**2** Fit the coped edge of the baseboard over another section that is butted squarely into the corner of the wall. Drill pilot holes and attach the baseboard with 6d finish nails driven at stud locations.

**3** Fit outside corners by cutting the ends of baseboard at opposite 45° miters, using a miter saw. Drill pilot holes and attach baseboards with 6d finishing nails. Drive all nail heads below the wood surface, using a nail set. Fill all the nail holes with wood putty.

## How to Install Moldings for Windows & Doors

**1** On each jamb, mark a setback line 1/8" from the inside edge. Moldings will be installed flush with these lines. NOTE: On double-hung windows, moldings usually are installed flush with the edge of the jambs, so no setback line is needed.

**2** Place a length of molding along one side jamb, flush with the setback line. At the top and bottom of the molding, mark the points where horizontal and vertical setback lines meet. (When working with doors, mark molding at the top only.)

**3** Cut the ends of the molding at 45° angles, using a miter saw. Measure and cut the other vertical molding piece, using the same method.

**4** Attach the vertical moldings with 4d finish nails driven through the moldings and into the jambs, and with 6d finish nails driven into framing members near the outside edge of the case molding. Drill pilot holes to prevent splitting, and space nails every 12".

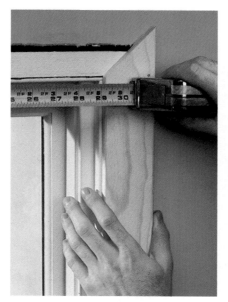

**5** Measure between the installed moldings on the setback lines, and cut top and bottom moldings with ends mitered at 45°. If window or door unit is not perfectly square, make test cuts on scrap pieces to find the correct angle for the joints. Drill pilot holes and attach with 4d and 6d finish nails.

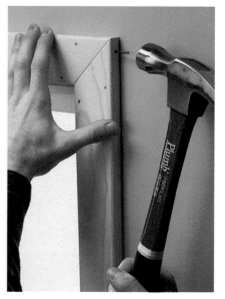

**6** Lock-nail corner joints by drilling pilot holes and driving a 4d finishing nail through each corner, as shown. Drive all nail heads below the wood surface, using a nail set, then fill the nail holes with wood putty.

201

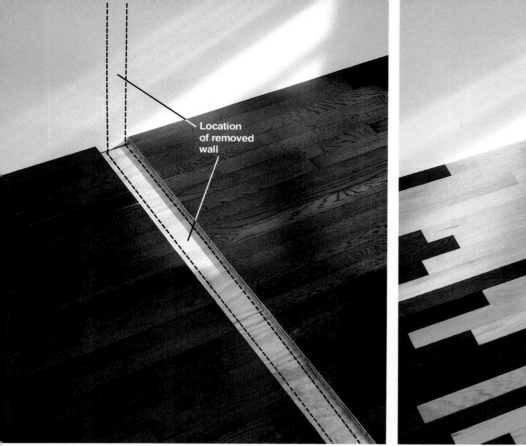

**When patching a wood-strip floor**, remove all of the floor boards that butt against the flooring gap, using a pry bar, and replace them with boards cut to fit. This may require that you trim the tongues from some tongue-and-groove floorboards. Sand and refinish the entire floor, so the new boards match with the old.

**A quick, inexpensive solution** is to install T-molding to bridge a gap in a wood strip floor. T-moldings are especially useful when the surrounding boards run parallel to the gap. T-moldings are available in several widths, and can be stained to match the flooring.

Completing the Project
# Patching Flooring

When an interior wall or section of wall has been removed during remodeling, you will need to patch gaps in the flooring where the wall was located. There are several options for patching floors, depending on your budget and the level of your do-it-yourself skills.

If the existing flooring shows signs of wear, consider replacing the entire flooring surface. Although it can be expensive, new flooring will completely hide any gaps in the floor, and will provide an elegant finishing touch for your remodeling project.

If you choose to patch the existing flooring, be aware that it is difficult to hide patched areas completely, especially if the flooring uses unique patterns or finishes. A creative solution is to intentionally patch the floor with material that contrasts with the surrounding flooring (page opposite).

## How to Use Contrasting Flooring Material

**Fill gaps in floors** with materials that have a contrasting color and pattern. For wood floors, parquet tiles are an easy and inexpensive choice (above, left). You may need to widen the flooring gap with a circular saw to make room for the contrasting tiles. To enhance the effect, cut away a border strip around the room and fill these areas with the same contrasting flooring material (above, right).

## Tips for Patching Floors

**Build up the subfloor** in the patch area, using layers of thin plywood and building paper, so the new surface will be flush with the surrounding flooring. You may need to experiment with different combinations of plywood and paper to find the right thickness.

**Make a vinyl or carpet patch,** by laying the patch material over the old flooring, then double-cutting through both layers. When the cut strip of old flooring is removed, the new patch will fit tightly. If flooring material is patterned, make sure the patterns are aligned before you cut.

**Install a carpet patch** using heat-activated carpet tape and a rented seam iron. Original carpet remnants are ideal for patching. New carpet—even of the same brand, style and color—seldom will match the old carpet exactly.

# Landscape
# Construction
# Projects

**Plan ahead** and be patient when designing your new landscape. Remember that plants grow and spread, and stone and wood structures change appearance as they weather. Landscape designers say that it takes at least five years for a landscape to reach its finished look. In the landscape shown above (inset), the owner chose to plant a few well-spaced shrubs and perennials. Several years later (larger photo), this attractive yard is approaching maturity without being overcrowded.

# Landscape Planning

Once you have reviewed some basic landscape design ideas, you are ready to plan your own yard. A detailed landscape plan takes time to develop, but helps ensure smooth work and successful results. Your finished plans should include detailed drawings, an accurate budget, a list of materials, and a realistic time schedule.

Evaluate your existing landscape carefully as you begin to plan. To save money and time, plan the new landscape so it makes use of existing features that are both attractive and functional—a favorite flower garden, a garden walk, or a healthy tree, for example. You can transplant many hardy bushes and most perennial flowers from one part of your yard to another to fit a new landscape plan.

Although most of the projects shown in this book can be done without a work permit, always check with the local inspections office before you begin. If a building permit is required, you will need to have the inspector check your work.

Follow these steps when creating your landscape plan:

# Tips for Landscape Planning

**Obey local "setback" regulations** when planning fences, walls, and other landscape structures. The setback distance, determined by the local Building Code, prevents you from building any structure too close to property lines. Call your community inspections office to learn about any other restrictions on how and where you can build landscape structures.

**Talk to your neighbors** about your landscaping plans. Many projects, like building a fence, or planting a large shade tree or hedge, will affect neighbors as well as yourself. Keep the peace and avoid legal disputes by making sure your neighbors do not object to your plans.

**Locate buried utility lines.** Public utilities, like power, telephone, gas, and water companies, are required by law to inspect your site on request and mark locations of all buried lines. If your project requires digging or excavation, make sure your work will not interfere with underground utility lines.

**Measure your yard**, including the locations of all permanent landscape features. Accurate yard measurements are essential for drawing plans and estimating the quantities and costs of materials.

# Testing Landscape Ideas

Making simple sketches is the traditional method for testing landscape ideas, but you will get a better idea of how your landscape will look if you also go outdoors and model your plans in the yard itself. For example, you can use stakes and sheets of cardboard to illustrate how a fence, trellis, or free-standing wall will look.

While testing your ideas, look at your landscape from many different angles. View the yard from downstairs and upstairs windows, from the front sidewalk and the street, and from neighboring yards. Consider how time-of-day and seasonal changes will affect shade patterns in the yard.

**Use a garden hose** to test the layout of walkways, patios, planting beds, ponds, and other landscape features. When planning a curved walkway (above), use pieces of wood lath cut to the same length to maintain an even width.

**Buy or borrow sample materials,** like interlocking blocks or brick pavers, and arrange them on-site to see which materials complement the existing materials in your yard and house.

## Tips for Testing Landscape Ideas

**Make simple sketches** by enlarging a photograph of your yard on a photocopier, then copying the outline onto tracing paper. Next, find magazine or catalog photos of plants and landscape structures, and trace them onto the drawing to see how they might look in your yard. If necessary, use a photocopier to shrink or enlarge the photos to the proper scale before tracing them.

**Use brown wrapping paper** to model patios, walkways, and other paved surfaces on your yard. You can test different paver patterns by tracing the designs on the paper with colored chalk.

**Test layouts** for planting areas using potted plants and shrubs. This also can help you determine which plant species look best in your yard.

## Landscape Planning
# Drawing a Plan

Accurate and detailed drawings of your landscape plan help you organize your work and make it easier to estimate quantities and costs of materials. If your project needs a building permit, the inspector who issues the permit will ask to see your drawn plans.

If you do not know the exact locations of property lines, prevent possible legal disputes by having your property surveyed.

If you are planning a large project that will be completed in stages, draw a separate plan for each stage of the project. These drawings are especially helpful if you consult a landscape designer. Many nurseries have designers on staff who review plans and offer free advice to customers.

**Use an original blueprint**, if you have one, and copy the outline of your house and yard onto tracing paper. If you do not have a blueprint, use drafting paper (inset), available at art supply stores, to draw a scaled plan.

## Landscape Plan Symbols

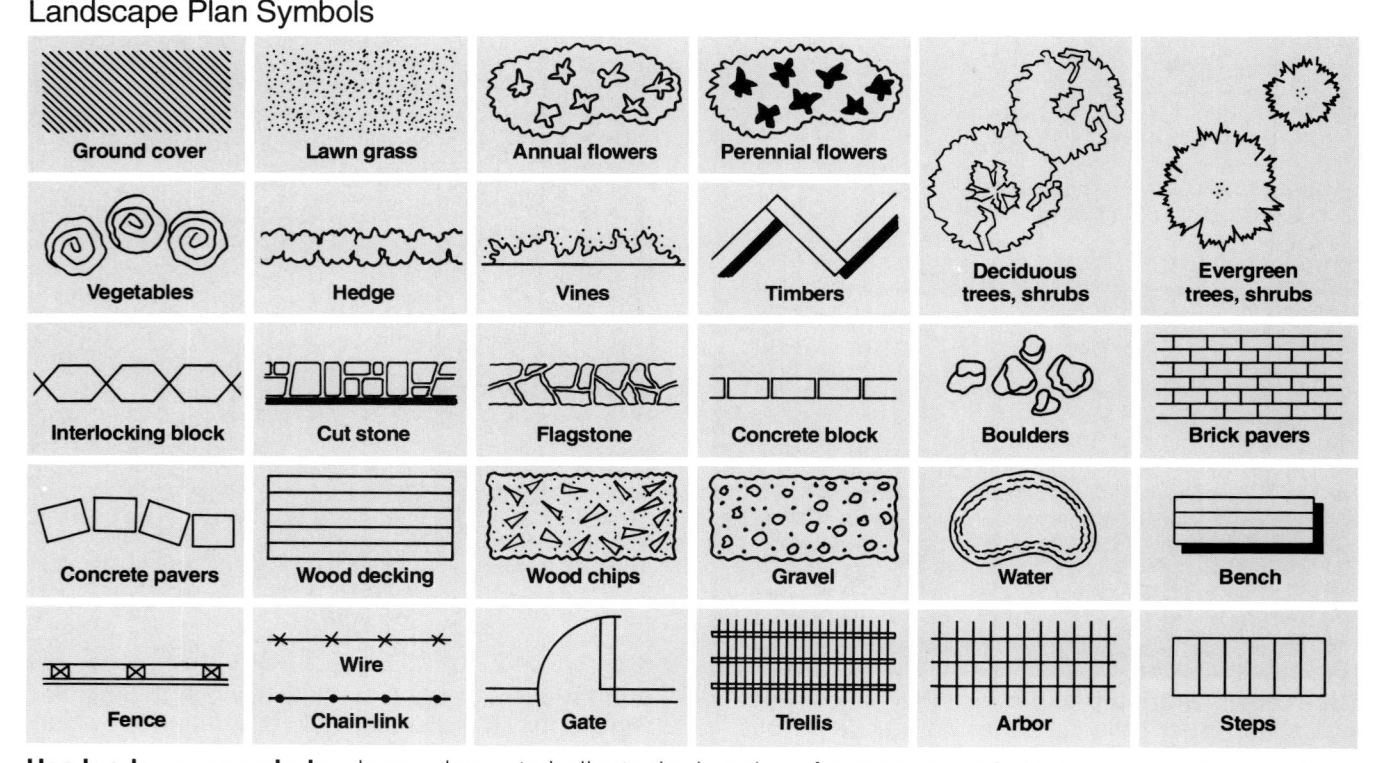

| | | | | | |
|---|---|---|---|---|---|
| Ground cover | Lawn grass | Annual flowers | Perennial flowers | Deciduous trees, shrubs | Evergreen trees, shrubs |
| Vegetables | Hedge | Vines | Timbers | | |
| Interlocking block | Cut stone | Flagstone | Concrete block | Boulders | Brick pavers |
| Concrete pavers | Wood decking | Wood chips | Gravel | Water | Bench |
| Fence | Wire / Chain-link | Gate | Trellis | Arbor | Steps |

**Use landscape symbols,** shown above, to indicate the location of structures and plants on your plan drawing. These standard symbols are used by landscape professionals and building inspectors.

## How to Draw a Plan

**1** Draw an outline of your property to scale on drafting paper, or trace the outline from an original blueprint. Make sure the property lines are accurate (consult a surveyor, if necessary). Mark all underground and overhead utility lines on the plan.

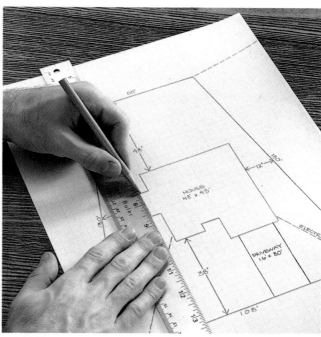

**2** Add the buildings, driveways, sidewalks, and other main features of your property to the plan. Include accurate measurements of the features.

**3** Show any existing yard features that will be retained in the new landscape. Mark low spots, hills, and contours with pencil shading, and show the shade patterns of trees and buildings. Compass directions on the plan will be helpful if you choose to consult a designer.

**4** Add all the proposed structures and plants. Make a list of all the materials you will need.

# Budgeting Your Time & Money

For large landscaping projects, you may want to spread out the expense and time by dividing the project into smaller jobs that can be completed over a period of months or even years. If you choose to work this way, make sure you begin with a good overall landscaping plan. First do the large projects, like retaining walls, then move to the smaller structures and planting projects.

Make accurate estimates of the materials you need, because leftover materials like concrete, brick, and stone usually cannot be returned to suppliers. To save money, try to coordinate your landscape projects with those of neighbors so you can take advantage of volume discounts on brick, stone, sod, and other materials.

**Save time by hiring a professional** to do difficult, time-consuming chores, or to haul large amounts of gravel, sand, or topsoil. Professionals have special equipment to do these jobs quickly.

## Tips for Saving Money

**Collect free materials.** For example, you can get wood chips, suitable for mulching planting areas or covering pathways, from tree trimmers, power companies, and other utility companies. Farmers or housing developers may let you collect rubble stone. Paving brick may be salvaged from demolition sites. Neighbors who are avid gardeners sometimes have extra flower bulbs and other perennials. If you are removing old landscape structures, consider reusing the materials.

**Save money** by hauling materials yourself with a pickup truck or trailer. Shipping charges for small volumes of gravel, sand, or topsoil can be more expensive than the materials themselves.

212

# Estimating & Ordering Materials

Use this chart to help you estimate the materials you will need for landscaping projects. Sizes and weights of materials may vary, so consult your supplier for more detailed information on estimating materials.

If you are unfamiliar with the gravel and stone products available in your area, visit a sand-and-gravel supplier to see the products first-hand.

When sand, gravel, and other bulk materials are delivered, place them on a tarp to protect your yard. Make sure the tarp is as close to the work area as possible.

## Methods for Estimating Materials

| | |
|---|---|
| Sand, gravel, topsoil (2" layer) | surface area (sq. ft.) ÷ 100 = tons needed |
| Standard brick pavers (4" × 8") | surface area (sq. ft.) × 5 = number of pavers needed |
| Poured concrete (4" layer) | surface area (sq. ft.) × .012 = cubic yards needed |
| Flagstone | surface area (sq. ft.) ÷ 100 = tons of stone needed |
| Interlocking block (6" × 16" face) | area of wall face (sq. ft.) × 1.5 = number of stones needed |
| Retaining wall timbers (5" × 6" × 8 ft.) | area of wall face (sq. ft.) ÷ 3 = number of timbers needed |
| Cut stone for 1-ft.-thick walls | area of wall face (sq. ft.) ÷ 15 = tons of stone needed |
| Rubble stone for 1-ft.-thick walls | area of wall face (sq. ft.) ÷ 35 = tons of stone needed |
| 8 × 8 × 16 concrete block for free-standing walls | height of wall (ft.) × length of wall × 1.125 = number of blocks |

# Using Landscape Professionals

Using landscape professionals can save work time and simplify large, complicated projects. Professional designers can help you plan and budget your project, and contractors can save you work time on large, difficult tasks.

The abilities and reputations of designers and contractors vary greatly, so always check references and insist on viewing samples of previous work before hiring a professional. Make sure to get a written, itemized estimate; terms for payment; and proof of bonding and insurance.

## Landscape Professionals

**Landscape architect:** a licensed structural designer who is qualified to plan large, highly technical structures, like a tall retaining wall or free-standing garden wall, an in-ground swimming pool, or gazebo.

**Landscape designer:** a general-purpose design professional, often affiliated with a large nursery. Reputable landscape designers are the best choice for designing and planning help.

**Garden designer:** usually employed at a garden center or nursery. Garden designers can help you choose plants and plan gardening areas.

**Landscape contractor:** supplies workers and supervises labor for a wide range of landscaping projects. Landscaping contractors range from small one- and two-man crews to large, well-established companies that can oversee all stages of a landscape project.

**Excavating contractor:** provides labor and machinery required for large digging and excavation projects. Make sure utility companies locate and mark underground lines before the contractor begins work.

**Concrete contractor:** a specialized professional skilled at pouring and finishing concrete patios, driveways, sidewalks, steps, and walls.

**Interlocking block** (below) is made from molded concrete that is split to provide a rough face resembling natural stone. Available in several colors and sizes, interlocking block is used for both straight and curved retaining walls, terraces, and raised planting beds. Interlocking-block walls create bold geometric patterns.

**Concrete block** is available in plain or decorative types. This durable building material is used often for free-standing garden walls. The hard, plain look of a concrete block wall can be softened with climbing plants or a surface application of stucco or stone veneer.

**Poured concrete** is durable and less expensive than other paving products. Although concrete is plain in appearance, it is easy to maintain, making it a popular choice for walkways, patios, walls, and steps.

## Landscape Design
# Materials

Stone, masonry, and wood are primary building materials for landscape construction. Stone and masonry give your landscape structures a feeling of permanence. Wood has a natural, warm look, is easy to shape, and can be painted or stained to match existing structures.

Whenever possible, choose landscape materials that either match or complement the materials already used on your home. For example, if you have a brick home, a patio made from similar brick will be more appealing than a poured concrete slab. Or, if you have a Tudor-style house

with exposed beams, a retaining wall built from rough timbers is more appropriate than a wall built from interlocking concrete blocks.

Man-made stone products cast from concrete are a good choice for landscape structures, considering the increasing price and dwindling supplies of forest timber and natural stone. Interlocking concrete block, brick pavers, and other manufactured stone products are widely available, easy to install, and very durable.

If you prefer the look of natural stone, try to select a type of rock that is common in your geographic region. Local stone makes your landscape look natural, and it is much less expensive than stone that must be shipped long distances.

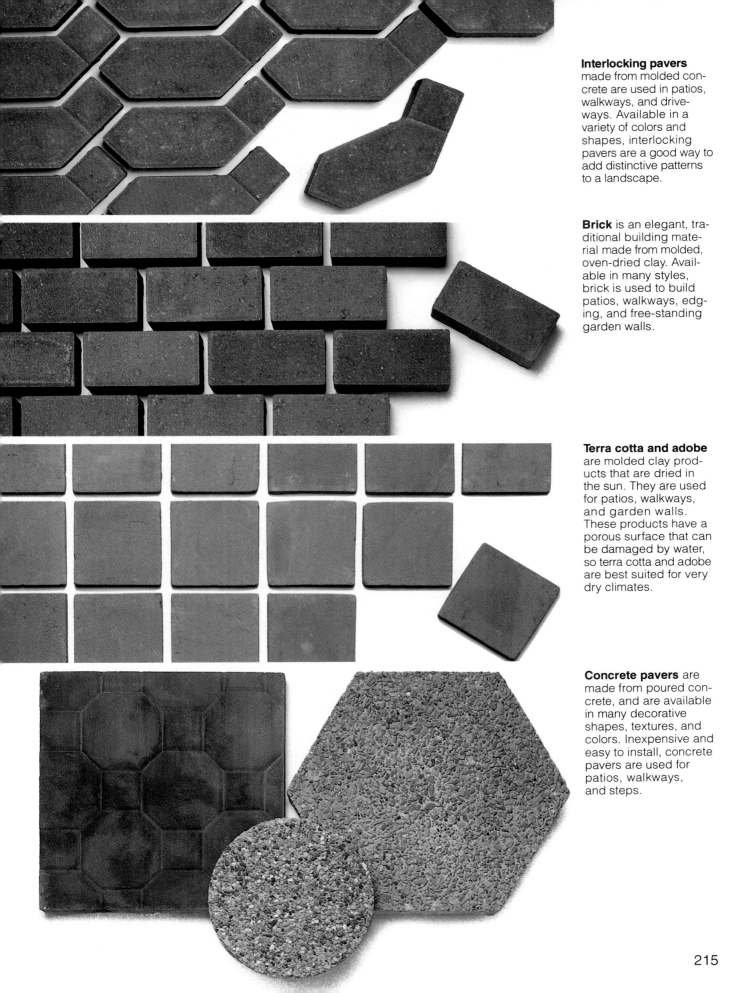

**Interlocking pavers** made from molded concrete are used in patios, walkways, and driveways. Available in a variety of colors and shapes, interlocking pavers are a good way to add distinctive patterns to a landscape.

**Brick** is an elegant, traditional building material made from molded, oven-dried clay. Available in many styles, brick is used to build patios, walkways, edging, and free-standing garden walls.

**Terra cotta and adobe** are molded clay products that are dried in the sun. They are used for patios, walkways, and garden walls. These products have a porous surface that can be damaged by water, so terra cotta and adobe are best suited for very dry climates.

**Concrete pavers** are made from poured concrete, and are available in many decorative shapes, textures, and colors. Inexpensive and easy to install, concrete pavers are used for patios, walkways, and steps.

**Crushed gravel**

**Smooth river gravel**

**Cut stone (granite)**

**Flagstone**

**Glacial rubble stone**

**Accent rock (quartz blend)**

# Natural Stone

**Gravel** comes in two forms: rough gravel made by crushing larger rocks, and smooth gravel usually dredged from rivers. Gravel is sorted by size, and has many landscape uses. Applied as a loose layer, gravel makes an informal, easy-to-maintain pathway. Laid in large beds, gravel lends a relaxed feeling to a landscape while providing texture and color.

**Cut stone,** sometimes call ashlar, is natural stone that has been cut into cubic shapes. Marble, hard limestone, and granite (shown here) are popular for cut stone. Cut stone is used for both mortared or unmortared walls, patios or walkways. It is an expensive, top-quality building material that gives landscape structures an elegant, timeless appearance.

**Flagstone** is uncut sedimentary stone that has naturally flat surfaces. Limestone, slate, and shale are common types of flagstone. Flagstone works well with large, expansive landscapes, and is used for walkways, patios, and steps. It is a durable, but expensive, paving material.

**Rubble stone** is any type of irregular, uncut rock collected from fields, gullies, or stream beds. It can include boulders, glacial debris, rough pieces of quartz or granite, random pieces of limestone or sandstone, or even volcanic rock. Rubble stone often is used in garden walls and retaining walls, and works best in informal, rustic landscapes. Rubble stone is cheaper than cut stone.

**Accent rock** is distinctive natural stone used as decoration rather than as a building material. Large, colorful rocks can be partially buried in a planting area or lawn to add visual interest. Accent rocks can range in size from small 20-lb. pieces to enormous boulders weighing more than a ton.

# Wood

**Wood and bark chips** are used for loose-fill on soft pathways or as a ground cover for planting areas. Wood and bark chips are inexpensive and lend a relaxed, casual look to a landscape.

**Pressure-treated pine** contains pesticides and wood preservatives to make it last. Less expensive than cedar and redwood, pressure-treated pine is used to build fences, retaining walls, raised planting beds, and garden steps. Most pressure-treated pine is green when new, but gradually weathers to a neutral gray. Or, it can be stained to resemble redwood or cedar. In some areas, treated pine also is available in a dark-brown color.

**Cedar** is a soft wood with a rough texture. It has natural resistance to decay and insect damage, and is used for fences, trellises, and arbors. Use cedar in above-ground structures only: where wood will be in contact with the ground, use pressure-treated lumber instead.

**Redwood** is a smooth-grained wood with a natural resistance to insects and decay. It is used for above-ground structures, like fences, trellises, and overhead arbors. Avoid using redwood where a structure will be in contact with the ground: for these applications, use pressure-treated wood instead. Because of high demand and dwindling supplies, redwood is becoming more expensive.

Redwood bark chips

Pressure-treated pine

Wood chips

Cedar

Redwood

**Common supplies** for landscape construction include: (A) sheet plastic, (B) landscape fabric, (C) burlap, (D) stucco lath, (E) bendable rigid plastic edging, (F) post caps, (G) wood sealer-preservative, (H) mason's string, (I) rigid plastic edging, (J) flexible plastic edging, (K) rope, (L) perforated drain pipe, (M) masonry sealer, (N) splash block for runoff water.

# Landscaping Supplies

In addition to the visible design materials used in a landscape (pages 214 to 217), there are many hidden, structural supplies that are equally important to successful landscaping projects.

Because landscape structures are exposed to weather extremes, make sure to invest in the best materials you can afford. Buying cheap materials to save a few dollars can shorten the life span of a landscape structure by many years.

Metal connecting materials, including nails, screws, fence hardware, and post anchors should be made from aluminum or galvanized steel, which will not rust.

**Check grade stamps** on pressure-treated lumber. Look for lumber treated with chromated copper arsenate, identified by the "CCA" label printed on the grade stamp. For above-ground and ground-contact applications, choose lumber graded "LP-22" or ".40 retention." If wood will be buried, use lumber graded "FDN" or ".60 retention," if it is available.

**Base materials** for landscape walls and paved surfaces include: (A) sand, (B) seed gravel, (C) compactible gravel subbase containing a large amount of clay and lime, (D) topsoil, (E) coarse gravel, used as backfill, (F) mortar mix, and (G) concrete mix.

**Connecting materials** for landscape construction include: (A) galvanized common nails, (B) galvanized finish nails, (C) self-tapping masonry anchors, (D) galvanized utility screws, (E) 12" galvanized spikes, (F) concrete reinforcement bars, (G) lead masonry anchors, (H) metal pipes for anchoring timbers, (I) lag screws with washers, (J) construction adhesive, (K) J-bolts, (L) galvanized post anchor, (M) rafter strap, (N) fence bracket.

**Basic yard and garden tools** used in landscape construction and maintenance include: (A) garden shovel, (B) hand shears, (C) pruning shears, (D) garden rake, (E) spade, (F) power trimmer, (G) hoe, (H) garden hose, (I) bow saw, (J) line-feed trimmer, (K) pressure sprayer.

# Tools for Landscape Construction

Most landscape construction projects can be done with ordinary garden tools and workshop tools you already own. If you need to buy new tools, always invest in high-quality products. A few specialty tools, most of which can be borrowed or rented, make some jobs easier.

When using power tools outdoors, always use a GFCI (ground-fault circuit-interrupter) extension cord for safety. After each use, clean and dry metal tools to prevent rust.

**A sturdy wheelbarrow** is an essential tool for landscape construction and maintenance. Better wheelbarrows have inflatable rubber tires and wooden handles.

**Basic hand and power tools** used in landscape construction include: (A) reciprocating saw, (B) hammer, (C) hand maul, (D) rubber mallet, (E) pencil, (F) circular saw, (G) eye protection, (H) drill with bits, (I) line level, (J) carpenter's level, (K) carpenter's square, (L) plumb bob and chalk line, (M) tape measures, (N) GFCI extension cord, (O) particle mask, (P) work gloves, (Q) caulk gun, (R) hearing protectors.

**Specialty tools you can rent** include: (A) tamping machine, (B) "jumping jack" tamping machine, (C) sod cutter, (D) power auger, (E) hand tamper, (F) chain saw.

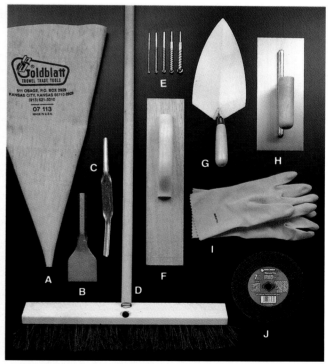

**Tools for masonry work** include: (A) mortar bag, (B) masonry chisel, (C) V-shaped mortar tool, (D) stiff broom, (E) masonry drill bits, (F) concrete float, (G) pointed trowel, (H) standard trowel, (I) rubber gloves, (J) masonry saw blade.

# Grading & Contouring Your Yard

Reshaping, removing, or adding soil is an important step in many landscaping projects. If you are installing a patio, for example, you may need to first create a large area that is very flat. Or you may want to put a finishing touch on a landscape by adding raised contours or planting areas to the yard.

Consider how the overall slope affects drainage in your yard. Make sure your finished landscape is graded so it directs runoff water away from buildings and minimizes low-lying areas that can trap standing water. To identify drainage problems, examine your yard immediately after a heavy rain, or after watering it thoroughly, and look for areas where water collects or flows toward building foundations.

Before digging, contact utility companies to pinpoint and mark the location of underground wires or pipes. You can arrange to have utility lines rerouted if there is no way to work around them.

**Build contours** to create visual interest in a flat landscape. Contours should have gentle slopes and irregular shapes that accent the surrounding yard. Contours can be used to create a visual barrier, or to provide planting areas (pages 294 to 295).

**Hire an excavating contractor** if you need to move large amounts of soil. Small front-end loaders are available for daily rental, but using them successfully requires some practice.

## Everything You Need:

Tools: hose, shovel, tape measure, garden rake, wheelbarrow, hammer or maul, line level.

Materials (as needed): edging material, topsoil, gravel, string, stakes, perforated drain pipe, splash block, sod, landscape fabric.

## How to Create a Landscape Contour

**1** Create an outline of the planned contour on your lawn, using a hose or rope. If the contour will be used as a planting area, install edging material along the outline.

**2** Fill the outlined area with topsoil. Use a rake to shape the soil into a smooth mound no more than 18" high, then tamp and water the soil to compress it. Landscape contours can be finished with sod or used as planting areas (pages 294 to 295).

## How to Grade Soil Around Foundations

**Prevent water damage to foundations** by grading soil so there is a smooth, gradual slope away from the building. For proper drainage, the ground within 6 ft. of a foundation should drop 3/4" for each foot of distance. To check the grade, attach a string to a pair of stakes and adjust the string so it is level. Measure down from the string at 1-ft. intervals to determine the grade. If necessary, add extra soil and shape it with a garden rake to get the proper grade.

## Tips for Solving Drainage Problems

**Fill small low-lying areas** by top-dressing them with black soil. Spread the new soil into an even layer, then compress it with a hand tamper.

**Improve drainage in a large low-lying area** by creating a shallow ditch, called a drainage swale, to carry runoff water away. If your region receives frequent heavy rainfalls, or if you have dense soil that drains poorly, you may need to lay a perforated drain pipe and a bed of gravel under the swale to make it more effective (page opposite).

## How to Make a Drainage Swale

**1** After identifying the problem area, use stakes to mark a swale route that will direct water away from the site toward a runoff area. The outlet of the swale must be lower than any point in the problem area.

**2** Dig a 6"-deep, rounded trench along the swale route. If you remove the sod carefully, you can lay it back into the trench when the swale is completed.

**3** Shape the trench so it slopes gradually downward toward the outlet, and the sides and bottom are smooth.

**4** Complete the swale by laying sod into the trench. Compress the sod, then water the area thoroughly to check the drainage.

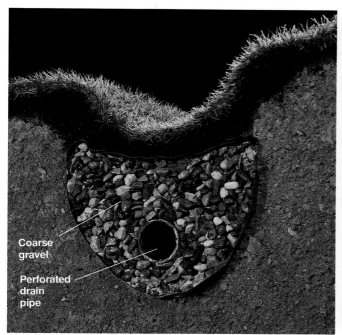

Coarse gravel

Perforated drain pipe

Splash block

**OPTION:** For severe drainage problems, dig a 1-ft.-deep swale angled slightly downward to the outlet point. Line the swale with landscape fabric. Spread a 2" layer of coarse gravel in the bottom of the swale, then lay perforated drain pipe over the gravel. Cover the pipe with a 5" layer of gravel, then wrap the landscape fabric over the top of the gravel. Cover the swale with soil and fresh sod. Set a splash block at the outlet to distribute the runoff and prevent erosion.

**Cut stone** is a top-quality, expensive building material used for retaining walls (shown above) and free-standing garden walls. For retaining walls, cut stone is laid without mortar to improve drainage, except for the top row, which can be anchored with mortar for extra strength. Retaining wall designs often include garden steps. For free-standing garden walls, cut stones usually are mortared. When built correctly, cut-stone walls can last for generations. See pages 236 to 237.

# Landscape Walls

Landscape walls include retaining walls and free-standing walls. They can define outdoor areas, increase the amount of level yard area, stop soil erosion, and improve the appearance of your yard and home.

Many stone, concrete, and wood products can be used to build landscape walls. When choosing materials, consider style, cost, ease of installation, and durability. Refer to pages 214 to 217 for more information on materials commonly used in landscape construction.

Wherever possible, limit the height of your landscape walls to 3 ft. Local Building Codes usually require deep concrete footings and special construction techniques for taller landscape walls.

**Retaining walls** are subject to enormous pressure from the weight of the soil behind the wall. To offset this pressure, build the retaining wall so each row of materials is set slightly behind the previous row. The backward angle of a retaining wall (at least 1" for every foot in height) is called the "batter." For maximum strength, some landscape contractors tilt the entire wall back into the hillside.

## Common Materials Used for Landscape Walls

**Landscape timbers** are inexpensive and easy to cut at any angle, but are less durable than stone or masonry. A well-built timber retaining wall made with good-quality pressure-treated lumber will last for 15 to 20 years in most climates. See pages 234 to 235.

**Rubble stone** is used for both retaining walls and free-standing garden walls, and usually is laid without mortar. Building rubble-stone walls requires patience, but the materials are less expensive than cut stone or interlocking block. See page 236.

**Interlocking block** made from cast concrete is the easiest of all materials to work with. It makes very strong and durable retaining walls, and is less expensive than cut stone. Interlocking block is especially useful for curved retaining walls. See pages 231 to 233.

**Concrete block** is inexpensive and is available in decorative and plain styles. Concrete block requires mortar, and makes a very sturdy free-standing garden wall. But because the mortared joints hinder drainage, concrete block is a poor choice for retaining walls. See pages 238 to 243.

**Terraced retaining walls** work well on steep hillsides. Two or more short retaining walls are easier to install and more stable than a single, tall retaining wall. Construct the terraces so each wall is no higher than 3 ft.

# Building a Retaining Wall

The main reason to build retaining walls is to create level planting areas or prevent erosion on hillsides. But if you have a flat yard, you also can build low retaining wall structures to make decorative raised planting beds and add visual interest to the landscape.

No matter what material is used, a retaining wall can be damaged if water saturates the soil behind it. To ensure its durability, make sure your wall contains the proper drainage features (page opposite).

Retaining walls taller than 3 ft. are subject to thousands of pounds of pressure from the weight of the soil and water, so they require special building techniques that are best left to a professional. If you have a tall hillside, it is best to terrace the hill with several short walls (photo, above).

Before excavating for a retaining wall, **check with local utility companies** to make sure there are no underground pipes or cables running through the site.

> **Everything You Need for Retaining Walls:**
>
> Tools: wheelbarrow, shovel, garden rake, line level, hand tamper, rented tamping machine, small maul, masonry chisel, eye protection, hearing protectors, work gloves, circular saw, level, tape measure, marking pencil.
>
> Materials: stakes, mason's string, landscape fabric, compactible gravel subbase, perforated drain pipe, coarse backfill gravel.
>
> Added supplies for interlocking block walls: masonry blade for circular saw, caulk gun, construction adhesive.
>
> Added supplies for stone walls: masonry chisel, masonry blade for circular saw, trowel, mortar mix.
>
> Added supplies for timber walls: chain saw or reciprocating saw, drill and 1" spade bit, 12" galvanized spikes.

## Options for Positioning a Retaining Wall

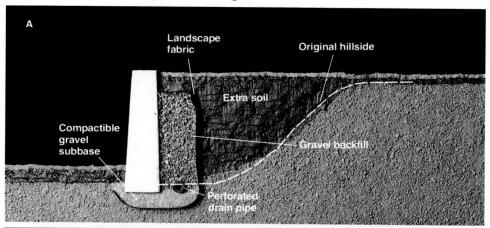

A — Landscape fabric, Original hillside, Extra soil, Compactible gravel subbase, Gravel backfill, Perforated drain pipe

B — Soil removed from base of hill, Original hillside, Compactible gravel subbase, Landscape fabric, Gravel backfill, Perforated drain pipe

**(A) Increase the level area** above the wall by positioning the wall well forward from the top of the hill. Fill in behind the wall with extra soil, available from sand-and-gravel companies.

**(B) Keep the basic shape** of your yard by positioning the wall near the top of the hillside. Use the soil removed at the base of the hill to fill in near the top of the wall.

Structural features for all retaining walls include: a compactible gravel subbase to make a solid footing for the wall, coarse gravel backfill and a perforated drain pipe to improve drainage behind the wall, and landscape fabric to keep the loose soil from washing into the gravel backfill.

## Providing Drainage for Retaining Walls

**Backfill with gravel** and install a perforated drain pipe near the bottom of the gravel backfill. Vent the pipe to the side or bottom of the retaining wall, where runoff water can flow away from the hillside without causing erosion.

**Dig a swale,** a shallow ditch 1 ft. to 2 ft. away from the top of the wall, to direct runoff water away from the retaining wall (see pages 224 to 225). This technique is useful for sites that have very dense soil that does not drain well.

## How to Prepare a Retaining Wall Site

**1** Excavate the hillside, if necessary, to create a level base for the retaining wall. For interlocking blocks or stone walls, allow at least 12" of space for gravel backfill between the back of the wall and the hillside. For timber walls, allow at least 3 ft. of space. When excavating large areas, rent earth-moving equipment or hire a contractor.

**2** Use stakes to mark the front edge of the wall at the ends and at any corners and curves. Connect the stakes with mason's string. Use a line level to check the string, and, if necessary, adjust the string so it is level.

**3** Dig a trench for the first row of building materials, measuring down from the mason's string to maintain a level trench. Make the trench 6" deeper than the thickness of one layer of building material. For example, if you are using 6"-thick interlocking blocks, make the trench 12" deep.

**4** Line the excavation with strips of landscape fabric cut 3 ft. longer than the planned height of the wall. Make sure seams overlap by at least 6".

# Building a Retaining Wall Using Interlocking Block

Several styles of interlocking block are available at building and outdoor centers. Most types have a natural rock finish that combines the rough texture of cut stone with the uniform shape and size of concrete blocks.

Interlocking blocks weigh up to 80 lbs. each, so it is a good idea to have helpers when building a retaining wall. Suppliers offer substantial discounts when interlocking block is purchased in large quantities, so you may be able to save money if you coordinate your own project with those of your neighbors.

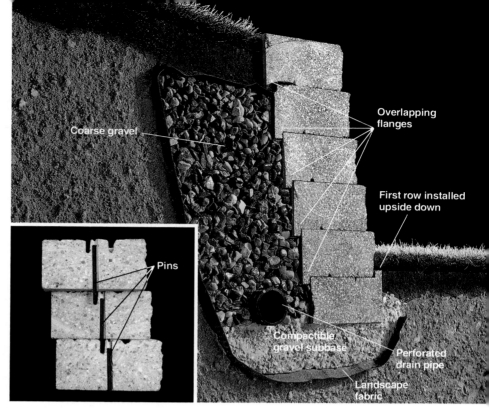

**Interlocking wall blocks** do not need mortar. Some types are held together with a system of overlapping flanges that automatically set the backward angle (batter) as the blocks are stacked. Other types of blocks use a pinning system (inset).

## Tips for Building a Retaining Wall Using Interlocking Block

**Make a stepped trench** when the ends of a retaining wall must blend into an existing hillside. Retaining walls often are designed so the ends curve or turn back into the slope.

**Make half-blocks** by scoring full blocks with a circular saw and masonry blade, then breaking the blocks along the scored line with a maul and chisel. Half-blocks are used when making corners, and to ensure that vertical joints between blocks are staggered between rows.

## How to Build a Retaining Wall Using Interlocking Block

**1** Spread a 6" layer of compactible gravel subbase into the trench and pack thoroughly. A rented tamping machine, sometimes called a "jumping jack," works better than a hand tamper (step 7) for packing the subbase.

**2** Lay the first row of blocks into the trench, aligning the front edges with the mason's string. When using flanged blocks, place the first row of blocks upside down and backward. Check the blocks frequently with a level, and adjust, if necessary, by adding or removing subbase material below the blocks.

**3** Lay the second row of blocks according to manufacturer's instructions. On flanged blocks, the blocks should be laid so the flanges are tight against the underlying blocks. Check regularly to make sure the blocks are level.

**4** Add 6" of gravel behind the blocks, making sure the landscape fabric remains between the gravel and the hillside. Pack the gravel thoroughly with a hand tamper.

**5** Place perforated drain pipe on top of the gravel, at least 6" behind wall, with perforations facing down. Make sure that at least one end of the pipe is unobstructed so runoff water can escape (page 229). Lay additional rows of blocks until the wall is about 18" above ground level. Make sure the vertical joints in adjoining rows are offset.

**6** Fill behind the wall with coarse gravel, and pack well. Lay the remaining rows of block, except for the cap row, backfilling with gravel and packing with a hand tamper as you go.

**7** Before laying the cap blocks, fold the end of the landscape fabric over the gravel backfill. Add a thin layer of topsoil over the fabric, then pack it thoroughly with a hand tamper.

**8** Fold any excess landscape fabric back over the soil, then apply construction adhesive to the blocks. Lay the cap blocks in place. Use topsoil to fill in behind the wall and to fill in the trench at the base of the wall. Install sod or other plants, as desired.

233

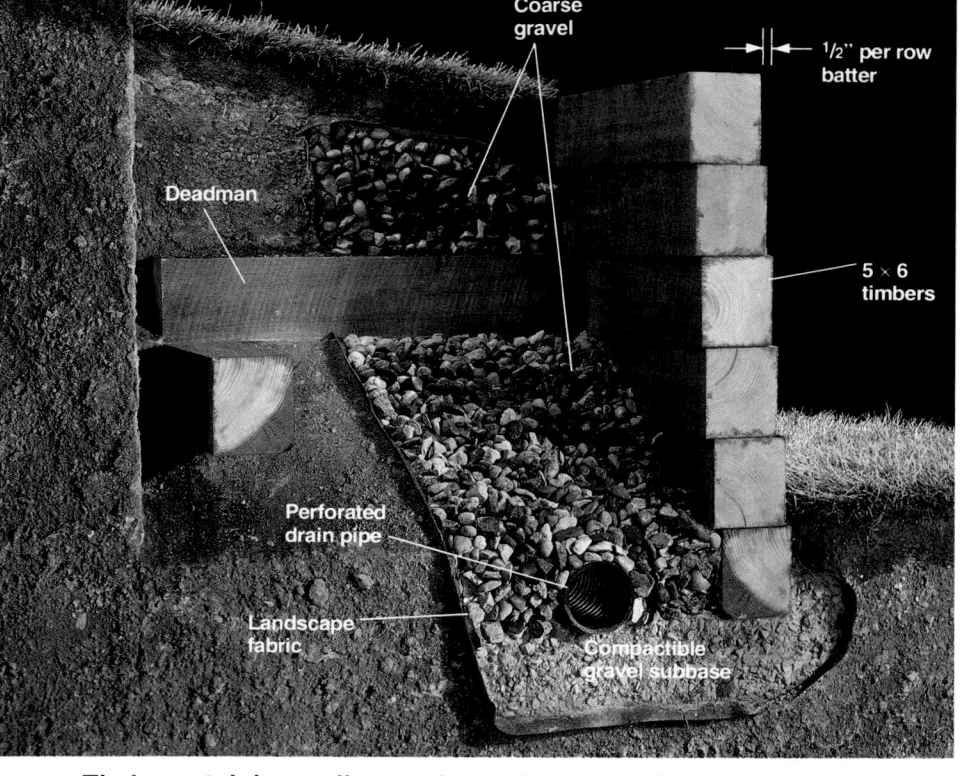

Coarse
gravel

½" per row
batter

Deadman

5 × 6
timbers

Perforated
drain pipe

Landscape
fabric

Compactible
gravel subbase

**Timber retaining walls** must be anchored with "deadmen" that extend from the wall back into the soil. Deadmen prevent the wall from sagging under the weight of the soil. For best results with timber retaining walls, create a backward angle (batter) by setting each row of timbers 1/2" behind the preceding row. The first row of timbers should be buried.

## Building a Retaining Wall Using Timbers

Timber walls have a life span of 15 to 20 years if built correctly. Use pressure-treated timbers at least 5 × 6 in size. Smaller timbers are not sturdy enough for retaining walls.

Use a chain saw or a reciprocating saw to cut landscape timbers. The pesticides used in treated lumber are toxic, so wear a particle mask, gloves, and long sleeves when cutting or handling pressure-treated lumber. Avoid using old timbers, like discarded railroad ties, that have been soaked in creosote. Creosote can leach into the soil and kill plants.

Before building the retaining wall, prepare the site as directed on page 230.

## Tips for Strengthening a Timber Retaining Wall

**Use metal reinforcement bars** instead of spikes for extra strength when connecting timbers. Cut 12" to 24" lengths of bar with sharp points, then drive them into pilot holes drilled through the top timber, spaced at 2-ft. intervals. This technique is especially useful if you have heavy, dense soil that drains poorly.

Timber depth
equal to
1/2 exposed
height

**Install vertical anchor posts** to reinforce the wall. Space the posts 3 ft. apart, and install them so the buried depth of each post is at least half the exposed height of the wall. Anchor posts are essential if it is not practical to install deadmen (photo, top).

234

# How to Build a Retaining Wall Using Timbers

**1** Spread a 6" layer of compactible gravel subbase into the prepared trench, then tamp the subbase and begin laying timbers, following the same techniques as with interlocking blocks (steps 1 to 7, pages 232 to 233). Each row of timbers should be set with a 1/2" batter, and end joints should be staggered so they do not align.

**2** Use 12" galvanized spikes or reinforcement bars to anchor the ends of each timber to the underlying timbers. Stagger the ends of the timbers to form strong corner joints. Drive additional spikes along the length of the timbers at 2-ft. intervals. If you have trouble driving the spikes, drill pilot holes.

**3** Install deadmen, spaced 4 ft. apart, midway up the wall. Build the deadmen by joining 3-ft.-long lengths of timber with 12" spikes, then insert the ends through holes cut in the landscape fabric. Anchor deadmen to wall with spikes. Install the remaining rows of timbers, and finish backfilling behind the wall (steps 6 to 8, page 233).

**4** Improve drainage by drilling weep holes through the second row of landscape timbers and into the gravel backfill, using a spade bit. Space the holes 4 ft. apart, and angle them upward.

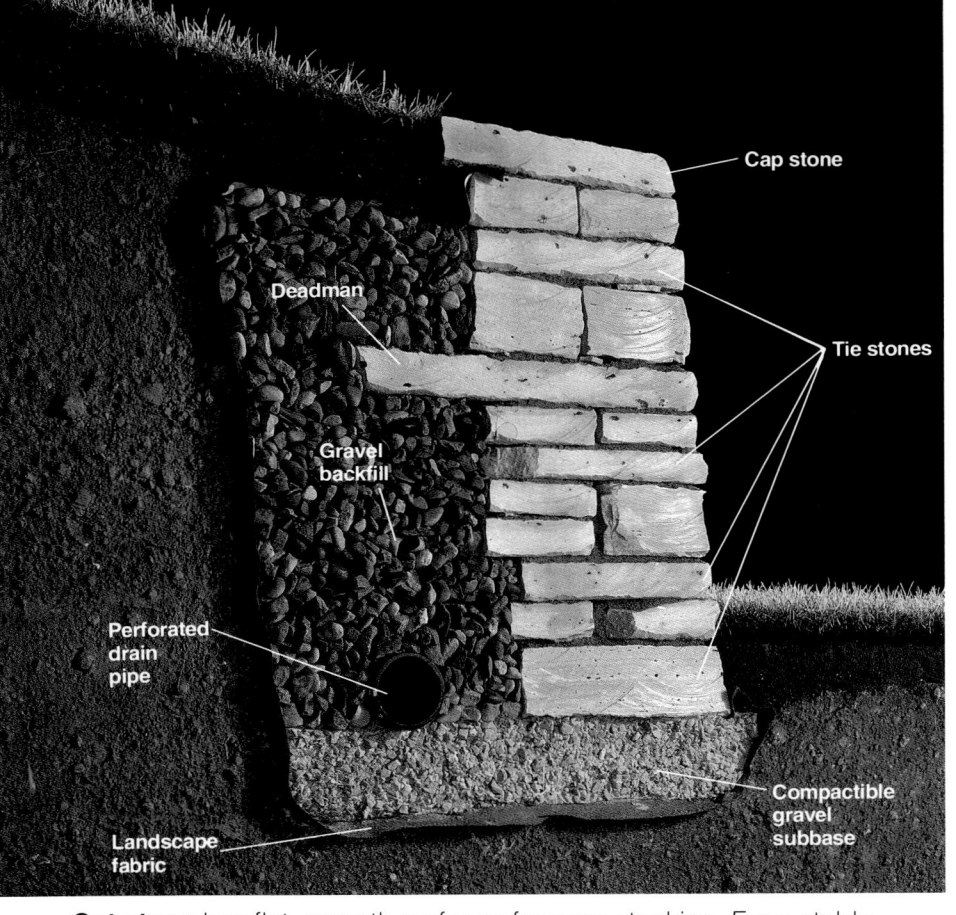

Labels on image: Cap stone · Deadman · Tie stones · Gravel backfill · Perforated drain pipe · Landscape fabric · Compactible gravel subbase

## Building a Retaining Wall Using Natural Stone

Retaining walls made from natural cut stone or rubble stone give a traditional, timeless look to a landscape. Natural stone walls usually are laid without mortar, although the last one or two rows can be mortared in place for greater strength. Unlike mortared stone or block walls (pages 238 to 243), unmortared stone walls require no concrete footings.

Before building the retaining wall, prepare the site as directed on page 230. Build the wall by placing the largest stones at the bottom and reserving the smoothest, flattest stones for the corners and the top (cap) row.

**Cut stone** has flat, smooth surfaces for easy stacking. For a stable retaining wall, alternate rows of "tie stones" that span the entire width of the wall with rows of smaller stones. Install extra-long stones (called deadmen) that extend back into gravel backfill, spaced every 4 to 6 ft.

## Retaining Wall Variations Using Rubble Stone

**Boulders** are large, uncut rocks, usually round in shape. The retaining wall site requires no subbase or backfill: simply dig out the hillside to fit the shape of the boulders and roll them into place. Boulders range in size from about 40 lbs. to several hundred lbs. For heavy boulders, you may want to hire a contractor to deliver and position the rocks.

**Field stone** refers to any irregular assortment of rough rock. You can gather field stone by hand or buy it from sand-and-gravel companies. Field-stone retaining walls do not need a subbase or backfill; but for better stability, build the wall so it tilts back into the hillside. Pack the open spaces between rocks with rock fragments or soil. If you wish, plant vines or groundcover in the exposed gaps.

## How to Build a Retaining Wall Using Cut Stone

**1** Spread a 6" layer of compactible gravel subbase into the prepared trench (step 1, page 232), then sort the stones by size and shape so they can be located easily as you build. Make sure you have enough long stones to serve as tie stones, deadmen, and cap stones.

**2** Trim irregular stones, if needed, to make them fit solidly into the wall. Always wear eye protection and hearing protectors when cutting stone. Score the stone first using a masonry blade and circular saw set to ¹/8" blade depth, then drive a masonry chisel along the scored line until the stone breaks.

**3** Lay rows of stones, following the same techniques for backfilling as for interlocking blocks (steps 2 to 7, pages 232 to 233). Build a backward slant (batter) into the wall by setting each row of stones about 1/2" back from the preceding row. For stability, work tie stones and deadmen into the wall at frequent intervals.

**4** Before laying the cap row of stones, mix mortar according to manufacturer's directions and apply a thick bed along the tops of the installed stones, keeping the mortar at least 6" from the front face of the wall. Lay the cap stones, and press them into the mortar. Because the mortar is not visible, this technique is called "blind mortaring." Finish backfilling behind the wall (step 8, page 233).

**A stucco finish and latice panels** turn a plain concrete block wall into a durable, attractive privacy wall. See pages 244 to 245 for these finishing techniques.

## Other Options for Finishing a Concrete Block Wall

**Stone veneer** (sometimes called cultured stone) copies the look of natural stone at a fraction of the cost. Available in dozens of different styles, stone veneer kits come with an assortment of flat pieces and corner pieces. The veneer is held in place with a layer of standard mortar (page 245).

**Decorative block** adds visual interest to a plain concrete block wall. Check with your local building inspector before adding block to a wall, since the added height may require extra reinforcement. Decorative block also may be used to build an entire wall (page 227).

# Building a Free-standing Wall

A free-standing wall serves the same function as a hedge or fence, but is much sturdier. Walls are popular in areas where growing shrubs and hedges is difficult. Free-standing walls can train climbing plants or support trellises or container plants. Low walls may be used as garden benches.

Most free-standing walls are built by mortaring concrete block, brick, or natural stone. The following pages show how to build a concrete block wall, but similar techniques can be used for any mortared wall.

Free-standing walls also can be built from unmortared stones, using techniques similar to those used in building a stone retaining wall (pages 236 to 237).

Limit your walls to 3 ft. in height. Taller walls need deep footings and extra reinforcement. Increase privacy by adding a trellis to the wall (photo, top left). Many local Building Codes limit the total height of the wall and trellis to 6 ft.

**Everything You Need:**

Tools: tape measure, rake, hammer, level, shovel, wheelbarrow, old paint brush, chalk line, trowel, rubber gloves, pencil, line level, masonry chisel, masonry hammer, V-shaped mortar tool, garden hoe, level.

Materials: rope, stakes, 2 × 6 lumber, compactible gravel subbase, reinforcement rods, oil, premixed concrete, concrete blocks, sheet plastic, 3/8"-thick wood strips, mortar mix, mason's string.

## How to Install a Footing for a Free-standing Wall

**1** Lay out the rough position of the wall, using a rope.

**2** Outline the wall footing, using stakes and mason's string. Check the string with a line level and adjust as needed. The footing should be twice as wide as the planned wall, and should extend 1 ft. beyond each end.

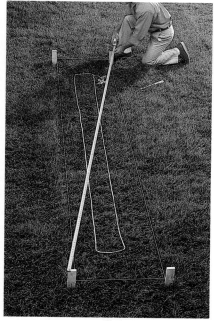

**3** Measure the diagonals to make sure the outline is square, and adjust as necessary. Dig a 1-ft.-deep trench for the footing, using the strings as a guide. Make sure the bottom of the trench is roughly level.

**4** Lay a 6" layer of compactible gravel subbase into the trench. Tamp the subbase thoroughly (page 233). NOTE: Follow local Building Code guidelines for footing depth.

**5** Build a wood form using 2 × 6 lumber, and set it in the trench. Add or remove subbase material to level the form. Drive stakes along the outside of the form to anchor it.

**6** Lay reinforcement bars inside the form to make the footing more crack-resistant. Set the bars on 2 × 4 scraps, a few inches inside the form. Coat the inside of the form with oil for easy removal.

(continued next page)

## How to Build a Free-standing Wall Using Concrete Block

**1** Test-fit a row of blocks on the footing, using smooth-sided end blocks at the ends. You may need to use half-blocks on one end to achieve the desired wall length. Use 3/8"-thick wood strips or dowels as spacers to maintain an even gap for mortar between the blocks.

Reference lines

**2** Draw pencil lines on the concrete to mark the ends of the test-fitted row. Extend the line well past the edges of the block. Use a chalk line to snap reference lines on each side of the footing, 3" from the blocks. These reference lines will serve as a guide when setting the blocks into mortar.

## How to Install a Footing for a Free-standing Wall (continued)

**7** Fill the form up to the top of the boards with concrete. Work the concrete with a shovel just enough to remove air pockets.

**8** Smooth off (screed) the surface of the concrete by dragging a short 2 × 4 along the top of the form. Add concrete to any low areas, and screed again.

**9** When concrete is hard to the touch, cover it with plastic and let it cure for 2 or 3 days. When surface has cured, pry the forms loose with a shovel.

**3** Remove the blocks and set them nearby. Mix mortar in a wheelbarrow or large pail, following manufacturer's directions. Mortar should be moist enough to hold its shape when squeezed.

**4** Trowel thick lines of mortar, slightly wider and longer than the base of the end block, onto the center of the footing. If the footing has cured for over a week, dampen it before mortaring.

**TIP:** When positioning concrete blocks, make sure the side with the wider flanges is facing upward. The wider flanges provide more surface for applying mortar.

**5** Set an end block into the mortar, so the end is aligned with the pencil mark on the footing. Set a level on top of the block, then tap the block with a trowel handle until it is level. Use the chalkline as a reference point for keeping the block in line.

**6** Apply mortar, then set and level the block at the opposite end of the footing. Stake a mason's string even with the top outside corners of the blocks. Check the string with a line level, then adjust the blocks to align with the string. Remove excess mortar, and fill the gaps beneath the end blocks (inset).

(continued next page)

**7** Apply mortar to the vertical flanges on one side of a standard block (inset) and to the footing, using a trowel. Set the block next to the end block, leaving a 3/8" layer of mortar between blocks. Tap the block into position with a trowel handle, using the string as a guide to align the block.

**8** Install the remaining blocks, working back and forth from opposite ends. Be careful to maintain 3/8" joints to ensure that the last block in the row will fit. Make sure the row is level and straight by aligning the blocks with the mason's string and checking them with a carpenter's level.

**9** At the middle of the row, apply mortar to the vertical flanges on both sides of the last block, then slide the block down into place. Align the last block with the mason's string.

**10** Apply a 1" layer of mortar to the top flanges of the end blocks. Scrape off any mortar that falls onto the footing.

**11** Begin laying the second row. Use half-size end blocks to create staggered vertical joints. Check with a straightedge to make sure the new blocks are aligned with the bottom blocks.

**VARIATION:** If your wall has a corner, begin the second row with a full-sized end block that spans the vertical joint formed where two sides of the wall meet. This creates staggered vertical joints.

**12** Insert a nail into the wet mortar at each end of the wall. Attach a mason's string to one nail, then stretch the string up over the corners of the end blocks and tie it to the nail at the opposite end.

**13** Install the second row of blocks, using the same method as with the first row. When the second row is completed, remove the nails and mason's string. Scrape off excess mortar, and finish the joints with a V-shaped mortar tool. Install each additional row of blocks by repeating steps 11 to 13. Finish the joints as each row of blocks is completed.

**14** Complete the wall with a row of cap blocks. Cap blocks are very heavy, and must be laid gently to keep mortar from being squeezed out. If you are adding lattice panels to the top of the wall, insert J-bolts into the joints between the cap blocks while mortar is still wet (page 244).

## How to Add Lattice Panels to a Block Wall

**1** While mortar is still wet, install ³/8"-diameter J-bolts into the center of the cap row joints at post locations. About 1" of the bolt should protrude. Pack mortar around the bolt and let it harden. (If mortar already has hardened, see OPTION, step 2.)

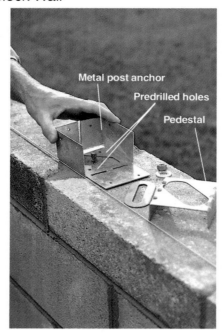

**2** Align and attach a metal post anchor at each post location. Slip an oval washer over each J-bolt, then attach a nut. OPTION: Attach metal post anchors by driving self-tapping masonry anchors through the predrilled holes in the bottom of the post anchor.

**3** Set a metal pedestal into each anchor. The top of the J-bolt should be below the pedestal.

**4** Cut a 4 × 4 post for each anchor. Set the post on the pedestal, then bend the open flange up against the post. Make sure the post is plumb, then attach it with 6d galvanized nails.

**5** Assemble and install lattice panels between posts, as directed on page 285. Most lattice panels are 8 ft. long, and can be cut to fit if your posts are spaced less than 8 ft. apart.

## How to Finish a Block Wall with Stucco

**1** Attach wire lath to the entire surface of all wall faces, using self-tapping masonry anchors. Lath provides a surface for application of stucco or mortar (step 1, below).

**2** Mix stucco, using a ratio of 3 parts sand and 2 parts portland cement, adding enough water so the mixture holds its shape when squeezed. Trowel a 3/8"-thick layer directly onto the metal lath. Scratch grooves into the surface of the stucco, then let the coat cure for two days. Dampen a few times daily.

**3** Apply a second 3/8" layer of the same stucco mixture over the first coat. Do not scratch this layer. Let stucco cure for two days. Dampen a few times daily.

**4** Mix a finish stucco coat, using 1 part lime, 3 parts sand, and 6 parts white cement. Dampen walls, and dab a finish coat onto the wall, using a whisk broom.

**5** Flatten the surface of the finish coat with a trowel. Dampen the wall daily for three or four days to complete the curing.

## How to Apply Stone Veneer to a Block Wall

**1** Prepare wall with wire lath (step 1, above), then apply a 1/2"-thick layer of standard mortar to the wall. Scratch grooves into the damp mortar, using the trowel tip, then allow to dry overnight. Beginning at the bottom of the wall, apply mortar to the back of each veneer piece, then press it onto the wall with a twisting motion. Keep a 1/2" gap between pieces.

**2** After mortar has dried for a day, fill the joints with fresh mortar, using a mortar bag. Use a V-shaped mortar tool to finish the joints (step 13, page 243).

**Flagstone** walkways combine charm with durability, and work well in both casual and formal settings. Also a popular material for patios, flagstone can be set in sand, or it can be mortared in place. See pages 250 to 251. TIP: Prevent damage to the edging material by trimming near the walkway with a line-feed trimmer instead of a mower.

# Building Walkways & Paths

Walkways and paths serve as "hallways" between heavily used areas of your yard, and can be used to direct traffic toward a favorite landscape feature, like a pond. Walkways also create a visual corridor that directs the eye from one area to another.

Curved paths give a softer, more relaxed look to a landscape, but straight or angular paths and walkways fit well in contemporary landscape designs.

Garden paths often are made from loose materials, like crushed rock or bark, held in place by edging. Walkways are more durable when made from stone or brick paving materials set in sand or mortar. Poured concrete sidewalks are practical and the most durable, but unless you have a lot of experience pouring and curing concrete, do not attempt to build them yourself. Most paving techniques used in patio construction (pages 262 to 271) can be used for walkways as well.

**Everything You Need:**

Tools: tape measure, spade, garden rake, rubber mallet, circular saw with masonry blade, masonry chisel, masonry hammer.

Materials: landscape fabric, garden hose, edging material (page 248), walkway surface materials, galvanized screws, 2 × 6 lumber. Added supplies for mortared brick walkways: mortar, mortar bag, V-shaped mortar tool, trowel.

**Loose materials**, such as gravel, crushed rock, wood chips and bark, make informal, inexpensive pathways that are well suited for light-traffic areas. Build loose-material paths with the surface material slightly above ground level, to keep it from being washed away.

**Brick pavers** provide stately charm to a main walkway, making a house more appealing from the street. Because pavers are very durable, they are ideal for heavy-traffic areas. Brick pavers can be set in sand, or mortared in place over an old concrete surface. Pavers used for mortared walkways often are thinner than those designed for sand installation.

## Tips for Building a Walkway

**Use a sod cutter** to strip grass from your pathway site. Available at most rental centers, sod cutters excavate to a very even depth. The cut sod can be replanted in other parts of your lawn.

**Install stakes and strings** when laying out straight walkways made from stone paving materials, and measure from the strings to ensure straight sides and uniform excavation depth.

**Brick edging** makes a good boundary for both straight and curved paths made from loose materials. See page 249.

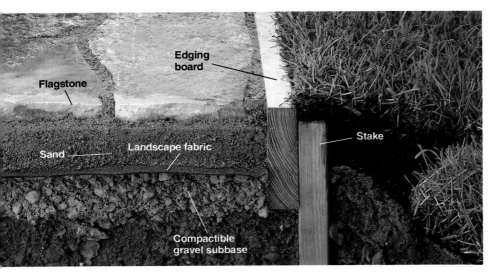

**Wood edging** makes a sturdy border for straight walkways made from flagstone or brick pavers set in sand. See pages 250 to 251.

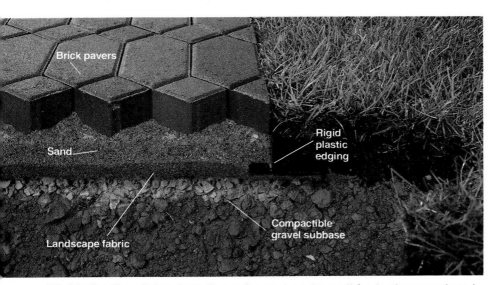

**Rigid plastic edging** installs easily, and works well for both curved and straight walkways made from paving stones or brick pavers set in sand. See pages 262 to 271.

## Types of Edging

Use edging to keep walkway materials in place. Consider cost, appearance, flexibility, and ease of installation when selecting an edging type.

**Brick edging** set in soil is good for casual, lightly traveled pathways, but should be used only in soil that is dense and well drained. (Bricks in loose or swampy soil will not hold their position.) Bricks can be set vertically, or tilted at an angle to make a saw-tooth pattern. Brick pavers also can be mortared to the sides of an old sidewalk to create a border for a new surface (pages 252 to 253).

**Wood edging** made from pressure-treated lumber, redwood, or cedar is inexpensive and easy to install. The tops of the boards are left exposed to create an attractive border. The wood edging boards are held in place by attaching them to recessed wood stakes spaced every 12" along the outside of the edging.

**Rigid plastic edging** is inconspicuous, durable, and easy to install. It was developed as an edging for brick pavers set in sand. Rigid plastic edging is held in place by the weight of the soil and with galvanized spikes driven through the back flange. Rolled vinyl edging is used most often to make boundaries for planting areas (pages 294 to 295), but also works as an edging for casual walkways. It is inexpensive and very flexible.

# How to Build a Path Using Loose Materials & Brick Edging

**1** Outline the path using a garden hose or rope (page 208), then excavate the site to a depth of 2" to 3", using a spade, hoe, or a rented sod cutter (page 247). Rake the site smooth.

**2** Dig narrow edging trenches about 2" deeper than the path site along both edges of the excavation, using a spade or hoe.

**3** Lay landscaping fabric between the edging trenches to prevent weeds from growing. Overlap sheets by at least 6".

**4** Set bricks on end into the edging trenches, with the tops slightly above ground level. Pack soil behind and beneath each brick, adjusting the bricks, if necessary, to keep the rows even.

**5** Finish the path by spreading loose material (gravel, crushed rock, bark, or wood chips) between the rows of edging bricks. Level the surface with a garden rake. The loose material should be slightly above ground level. Tap each brick lightly on the inside face to help set it into the soil. Inspect and adjust the bricks yearly, adding new loose material as needed.

## How to Build a Flagstone Walkway Using Wood Edging

**1** Outline the walkway site and excavate to a depth of 6". Allow enough room for the edging and stakes (step 2). For straight walkways, use stakes and strings to maintain a uniform outline (page 247). Add a 2" layer of compactible gravel subbase, using a rake to smooth the surface.

**2** Install 2 × 6 edging made from pressure-treated lumber around the sides of the site. Drive 12" stakes on the outside of the edging, spaced 12" apart. Tops of the stakes should be below ground level. Attach the edging to the stakes using galvanized screws.

**3** Test-fit the flagstones to find an efficient, attractive arrangement of stones. Arrange the stones to minimize the number of cuts needed. Leave a gap between stones that is at least 3/8", but no more than 2" wide. Use a pencil to mark stones for cutting, then remove the stones and set them nearby.

**4** Cut flagstones by scoring along the marked lines with a circular saw and masonry blade set to 1/8" blade depth. Set a piece of wood under the stone, just inside the scored line, then use a masonry chisel and hammer to strike along the scored line until the stone breaks.

**5** Lay sheets of landscape fabric over the walkway site to prevent plants and grass from growing up between the stones. (Omit the landscape fabric if you want to plant grass or ground cover to fill the cracks.) Spread a 2" layer of sand over the landscape fabric to serve as the base for the flagstones.

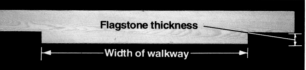

**6** Make a "screed" for smoothing the sand by notching the ends of a short 2 × 6 to fit inside the edging (see inset). The depth of the notches should equal the thickness of the stones, usually about 2". Screed the base by pulling the 2 × 6 from one end of the walkway to the other. Add more sand as needed until the base is smooth.

**7** Beginning at one corner of the walkway, lay the flagstones onto the sand base so the gap between stones is at least ³/8", but no more than 2". If needed, add or remove sand beneath stones to level them. Set the stones by tapping them with a rubber mallet or a length of 2 × 4.

**8** Fill the gaps between stones with sand. (Use soil if you are planting grass or ground cover in the cracks.) Pack the sand with your fingers or a piece of scrap wood, then spray the walkway lightly with water to help the sand settle. Add new sand as necessary until gaps are filled.

# How to Resurface a Sidewalk Using Mortared Brick Pavers

**1** Select a paver pattern (page 263), then dig a trench around the concrete, slightly wider than the thickness of one paver. Dig the trench so it is about 3½" below the concrete surface. Soak the pavers with water before mortaring. Dry pavers absorb moisture, weaking the mortar strength.

**2** Sweep the old concrete, then hose off the surface and sides with water to clear away dirt and debris. Mix a small batch of mortar according to manufacturer's directions. For convenience, place the mortar on a scrap of plywood.

**3** Install edging bricks by applying a ½" layer of mortar to the side of the concrete slab and to one side of each brick. Set bricks into the trench, against the concrete. Brick edging should be ½" higher than the thickness of the brick pavers.

**4** Finish the joints on the edging bricks with a V-shaped mortar tool (step 9), then mix and apply a ½"-thick bed of mortar to one end of the sidewalk, using a trowel. Mortar hardens very quickly, so work in sections no larger than 4 sq. ft.

**5** Make a "screed" for smoothing mortar by notching the ends of a short 2 × 4 to fit between the edging bricks (page 251). Depth of the notches should equal the thickness of the pavers. Drag the screed across the mortar bed until the mortar is smooth.

**6** Lay the paving bricks one at a time into the mortar, maintaining a ½" gap between pavers. (A piece of scrap plywood works well as a spacing guide.) Set the pavers by tapping them lightly with a rubber mallet.

**7** As each section of pavers is completed, check with a straightedge to make sure the tops of the pavers are even.

**8** When all the pavers are installed, use a mortar bag to fill the joints between the pavers with fresh mortar. Work in 4-sq.-ft. sections, and avoid getting mortar on the tops of the pavers.

**9** Use a V-shaped mortar tool to finish the joints as you complete each 4-sq.-ft. section. For best results, finish the longer joints first, then the shorter joints. Use a trowel to remove excess mortar.

**10** Let the mortar dry for a few hours, then scrub the pavers with a coarse rag and water. Cover the walkway with plastic and let the mortar cure for at least 24 hours. Remove plastic, but do not walk on the pavers for at least three days.

**Riser**

**Tread**

**Simple garden steps** can be built by making a series of concrete platforms framed with 5 × 6 timbers. Garden steps have shorter vertical risers and deeper horizontal treads than house stairs. Risers for garden stairs should be no more than 6", and treads should be at least 11" deep.

# Building Garden Steps

Garden steps make sloping yards safer and more accessible. They also add visual interest by introducing new combinations of materials into your landscape design.

You can build garden steps with a wide variety of materials, including flagstone, brick, timbers, concrete block, or poured concrete. Whatever materials you use, make sure the steps are level and firmly anchored. They should be easy to climb and have a rough texture for good traction.

### Everything You Need:

Tools: chain saw or reciprocating saw with 12" wood-cutting blade, tape measure, level, masonry hammer, shovel, drill with 1" spade bit and bit extension, rake, wheelbarrow, hoe, concrete float, edging tool, stiff brush.

Materials: 2 × 4 lumber, 5 × 6 landscape timbers, mason's string, 3/4" I.D. (interior diameter) black pipe, 12" galvanized spikes, premixed concrete, compactible gravel subbase, seed gravel (1/2" maximum diameter), sheet plastic, burlap.

## Tips for Mixing Concrete

**For large amounts** (more than 1/2 cubic yard), mix your own dry ingredients in a wheelbarrow or rented mixer. Use a ratio of 1 part portland cement (A), 2 parts sand (B), and 3 parts gravel (C). See page 213 to estimate the amount of concrete needed.

**For small amounts** (less than 1/2 cubic yard), buy premixed bags of dry concrete. A 60-lb. bag of concrete creates about 1/2 cubic foot of concrete. A special hoe with holes in the blade is useful for mixing concrete.

## Tips for Building Garden Steps

1/8" downward pitch per foot

**Build a slight downward pitch** into outdoor steps so water will drain off without puddling. Do not exceed a pitch of 1/8" per foot.

**Order custom-cut timbers** to reduce installation time if the dimensions of each step are identical. Some building supply centers charge a small fee for custom-cutting timbers.

## How to Plan Garden Steps

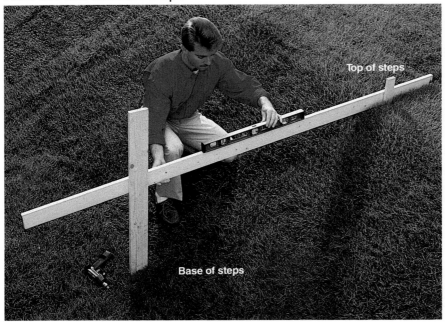

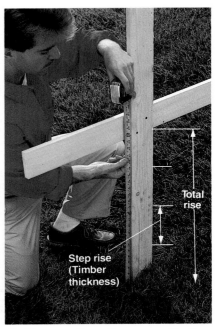

**1** Drive a tall stake into the ground at the base of the stairway site. Adjust the stake so it is exactly plumb. Drive a shorter stake at the top of the site. Position a long, straight 2 × 4 against the stakes, with one end touching the ground next to the top stake. Adjust the 2 × 4 so it is level, then attach it to the stakes with screws. (For long spans, use a mason's string instead of a 2 × 4.)

**2** Measure from the ground to the bottom of the 2 × 4 to find the total vertical **rise** of the stairway. Divide the rise by the actual thickness of the timbers (6" if using 5 × 6 timbers) to find the number of steps required. Round off fractions to the nearest full number.

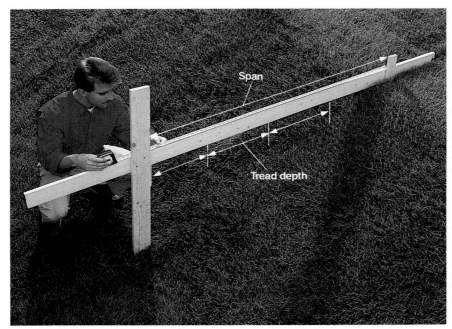

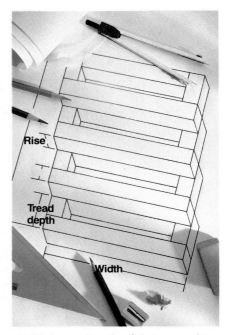

**3** Measure along the 2 × 4 between the stakes to find the total horizontal **span**. Divide the span by the number of steps to find the depth of each step tread. If depth is less than 11", revise the step layout to extend the depth of the step treads.

**4** Make a sketch of the step site, showing rise, tread depth, and width of each step. Remember that actual timber dimensions may vary from the nominal measurements.

# How to Build Garden Steps Using Timbers & Concrete

**1** Mark the sides of the step site with stakes and string. The stakes should be positioned at the front edge of the bottom step and the back edge of the top step.

**2** Add the width of a timber (5") to the tread depth, then measure back this distance from the stakes and drive additional stakes to mark the back edge of the first step. Connect these stakes with string to mark the digging area for the first step.

**3** Excavate for the first step, creating a flat bed with a very slight forward slope, no more than 1/8" from back to front. Front of excavation should be no more than 2" deep. Tamp the soil firmly.

**4** For each step, use a chain saw or reciprocating saw to cut a front timber equal to the step width, a back timber 10" shorter, and two side timbers equal to the tread depth.

(continued next page)

## How to Build Garden Steps Using Timbers & Concrete (continued)

**5** Arrange the timbers to form the step frame, and end-nail them together with 12" spikes.

**6** Set the timber frame in position. Use a carpenter's square to make sure the frame is square, and adjust as necessary. Drill two 1" guide holes in the front timber and the back timber, 1 ft. from the ends, using a spade bit and bit extension.

**7** Anchor the steps to the ground by driving a 2 1/2-ft. length of 3/4" pipe through each guide hole until the pipe is flush with the timber. When pipes are driven, make sure the frame is level from side to side and has the proper forward pitch. Excavate for the next step, making sure the bottom of the excavation is even with top edge of the installed timbers.

Drive pipes here

**8** Build another step frame and position it in the excavation so the front timber is directly over the rear timber on the first frame. Nail the steps together with three 12" spikes, then drill guide holes and drive two pipes through only the back timber to anchor the second frame.

**9** Continue digging and installing the remaining frames until the steps reach full height. The back of the last step should be at ground level.

**10** Staple plastic over the timbers to protect them from wet concrete. Cut away the plastic so it does not overhang into the frame opening.

**11** Pour a 2" layer of compactible gravel subbase into each frame, and use a 2 × 4 to smooth it out.

**12** Mix concrete in a wheelbarrow, adding just enough water so the concrete holds its shape when sliced with a trowel. NOTE: To save time and labor, you can have ready-mix concrete delivered to the site. Ready-mix companies will deliver concrete in amounts as small as 1/3 cubic yard (enough for three steps of the type shown here).

**13** Shovel concrete into the bottom frame, flush with the top of the timbers. Work the concrete lightly with a garden rake to help remove air bubbles, but do not overwork the concrete.

(continued next page)

# How to Build Garden Steps Using Timbers & Concrete (continued)

**14** Smooth (screed) the concrete by dragging a 2 x 4 across the top of the frame. If necessary, add concrete to low areas and screed again until the surface is smooth and free of low spots.

**15** While the concrete is still wet, "seed" it by scattering mixed gravel onto the surface. Sand-and-gravel suppliers and garden centers sell colorful gravel designed for seeding. For best results, select a mixture with stones no larger than 1/2" in diameter.

**16** Press the seeded gravel into the surface of the concrete, using a concrete float, until the tops of the stones are flush with the surface of the concrete. Remove any concrete that spills over the edges of the frame, using a trowel.

**17** Pour concrete into remaining steps, screeding and seeding each step before moving on to the next. For a neater appearance, use an edging tool (inset) to smooth the cracks between the timbers and the concrete as each step is finished.

**18** When the sheen disappears from the poured concrete (4 to 6 hours after pouring), use a float to smooth out any high or low spots in each step. Be careful not to force seeded gravel too far into the concrete. Let the concrete dry overnight.

**19** After concrete has dried overnight, apply a fine mist of water to the surface, then scrub it with a stiff brush to expose the seeded gravel.

**VARIATION:** To save time and money, skip the seeding procedure. To create a nonslip surface on smooth concrete, draw a stiff-bristled brush or broom once across the concrete while it is still wet.

**20** Remove the plastic from the timbers, and cover the concrete with burlap. Allow concrete to cure for several days, spraying it occasionally with water to ensure even curing. NOTE: Concrete residue can be cleaned from timbers, using a solution of 5% muriatic acid and water.

# Building a Patio

A patio can serve as the visual centerpiece of your yard and as the focus of your outdoor life-style. To be functional, a patio should be as large as a standard room—100 square feet or more.

Brick pavers are the most common material used for patios, but you can also build a patio with flagstone, following the same methods used for flagstone walkways (pages 246 to 253).

The most important part of a patio project is ex-cavating and creating a flat base with the proper slope for drainage. This work is easier if you build your patio on a site that is relatively flat and level. On a hilly, uneven yard, you may be able to create flat space for a patio by building a retaining wall terrace (pages 228 to 237).

### Everything You Need

Tools: tape measure, carpenter's level, shovel, line level, rake, hand tamper, tamping machine.

Materials: stakes, mason's string, compactible gravel subbase, rigid plastic edging, land-scape fabric, sand, pavers, 1"-thick pipes.

**Interlocking brick pavers** come in many shapes and colors. Two popular paver styles include Uni-Decor™ (left) and Symmetry™ (right). Patios made with interlocking pavers may have a border row made from standard brick pavers (page opposite).

## Common Paving Patterns for Standard Brick Pavers

**Standard brick pavers** can be arranged in several different patterns, including: (A) running bond, (B) jack-on-jack, (C) herringbone, and (D) basketweave. Jack-on-jack and basketweave patterns require fewer cut pavers along the edges. Standard pavers have spacing lugs on the sides that automatically set the joints at $1/8$" width. See page 213 to estimate the number of pavers you will need for your patio.

## Installation Variations for Brick Pavers

**Sand-set:** Pavers rest on a 1" bed of sand laid over a 4" compactible gravel subbase. Rigid plastic edging holds the sand base in place. Joints are $1/8$" wide, and are packed with sand, which holds the pavers securely yet allows them to shift slightly as temperatures change.

**Dry mortar:** Installation is similar to sand-set patio, but joints are $3/8$" wide, and are packed with a mixture of sand and mortar, soaked with water, and finished with a V-shaped mortar tool. A dry-mortar patio has a more finished masonry look than a sand-set patio, but the joints must be repaired periodically.

**Wet mortar:** This method often is used when pavers are installed over an old concrete patio or sidewalk (see pages 252 to 253). Joints are $1/2$" wide. Wet mortar installation can also be used with flagstone. For edging on a wet-mortar patio, use rigid plastic edging or paver bricks set on end.

## How to Build a Sand-set Patio with Brick Pavers

**1** To find exact patio measurements and reduce the number of cut bricks needed, test-fit perpendicular rows of brick pavers on a flat surface, like a driveway. Lay two rows to reach the rough length and width of your patio, then measure the rows to find the exact size. (For a dry-mortar patio, put 3/8" spaces between pavers when test-fitting the rows.)

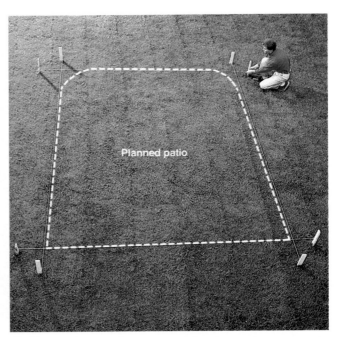

**2** Use stakes and mason's string to mark out a rectangle that matches the length and width of your patio. Drive the stakes so they are at least 1 ft. outside the site of the planned patio. The intersecting strings mark the actual corners of the patio site.

**3** Check the rectangle for squareness by measuring the diagonals (A-C, B-D). If the rectangle is square, the diagonals will have the same measurement. If not, adjust the stakes and strings until the diagonals are equal. The strings will serve as a reference for excavating the patio site.

**4** Using a line level as a guide, adjust one of the strings until it is level. When the string is level, mark its height on the stakes at each end of the string.

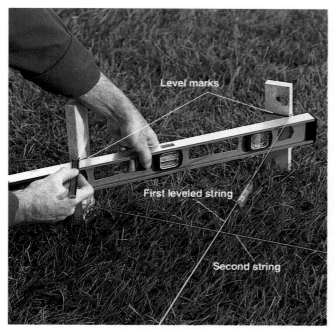

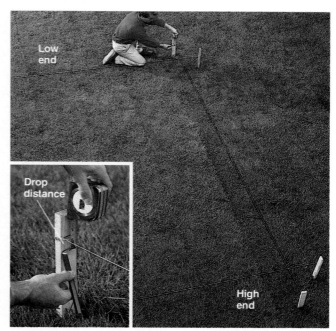

**5** To adjust each remaining string so it is level and even with the first string, use a carpenter's level as a guide for marking adjacent stakes, then adjust the strings to the reference marks. Use a line level to make sure all strings are level.

**6** To ensure good drainage, choose one end of the patio as the low end. (For most patios, this will be the end farthest from the house.) Measure from the high end to the low end (in feet), then multiply this number by 1/8" to find the proper drop distance. Measure down from the level marks on the low-end stakes, and mark the drop distance (inset).

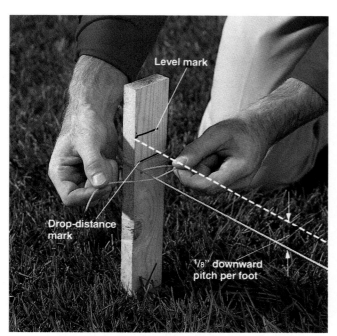

**7** Lower the strings at the low-end stakes so the strings are even with the drop-distance marks. Keep all strings in place as a guide while excavating the site and installing the edging.

**8** Remove all sod inside the strings and 6" beyond the edges of the planned patio. NOTE: If your patio will have rounded corners, use a garden hose or rope to outline the excavation.

(continued next page)

**9** Starting at the outside edge, excavate the patio site so it is at least 5" deeper than the thickness of the pavers. For example, if your pavers are 1³/4" thick, excavate to a depth of 6 ³/4". Try to follow the slope of the side strings, and periodically use a long 2 × 4 to check the bottom of the excavation site for high and low spots.

**10** Pour compactible gravel subbase over the patio site, then rake it into a smooth layer at least 4" deep. The thickness of the subbase layer may vary to compensate for unevenness in the excavation. Use a long 2 × 4 to check the surface of the subbase for high and low spots, and add or remove compactible gravel as needed.

**11** Pack the subbase using a tamping machine until the surface is firm and flat. Check the slope of the subbase by measuring down from the side strings (see step 14). The space between the strings and the subbase should be equal at all points.

**12** Cut strips of landscape fabric and lay them over the subbase to prevent weeds from growing up through the patio. Make sure the strips overlap by at least 6".

**13** Install rigid plastic edging around the edges of the patio below the reference strings. Anchor the edging by driving galvanized spikes through the predrilled holes and into the subbase. To allow for possible adjustments, drive only enough spikes to keep the edging in place.

**14** Check the slope by measuring from the string to the top of the edging at several points. The measurement should be the same at each point. If not, adjust the edging by adding or removing sub-base material under the landscape fabric until the edging follows the slope of the strings.

**15** For curves and rounded patio corners, use rigid plastic edging with notches on the outside flange. It may be necessary to anchor each section of edging with spikes to hold curved edging in place.

**16** Remove the reference strings, then set 1"-thick pipes or wood strips across the patio area, spaced every 6 ft., to serve as depth spacers for laying the sand base.

(continued next page)

## How to Build a Sand-set Patio with Brick Pavers (continued)

**17** Lay a 1"-thick layer of sand over the landscape fabric and smooth it out with a garden rake. Sand should just cover the tops of the depth spacers.

**18** Water the sand thoroughly, and pack it lightly with a hand tamper.

**19** Screed the sand to an even layer by resting a long 2 × 4 on the spacers embedded in the sand and drawing the 2 × 4 across the spacers using a sawing motion. Add extra sand to fill footprints and low areas, then water, tamp, and screed the sand again until it is smooth and firmly packed.

**20** Remove the embedded spacers along the sides of the patio base, then fill the grooves with sand and pat them smooth with the hand tamper.

**21** Lay the first border paver in one corner of the patio. Make sure the paver rests firmly against the rigid plastic edging.

**22** Lay the next border paver so it is tight against the previous paver. Set the pavers by tapping them into the sand with a mallet. Use the depth of the first paver as a guide for setting the remaining pavers.

**23** Working outward from the corner, install 2-ft.-wide sections of border pavers and interior pavers, following the desired pattern. Keep the joints between pavers very tight. Set each paver by tapping it with the mallet.

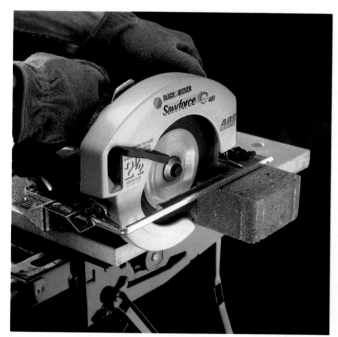

**24** If your patio pattern requires that you cut pavers, use a circular saw with a diamond-tipped blade or masonry blade to saw them to size. Always wear eye protection and work gloves when cutting pavers.

**25** After each section of pavers is set, use a straightedge to make sure the pavers are flat. Make adjustments by tapping high pavers deeper into the sand, or by removing low pavers and adding a thin layer of extra sand underneath them.

(continued next page)

## How to Build a Sand-set Patio with Brick Pavers (continued)

**26** Remove the remaining spacers when the installed surface gets near to them. Fill the gaps left by the spacers with loose sand, and pat the surface smooth with a hand tamper (inset).

**27** Continue installing 2-ft.-wide sections of border pavers and interior pavers. As you approach the opposite side of the patio, reposition the rigid plastic edging, if necessary, so full-sized pavers will fit without cutting.

**28** At rounded corners and curves, install border pavers in a fan pattern with even gaps between the pavers. Gentle curves may accommodate full-sized border pavers, but for sharper bends you may need to mark and trim wedge-shaped border pavers to make them fit.

**29** Lay the remaining interior pavers. Where partial pavers are needed, hold a paver over the gap, and mark the cut with a pencil and straightedge. Cut pavers with a circular saw and masonry blade (step 24). After all pavers are installed, drive in the remaining edging spikes and pack soil behind the edging.

**30** Use a long 2 × 4 to check the entire patio for flatness. Adjust uneven pavers by tapping high pavers deeper into the sand, or by removing low pavers and adding a thin layer of extra sand underneath them. After adjusting bricks, use a mason's string to check the rows for straightness.

**31** Spread a 1/2" layer of sand over the patio. Use the tamping machine to compress the entire patio and pack sand into the joints.

**32** Sweep up the loose sand, then soak the patio area thoroughly to settle the sand in the joints. Let the surface dry completely. If necessary, repeat step 31 until the gaps between pavers are packed tightly with sand.

**Dry-mortar option:** For a finished masonry look, install pavers with a 3/8" gap between bricks. Instead of sand, fill gaps with a dry mixture made from 4 parts sand and 1 part dry mortar. After spreading the dry mixture and tamping the patio, sprinkle surface with water. While mortar joints are damp, finish them with a V-shaped mortar tool (shown above). After mortar hardens, scrub pavers with water and a coarse rag.

# Fences, Arbors & Trellises

Screening structures like fences, arbors, and trellises serve many functions in a landscape. They can protect privacy, improve home security, block sunlight, or diffuse strong winds. They also let you add attractive wood colors and textures to your landscape design.

Moisture poses the greatest threat to outdoor wood structures, so always choose lumber suited for exposure to water. Redwood and cedar have natural resistance to decay and insect damage, but pressure-treated pine lumber is less expensive and more durable. For a more attractive appearance, stain pressure-treated lumber to make it resemble redwood or cedar. Use only rust-proof nails, screws, and metal connectors to assemble your wood structures.

A variety of preassembled wood panels (top photo, page opposite) is available to simplify construction of fences and other screening structures. Or, you can build your structures from standard dimension lumber. Whatever wood you choose, protect your investment by coating wood structures with a fresh coat of sealer-preservative or paint every two or three years.

**Preassembled panels** for landscape structures include: (A) lattice panels, (B) solid panels with lattice tops, (C) staggered board, (D) horizontal board, (E) modified picket, and (F) dog-eared board. Lattice panels, often used for trellises and arbors, are available in 2 × 8 and 4 × 8 sheets. The remaining panels, used for fences, are available in 4 × 8 and 6 × 8 sizes. Preassembled gates (inset) are available to match some panel styles. Cost of panels varies widely depending on the quality of the product.

## Tips for Building Wood Screening Structures

**Use metal connectors** to join wood components. Galvanized metal connectors simplify installation and help strengthen the structure. Exposed metal can be painted to make it less visible.

**Protect the tops of posts** from moisture by trimming them to a point so water will run off, or by covering them with metal or wood post caps.

**Apply sealer-preservative** to the end-grain of cut lumber as you build outdoor structures. The end-grain, even in pressure-treated lumber, is vulnerable to moisture and rot.

# Building a Wood Fence

A fence is as much a part of the neighborhood's landscape as your own. For this reason, local Building Codes and neighborhood covenants may restrict how and where you can build a fence.

In residential areas, for example, privacy fences usually are limited to 6 ft. in height. Remember that the fence you build to give you privacy also will obstruct the view of neighbors. Avoid hard feelings by discussing your plans with neighbors before building a fence. If you are willing to compromise, you may find that neighbors will share the work and expense.

Determine the exact property boundaries before you lay out the fence lines. You may need to call the city or county surveyor to pinpoint these boundaries. To avoid disputes, position your fence at least 6" inside the property line, even if there are no setback regulations (page 207).

To ensure sturdy construction, all screening fences should have posts anchored with concrete footings. When buying posts. remember that footing depths are determined by your local

Building Code. In cold climates, local Codes may require that fence footings extend past the winter frost line.

Many homes have chain-link fences that provide security but are not very attractive. To soften the look of chain-link, plant climbing vines, shrubs, or tall perennials against the fence.

**Everything You Need:**

Tools: tape measure, line level, plumb bob, rented power auger, circular saw, pencil, shovel, hammer, cordless screwdriver, paint brush, pressure sprayer.

Materials: 4 × 4 fence posts, stakes, mason's string, masking tape, coarse gravel, 2 × 4 lumber, premixed concrete, fence panels or boards, galvanized fence brackets, 4d galvanized nails, 3" galvanized utility screws, preassembled gate, gate hinges and latch, post caps, galvanized casing nails, liquid sealer-preservative.

# Wood Fence Variations

**A panel fence** is easy to build, and is well suited for yards that are flat or that have a steady, gradual slope. On a sloped lot, install the panels in a step pattern, trying to keep an even vertical drop between panels. It is difficult to cut most preassembled panels, so try to plan the layout so only full-width panels are used. See pages 276 to 279.

**A low fence** establishes boundaries and adds to the landscape design, but it does not block your view completely. Low fences work well for confining children or pets.

**A split-rail fence** is an inexpensive, easy-to-build alternative that complements rustic, informal landscapes. Building centers stock precut cedar rails and posts for split-rail fences.

**A board-and-stringer** fence is made with individually cut pieces of lumber. A board-and-stringer fence is a good choice if preassembled panels are unavailable, or if your yard has steep or irregular slopes. See pages 280 to 281.

## How to Install Fence Posts

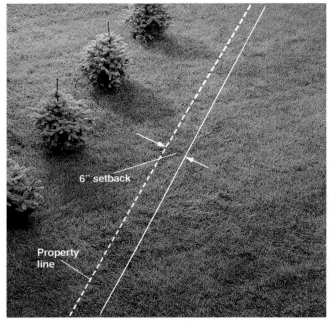

**1** Determine the exact property lines if your fence will adjoin your neighbor's property. Plan your fence line with a setback of at least 6" from the legal property line. (Local regulations may require a larger setback.)

**2** Mark the fence line with stakes and mason's string. Using a line level as a guide, adjust the string until it is level.

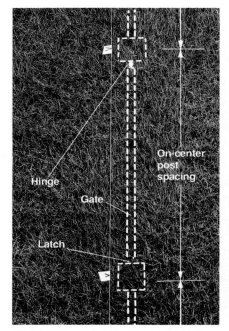

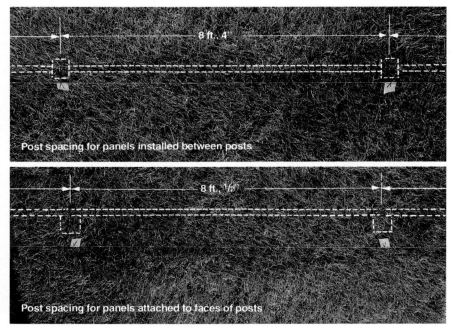

**3** Use masking tape to mark the string where the gate posts will be installed. Measure gate width, including hinges and latch hardware, then add 4" to find the on-center spacing between posts.

**4** Mark string at remaining post locations. For a panel fence, try to plan the layout so cut panels will not be needed. If your fence will use 8-ft-long panels installed between 4 × 4 posts, space the posts 8 ft., 4" apart, on-center (top). If panels will be attached to faces of posts, space the posts 8 ft., 1/2" apart, on-center (bottom). For a custom board-and-stringer fence, posts can be set closer together for greater strength.

**5** Use a plumb bob to pinpoint the post locations on the ground, then mark the locations with stakes and remove the string.

**6** Dig post holes with a power auger, available at rental centers. Holes should be 6" deeper than the post footing depth specified by your local Building Code. Pour a 6" layer of gravel into each hole to improve drainage.

**7** Position each post in its hole. Adjust the post until it is plumb, then brace it with scrap pieces of 2 × 4 driven into the ground and screwed to the sides of the post.

**8** When all posts are in position, use the mason's string to make sure the fence line is straight. Adjust the posts, if necessary, until the fence line is straight and the posts are plumb.

**9** Fill each post hole with premixed concrete. Overfill the holes slightly. Check posts to make sure they are plumb, then shape the concrete around the bottom of each post to form a rounded crown that will shed water (inset). Let concrete cure for 48 hours before continuing with fence construction.

## How to Install Preassembled Fence Panels

**1** After posts are installed (pages 276 to 277), test-fit the panels and gates to make sure they fit between the posts. If necessary, trim the edges of the panels slightly to improve the fit (inset).

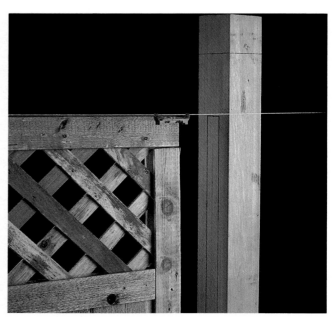

**2** Mark the position of fence panels on the sides of the posts. Make sure the bottom of the panels will be at least 2" above ground level. On level sites, use a line level to ensure that the outlines are at the same level. On a sloped site where panels will be installed step-fashion, try to maintain a uniform vertical drop with each panel.

**3** Attach three evenly spaced fence brackets inside each drawn outline on the sides of the posts, using 4d galvanized nails. The bottom bracket should be aligned against the bottom of the outline (inset). On the top two brackets, bend the bottom flange flat against the post. See VARIATION (next page) if panels will be attached to the front faces of the posts.

**4** Slide the fence panels into the brackets from above until they rest on the bottom flanges of the lowest brackets. Attach the panels from each side by driving 4d galvanized nails through the holes in the brackets (inset). NOTE: To provide easy access for delivering furniture or other large materials through your yard, attach one fence panel with screws so it can be removed easily.

**VARIATION:** To attach panels to the front faces of posts, position each panel so it is level, then anchor it by driving galvanized utility screws through panel frames and into the posts. Space the screws 18" apart.

**5** Attach three evenly spaced hinges to the gate frame, using galvanized screws. Follow the hardware manufacturer's directions, making sure the hinge pins are straight and parallel with the edge of the gate.

**6** Position the gate between the gate posts so the hinge pins rest against one post. Set the gate on wood blocks, then attach the hinges to the post with galvanized screws.

**7** Attach the latch hardware to the other gate post and to the gate, using galvanized screws. Open and close the gate to make sure the latch works correctly.

**8** Measure and trim the tops of the posts to a uniform height, using a reciprocating saw or handsaw. (If you are not using post caps, cut the posts to a point to help them shed water.)

**9** Cover flat post tops with decorative wood or metal caps, and attach them with galvanized casing nails. Coat the fence with sealer-preservative or paint.

## How to Build a Fence Using Boards & Stringers

**1** Install fence posts (pages 276 to 277). Mark cutoff lines on the end posts, 1 ft. below the planned height of the finished fence, then attach a chalk line to the height marks on the end posts, and snap a cutoff line across the posts. (Board-and-stringer fences usually are constructed so the vertical boards extend above the posts.)

**2** Trim off the posts along the marked cutoff lines, using a reciprocating saw or handsaw. Brush sealer-preservative onto the cut ends of the posts.

**3** Cut 2 × 4 top stringers and coat the ends with sealer-preservative. Center the end joints over the posts, then attach the stringers to the posts with galvanized screws or nails.

**4** Mark lines on each post to serve as references for installing additional stringers. Space the marks at 2-ft. intervals.

**5** At each stringer reference mark, use galvanized nails to attach a 2" fence bracket to the sides of the posts. Brackets should be flush with the front face of the posts.

**6** Position a 2 × 4 stringer between each pair of fence brackets. Hold or tack the stringer against the posts, then mark it for cutting by marking back side along the edges of posts. (If yard is sloped, stringers will be cut at angles.) Cut stringers 1/4" shorter than measurement so stringer will slide into brackets easily.

**7** Slide the stringers into the fence brackets and attach them with galvanized nails. If stringers are cut at an angle because of the ground slope, bend the bottom flanges on the fence brackets to match this angle before installing the stringers.

**8** Install vertical boards, beginning at an end post. To find board length, measure from the ground to the top edge of the top stringer, then add 10". Cut board to length, then use galvanized screws to attach it to post or rails. Boards should be plumb, and should extend 1 ft. above the top stringer, leaving a 2" gap at the bottom.

**9** Measure and cut the remaining fence boards, and attach them to the stringers with galvanized screws. Leave a gap of at least 1/8" between boards (a piece of scrap wood works well as a spacing guide). Each board should extend exactly 1 ft. above the top stringer, and should have a 2" gap at the bottom. At the corners and ends of the fence, you may need to rip-cut fence boards to make them fit.

**10** Attach a prebuilt gate as shown on page 279. Finish the fence by coating it with sealer-preservative or paint.

281

# Building Arbors & Trellises

Overhead arbors and vertical trellises provide airy, attractive ceilings and walls for outdoor living spaces. They can turn an exposed patio or deck into an intimate, sheltered living area.

Standing alone, a trellis or arbor structure serves as a distinctive focal point for your landscape. Simple trellises can improve the look of a plain surface, like a garage wall, or can effectively disguise a utility area such as a trash collection space or a compost container.

### Everything You Need:

Tools: tape measure, plumb bob, hammer, rented power auger, shovel, circular saw, miter saw, paint brush, T-bevel, pencil, drill and bits, ratchet wrench, cordless screwdriver, pressure sprayer.

Materials: stakes, mason's string, gravel, 4 × 4 posts, coarse gravel, premixed concrete, lumber (2 × 6s, 2 × 4s, 2 × 2s), 3" galvanized lag screws with washers, rafter ties, 3" galvanized utility screws, lattice panels and molding (as needed), 1" galvanized wire brads, sealer-preservative.

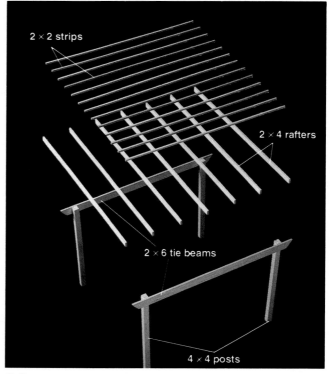

2 × 2 strips

2 × 4 rafters

2 × 6 tie beams

4 × 4 posts

**Arbor structure** is a simple arrangement of framing members joined to form a geometric pattern overhead. Four 4 × 4 posts support a pair of 2 × 6 tie beams, which in turn support 2 × 4 rafters. The "roof" pattern can be made with strips of 2 × 2, prebuilt grid panels, or lattice panels.

**Parallel ropes or wires** make a simple, inexpensive trellis that is ideal for training annual flowering vines, like morning glories. A simple trellis can improve the look of a plain wall.

**Lattice panels** are easy to install, and work well to provide privacy or to block sun. Lattice panels will support lightweight climbing vines, like some types of ivy, but are not well suited for heavier vines.

**Grid panels** provide an airy, open surface for trellises and arbors. Grid panels work well for holding heavy climbing plants, like clematis or climbing roses.

**Strips of 2 × 2** make sturdy arbors and trellises. This construction will support large hanging baskets of flowers, or heavy climbing vines, like wild grape.

## How to Build an Overhead Arbor

**1** Install 4 × 4 posts as directed on pages 276 to 277. Concrete footings for arbors should be at least 3 ft. deep. For arbors larger than 10 ft. × 10 ft., use 6 × 6 posts at the corners.

**2** Mark one post at the desired height of the arbor. Mark the remaining posts at the same height, using a line level as a guide.

**3** Measure and cut two 2 × 6s to use as tie beams. If you want the tie beams to extend past the posts, cut the bottom corners of the 2 × 6s at an angle.

**4** Position a tie beam against one pair of posts, flush with the marked lines on the posts, then attach the beam to each post with two countersunk 3" lag screws with washers. Attach the second tie beam to the other pair of posts.

**5** Mark the top of each tie beam at 2-ft. intervals. These marks will serve as a reference for installing rafters.

**6** Measure and cut 2 × 4 rafters. If the rafters will extend past the tie beams, cut the bottom corners of the rafters at an angle.

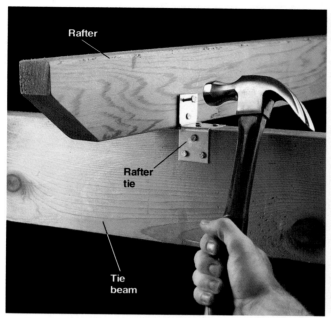

**7** Position the rafters over the tie beams and align them with the reference marks. Attach the rafters to the tie beams with rafter ties and galvanized nails. Use a reciprocating saw or handsaw to cut off any posts that extend above the rafters, and coat the cut ends with sealer-preservative.

**8** Finish the arbor by attaching 2 × 2 strips across the tops of the rafters, using galvanized screws. Space the strips evenly, no more than 18" apart. For denser shade, finish the arbor with lattice panels (below) instead of 2 × 2s.

## How to Build a Trellis Using Lattice Panels

**1** Build lattice panels by cutting sheets of lattice to size and framing them with miter-cut pieces of lattice molding. Attach the molding to the lattice with 1" galvanized wire brads.

**2** Install posts (pages 276 to 277) and trim them to the desired height. Mark the posts to show where lattice panels will fit, and install three fence brackets (inset) on the sides of the posts (steps 2 to 3, page 278).

**3** Slide the framed lattice panels into the brackets from above until the panels rest on the bottom flanges of the lowest brackets. Attach with galvanized nails. Apply sealer-preservative or stain to the entire structure.

# Building Garden Ponds

Garden ponds provide a focal point and create a feeling of serenity in any yard. Ponds also expand your planting options and attract new, unusual species of wildlife.

Modern materials have simplified pond-building and made ponds more affordable. Expensive pumps and filtration systems usually are not necessary in small ponds, although they do enable the pond to support more plants and fish.

Artificial garden ponds require pond liners, which are available in two basic types: liner shells and flexible liners. Fiberglass liner shells are easy to install—simply dig a hole and set them in the ground. They are inexpensive and available in many shapes and sizes, but they may crack in very cold weather.

Most garden ponds are built with soft, flexible liners that conform to any shape and size. Some flexible liners are made from polyvinyl chloride (PVC) fabric. PVC liners are economical, but they can become brittle in just a few years.

Better-quality flexible pond liners are made of rubber. Rubber liners are more costly, but also more durable than PVC liners or fiberglass shells.

## Everything You Need:

Tools: hose, garden spade, carpenter's level, hand spade or trowel.

Materials: pond liner, sand, mortar mix, flagstone coping stones, long 2 × 4.

| Sizing Chart for Flexible Liners | | |
|---|---|---|
| Liner Size | Maximum Pond Size | |
| | 18" deep | 24" deep |
| 8 × 10 | 4 × 6 | 3 × 5 |
| 10 × 10 | 6 × 6 | 5 × 5 |
| 10 × 15 | 6 × 11 | 5 × 10 |
| 15 × 15 | 11 × 11 | 10 × 10 |

**Flexible pond liners** (above) adapt to nearly any shape or size you want. A shallow shelf holds potted plants. **Fiberglass liner shells** (below) come in many sizes and shapes. Simply set them in the ground and they are ready to stock with fish and aquatic plants.

## Tips for Building & Maintaining a Garden Pond

Photo by Susan Roth

**Select a level site** for your garden pond. Sloping ground requires a lot of digging and does not provide a natural setting for the pond. Do not build a pond directly under a tree, since fallen leaves contaminate water and root systems make digging difficult. Ponds should not receive too much direct sunshine, however, so choose a site that is in the shadow of a tree or another landscape structure for at least half the day.

**Replenish water supply** regularly, especially during hot, dry weather. Ponds stocked only with hardy aquatic plants may be replenished with tap water from a garden hose. If the pond is stocked with fish, let water sit for at least three days so chlorine can evaporate before the water is added to the pond.

**Collect rainwater** in a barrel to replenish ponds that are stocked with fish or very delicate plants. Rainwater is preferable to city water, which contains chemical additives, like chlorine.

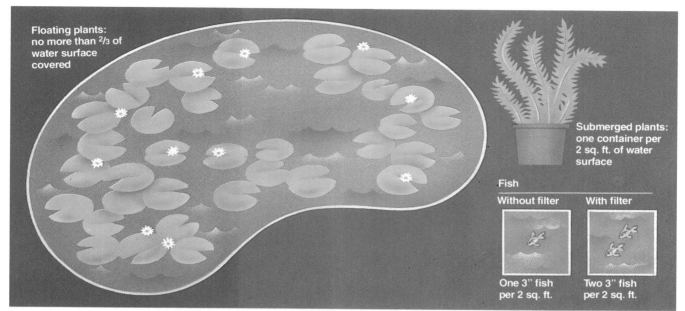

Floating plants:
no more than 2/3 of
water surface
covered

Submerged plants:
one container per
2 sq. ft. of water
surface

Fish

| Without filter | With filter |
| --- | --- |
| One 3" fish per 2 sq. ft. | Two 3" fish per 2 sq. ft. |

**Keep a balance of plants and fish** in your pond. Floating plants provide shade for fish and help inhibit algae, but should cover no more than 2/3 of the pond surface. Every pond should have at least one container of submerged plants, which provide oxygen for fish, for every two square feet of pond surface. (NOTE: aquatic plants are available at local nurseries or from mail-order suppliers. Taking aquatic plants from lakes and ponds is illegal in most areas.) Fish add interest to your pond and release carbon dioxide that can be used by plants. Stock no more than one 3" fish per two square feet of surface if your pond does not have an aeration and filtration system. After filling the pond, let water sit for at least one week before stocking it with plants and fish. Ponds with fish should be at least 24" deep.

Planter shown cutaway

Plastic planter

Aquarium gravel

Landscape fabric

Topsoil

1" holes

**Build containers** for aquatic plants by drilling 1" holes in plastic planters and lining them with landscape fabric. Holes allow water to circulate past the roots of the plants. Planters protect pond liners and simplify maintenance.

**Use chemicals sparingly.** Little maintenance other than a yearly cleaning is needed for balanced ponds. Water-quality problems, like algae buildup, can be treated with diluted chemical products sold in pet stores.

**Bring plants and fish indoors** if your pond freezes for more than a week or two during the winter. Cut away plant stems, then store the plants in a dry, dark location. Keep fish in an aerated aquarium during long periods of freezing weather.

## How to Install a Garden Pond with a Flexible Liner

**1** Select a site for the pond (see page 288) and outline the pond with a hose or heavy rope. Avoid sharp angles, corners, and symmetrical shapes. Ponds should have at least 15 square feet of surface area. Minimum depth is 18" for plants only, and 24" if fish will be added to the pond.

**2** Excavate the entire pond area to a depth of about 1 ft. The sides of the pond should slope slightly toward the center. Save some of the topsoil for use with aquatic plants (page 289).

**3** Excavate the center of the pond to maximum depth, plus 2" to allow for a layer of sand. Leave a 1-ft.-wide shelf inside the border to hold aquatic planters. The pond bed should be flat, with walls sloping downward from the shelf.

**4** Lay a straight board across the pond, then place a carpenter's level on the board. Check all sides to make sure the edges of the pond are level. If not, adjust the surrounding ground to level by digging, filling, and packing soil.

**5** Once the excavation is completed and the site is level, dig a shallow bed around the perimeter of the pond to hold the border flagstones (called coping stones).

**6** Remove all stones, roots, and sharp objects from the pond bed, then smooth out the soil base. Next, spread a 2" layer of wet sand on the level areas of the pond bed. Pack the sand with a tamper, then smooth it out with a length of 2 × 4.

**OPTION**: When using the more inexpensive (and more fragile) PVC pond liners, line the hole with cardboard or old carpeting pieces before installing the liner. The protective layer helps prevent puncturing and stretching of the liner.

**7** Place the liner into the pond bed, then fold and tuck the liner so it conforms to the shape of the hole. Smooth out the liner as much as possible, avoiding any sharp creases.

(continued next page)

**8** Set a few stones on the overhang to hold the liner in place. Too many stones will cause the liner to stretch, not settle into the hole, when it is filled with water.

**9** Fill the pond up to the top with water. Smooth out any large creases or wrinkles that develop as the water level rises. Remove the stones after the pond is full, and allow the liner to settle for one day.

**10** Using a scissors, trim the liner so it overhangs the top of the pond by about 12" all the way around the perimeter of the pond.

**11** Spread a mixture of 20 parts sand to one part dry mortar in a shallow layer on top of the liner overhang. Spray with a light mist. Set coping stones into the sand so they overhang the edge of the pond by about 2". Set one of the stones ½" lower than the rest, to serve as an overflow point for excess water.

## How to Install a Garden Pond with a Liner Shell

**1** Set the fiberglass liner shell in place, then use ropes to outline both the flat bottom and the outside edge of the liner on the ground. Use a level to make sure the outline is directly below the outside edge of the shell.

**2** Excavate the center of the site to maximum shell depth, then excavate the sides so they slope inward to the flat bottom. Test-fit the shell repeatedly, digging and filling until the shape of the hole matches the shell.

**3** Remove all stones and sharp objects, then set the shell into the hole. Check with a level to make sure the shell is level, and adjust the hole as necessary. The top of the shell should be slightly above ground level.

**4** Begin slowly filling the shell with water. As the water level rises, pack wet sand into any gaps between the shell and the sides of the hole.

**5** Dig a shallow bed around the perimeter of the liner to hold coping stones, if desired. Place the stones near the pond liner, but do not set them on the liner edges. Any weight on the edges of fiberglass shell could cause it to crack.

**Use edgings** around planting areas to define borders and reduce maintenance. Without edgings, lawn grass will spread into your planting area and loose-fill materials can spill out. The flexible plastic edging shown above is inexpensive and easy to install. Other edging options are shown below.

## Creating a Planting Area

Planting areas provide a natural finishing touch to a landscape. A planting area can hold an elaborate bed of flowers, a vegetable garden, a group of ornamental trees, or a simple shrub sur rounded by a bed of gravel or bark chips. Retain ing wall materials (pages 228 to 237) often are used to make raised or terraced planting areas.

Make your planting areas proportionate to your yard size. Some landscape designers advise that planting areas should occupy at least 50% of the total yard space.

Unless your soil is very rich, you probably will need to add fertilizer, peat moss, or mulch to make it more suitable for planting. The type of soil builders you add depends on the quality of your soil and the kinds of plants you want to grow. To find the best soil builders, take a sample of your soil to a local garden center or a university extension service for a soil analysis.

**Everything You Need:**

Tools: hose, shovel, garden rake, scissors, hand spade.

Materials: see photos below.

## Materials for Planting Areas

**Common edging materials** include: (A) standard brick pavers, (B) interlocking pavers set on edge, (C) cut-stone slabs, (D) rough stone, or (E) wood. To prevent weeds from sprouting, cover the planting area with landscape fabric (page 218) before planting, and cover the planting area with bark chips or another loose-fill material.

**Natural soil builders** improve the growing quality of soil without relying on hazardous chemicals. Composted manure is a mild, slow-release fertilizer ideal for all plants. Peat moss makes heavy, clay soil more workable, and it also neutralizes acidic or alkaline soil. Bone meal is high in phosphorus—an essential nutrient for fruits and vegetables.

## How to Make a Planting Area

**1** Outline the planting area, using a garden hose or rope. Cut away the existing lawn inside the outline to a depth of 3" to 4".

**2** Dig a narrow trench around the sides of the cutout area, and install the edging material so the top of the edging is just above ground level. Join the ends of flexible plastic edging with a plastic connector. Pack soil around the edging to hold it in place.

**3** Spread any necessary soil builders over the planting area. Use a shovel to loosen soil 12" deep and work the soil builders into the ground.

**4** Rake the surface smooth, and remove any rocks, sticks, and roots.

**5** Lay landscape fabric over the planting area, and trim away the edges with a scissors. Cut X-shaped slits in the fabric where each plant will be located, and dig a planting hole in the soil below.

**6** Transplant flowers from their containers to the planting area, then lay an even layer of loose-fill mulch over the landscape fabric and around the base of each plant. Water the area thoroughly.

# Maintaining a Landscape

Like the other areas of your home, your finished yard requires periodic maintenance. But most do-it-yourself home landscapers soon find that yard work is more like an enjoyable hobby than a tiresome chore. Watching your landscape mature and planning new projects is all the more enjoyable when the landscape was built by your own hands.

Keep a seasonal and weekly schedule for outdoor work. In addition to weekly mowing, watering, and weeding, plan on spending some time every two or three months to inspect and repair landscape structures and tend to the seasonal needs of plants. In particular, trees and shrubs need to be pruned occasionally to stimulate good growth.

Follow the simple maintenance tips on these pages to protect your landscape and ensure your continued enjoyment.

**Protect wood structures** by treating them every two or three years with sealer-preservative, stain, or exterior paint. Sealer-preservative can be applied with a pressure sprayer, but remember that these liquids are toxic. Take care not to breathe the vapors, and make sure the spray does not fall on living plants. Replace any rotted boards.

## How to Maintain a Brick Paver Patio

**1** Once a year, inspect the joints between the pavers, and remove any weeds, debris, or cracked mortar.

**2** Refill the joints by packing them with fine sand or dry mortar mix. Sweep the patio thoroughly.

**3** Seal the entire surface with liquid masonry sealer applied with a pressure sprayer. Sealers protect the pavers from water damage and prevent weeds from sprouting.

## How to Do Basic Pruning

**Remove dead branches** from all shrubs in the spring, using pruning shears. Also remove any branches touching the ground. Thin out the interior of the plant by cutting away branches that cross or rub together. Opening the interior of the plant to sunlight stimulates growth. Recommended pruning techniques vary depending on the species, so consult a nursery or arboretum for more detailed advice.

**Shape dense hedges and shrubs** using a power shears. Cutting back up to 1/3 of the new growth helps stimulate root and branch growth. To ensure that sunlight reaches all parts of a hedge, shape it so the top is narrower than the bottom. Avoid severe pruning and shearing on needle evergreens and on flowering bushes like azaleas, rhododendrons, and dogwood.

## How to Prune Tree Branches

**1** Make a shallow cut partway through the underside of the branch, several inches from the thickened "collar" at the end of the branch. Making the bottom cut first prevents the falling branch from stripping living bark off the tree trunk.

**2** Cut through the top side of the branch until it breaks away. Be very careful if you are working on a ladder.

**3** Remove the stump by cutting just outside the collar. Support the stump as you finish the cut so it does not strip away bark when it breaks free. **Do not** coat the wound with paint, tar, or sealer. These substances actually hinder the tree's ability to heal itself.

# Deck Basics

# Parts of a Deck

Structural parts of a deck include posts, beams, ledgers, and joists. They support and distribute the weight of the deck. For economy and durability, use pressure-treated lumber for these parts. The other parts of a deck include the decking, facing, railings, and stairway. Use redwood or cedar for these visible parts.

**Ledgers** anchor an attached deck to a house. Ledgers support one end of all joists.

**Concrete footings** with post anchors support the weight of the deck and hold the deck posts in place. They are made by pouring concrete into tube forms. Local climates and building codes determine depth of footings. **Post anchors** should be made of galvanized steel to resist corrosion.

**Posts** transfer the weight of the deck to the footings. They are attached to the post anchors with galvanized nails, and to the beam with lag screws.

**Beams** provide the main structural support for the deck. A beam is usually made from a pair of 2 × 8s or 2 × 10s attached to the deck posts.

**Joists** support the decking. For an attached deck, the joists are fastened at one end to the **ledger**, and at the other end to the **header joist**. The **outside joists** can be covered with redwood or cedar **facing** boards for appearance.

**Decking** is the main feature of any deck. The decking boards are attached to the joists with galvanized screws or nails.

**Railing parts** include **railing posts** and **balusters** attached to the header and outside joists, a horizontal **rail,** and a **cap.** Building codes may require railings on decks 24" or more above ground level.

**A stairway** is made from a pair of **stringers** fastened to the side of the deck, and a series of **treads** attached to the stringers with metal cleats.

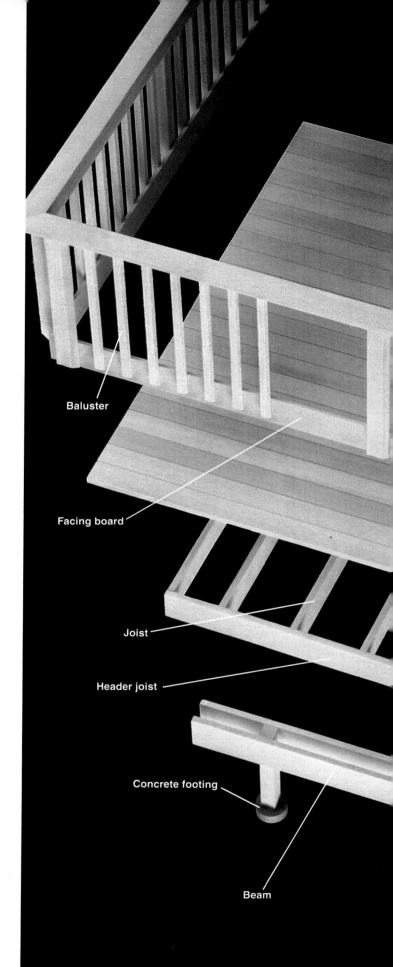

Baluster

Facing board

Joist

Header joist

Concrete footing

Beam

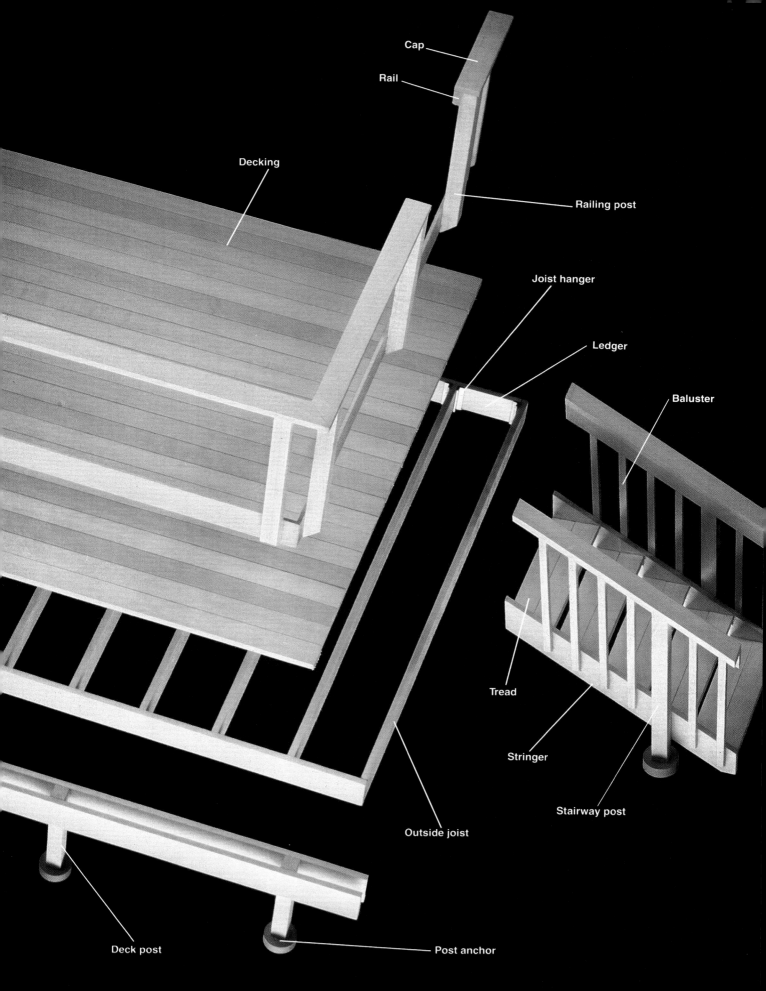

Cap

Rail

Decking

Railing post

Joist hanger

Ledger

Baluster

Tread

Stringer

Stairway post

Outside joist

Deck post

Post anchor

# Decking Patterns

Decking is an important element of a deck, and can be installed using a variety of board sizes and design patterns. The decking pattern determines the spacing and layout of the joists. For example, a normal, straight decking pattern requires joists that are spaced 16" on-center. A diagonal decking

**Diagonal pattern** adds visual interest to a deck. Diagonal patterns require joists that are spaced closer together than for straight patterns.

**Parquet pattern** requires double joists and blocking to provide a supporting surface for attaching the butted ends of decking boards.

pattern requires that the joist spacing be 12" on-center. Parquet patterns and some other designs may require extra support, like double joists or extra blocking. For sturdy, flat decking, use 2 × 4 or 2 × 6 lumber. Thinner lumber is more likely to twist or cup.

**Framed opening** for a tree requires extra blocking between joists. Short joists are attached to blocking with joist hangers.

**Border pattern** gives an elegant, finished look to a deck. Install trim joists to support the border decking.

# Stairways

**Platform steps** feature wide treads. Each step is built on a framework of posts and joists.

A stairway provides access to a deck from the yard or patio. Its position also helps establish traffic patterns across the deck.

Build the stairway with lumber that matches the rest of the deck. If possible, stair treads should use the same board pattern as the surface decking. On decks more than 24" high, local codes may require stairway handrails.

## Stairway Styles

**Open steps** have metal cleats that hold the treads between the stringers. The treads on this stairway are built with 2 × 6s to match the surface decking.

**Boxed steps,** built with notched stringers and solid risers, give a finished look to a deck stairway. Predrill ends of treads to prevent splitting.

**Long stairways** sometimes require landings. A landing is a small platform to which both flights of stairs are attached.

# Railings

Railings usually are required by building code on any deck that is more than 24" high. Select a railing design that fits the style of your home.

For example, on a low, ranch-style house, choose a deck railing with wide, horizontal rails. On a Tudor-style home with a steep roof, choose a railing with closely spaced, vertical balusters.

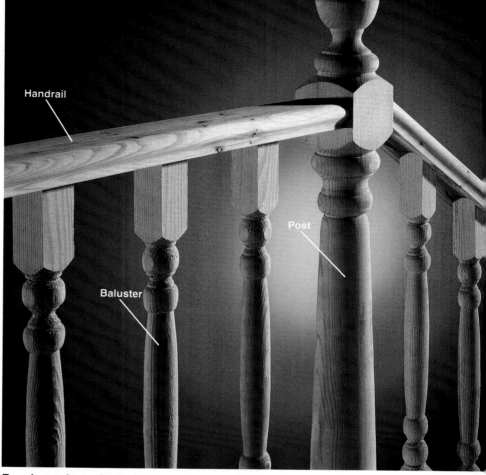

**Preshaped products** let you easily build decorative deck railings. Railing products include shaped handrails, balusters, and posts.

## Railing Styles

**Vertical balusters** with posts and rails are a good choice for houses with strong vertical lines. A vertical baluster railing like the one shown above is a good choice where children will be present.

**Horizontal railings** are often used on low, ranch-style homes. Horizontal railing is made of vertical posts, two or more wide horizontal rails, and a railing cap.

**Lattice panels** add a decorative touch to a deck. They also provide extra privacy.

# Lumber Basics

Lumber used to construct a deck must be resistant to rot and insect damage. The three types of wood recommended for deck construction are: heartwood grade redwood, heartwood cedar, and pressure-treated lumber.

The reddish heartwoods of both redwood and cedar have natural decay resistance. The sapwood of redwood and cedar is lighter in color than the heartwood and has less resistance to decay. Sapwood must be treated with a clear sealer-preservative if used outdoors.

Pressure-treated lumber is treated with chemical preservatives. The preservative most often used for decking lumber is chromated copper arsenate, identified by the label "CCA."

Inspect each piece of lumber, and return any pieces that are severely warped or cracked. Avoid any boards that have large knots, especially where strength is essential, like joists or stairways.

**Inspect lumber for flaws.** Sight along each board to check for warping and twisting. Return any boards with serious flaws. Check for large or loose knots. Boards used for structural parts should be knot-free (clear), or should have only small knots that are tight and ingrown.

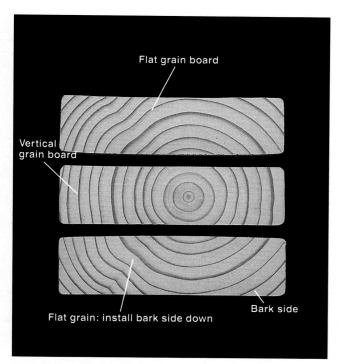

**Check end grain** of decking boards. Boards with flat grain should be installed so that the bark side faces down. Flat grain boards tend to "cup" toward the bark side and can trap standing water if not installed properly.

**Store lumber** so that it stays dry and warp-free. Use supports to keep the wood stack a few inches off the ground. Use spacer blocks to support each row of lumber, and to allow air circulation between boards. Cover the lumber stack with heavy plastic or a water-proof tarp.

**Seal cut edges** of all lumber, including pressure-treated wood, by brushing on clear liquid sealer-preservative. Chemicals used in pressure treatment do not always penetrate completely. Sealer-preservative protects all types of wood from rot.

# Pressure-treated Lumber

Pressure-treated lumber is the strongest and least expensive choice for deck lumber. Pressure-treated lumber resists rot and insects and is an excellent building material for outdoor use.

Treated lumber is created by forcing chemical preservatives into it under high pressure. The most common treatment uses chromated copper arsenate, identified by the label "CCA." The preservative usually gives the wood a green color, which fades with time. Or, you can stain pressure-treated wood in a variety of colors.

Pressure-treated lumber is rated by the amount of chemical retained by the wood. For decks, choose lumber with a retention level of .40, approved for direct ground contact. This is sometimes signified by the code "LP 22" stamped on the wood.

Pressure-treated lumber can be used to build the entire deck; or, it can be used only for posts, beams, and joists, with redwood or cedar used for decking, stairways, facing, and railings.

**Caution:**
The chemicals in pressure-treated lumber are toxic. Wear eye protection, a particle mask, and long sleeves and pants to avoid contact with sawdust from pressure-treated wood.

**Grade stamp** for pressure-treated lumber lists the type of preservative used and the chemical retention level of the wood. Look for "CCA" label indicating that chromated copper arsenate is the preservative. Make sure lumber carries the label "LP 22," or ".40 retention." Other information found on grade stamp includes proper exposure rating, and name and location of treating company.

# Redwood

Redwood is an attractive wood often used for outdoor structures. The heartwood has a brownish red color and is naturally resistant to decay. The cream-colored sapwood should be treated with wood preservative when used in a deck.

Quality redwood is somewhat expensive, so it is often used only for visible parts of the deck, like decking and railings.

Redwood is available in more than 30 grades. "Construction heart" or "merchantable heart" are medium-quality grades that are good choices for a deck.

# Cedar

The cedar species recommended for decks include red cedar and incense cedar. Cedar has a light brown appearance, with an attractive grain. Because it ages to a uniform silver-gray, cedar is often used where a weathered appearance is desired.

Heartwood cedar is naturally resistant to decay. Sapwood cedar is white or cream-colored, and should be treated with wood preservative when used in a deck.

Cedar can be used for the visible surfaces of the deck. For structural members like joists, beams, and posts, use pressure-treated lumber.

**Grade stamp** for redwood lists wood dryness, lumber grade, and membership association. Redwood should be certified "KILN DRIED" or "DRY"; and graded as clear redwood (CLR RWD), construction heartwood (CONST HT), merchantable heartwood (MERCH HT), or construction redwood (CONST RWD).

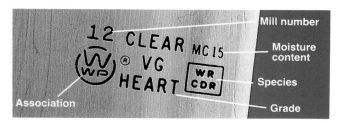

**Grade stamp** for cedar lists the lumber mill number, the moisture content, the species, the lumber grade, and membership association. Western red cedar (WRC) or incense cedar (INC) used in decks should be graded as heartwood (HEART) with a maximum moisture content of 15% (MC 15).

# Lumber Size & Deck Planning

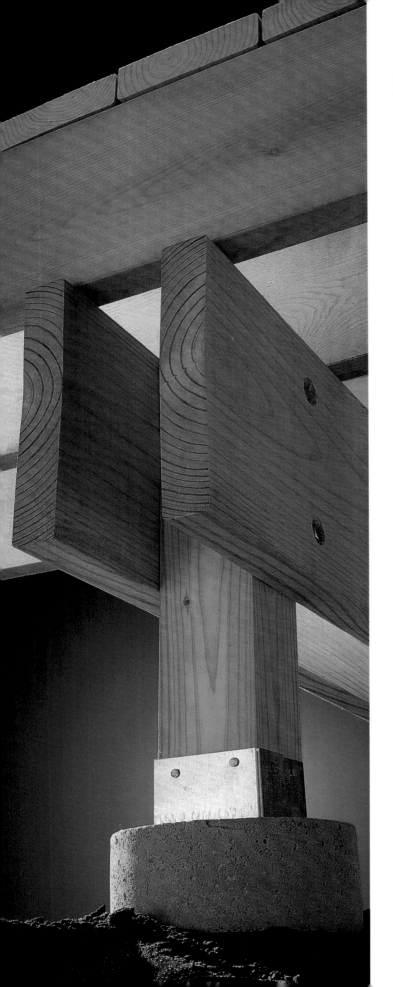

A deck has seven major structural parts: the **ledger, decking, joists,** one or more **beams, posts, stairway stringers,** and **stairway treads.** To create a working design plan, you must know the span limits of each part of the deck. The ledger is attached directly to the house and does not have a span limit.

A span limit is the safe distance a board can cross without support from underneath. The maximum safe span depends on the size of the board. For example, 2 × 6 joists spaced 16" on-center can safely span 9' 9", while 2 × 10 joists can span 16' 5".

Begin planning by first choosing size and pattern of the decking. Then determine the size and layout of the joists, beams, and posts, using the span tables on the opposite page. In general, a deck designed with larger-size lumber, like 2 × 12 joists and beams, requires fewer pieces, because the boards have a large span limit.

| Nominal | Actual |
|---------|--------|
| 1 × 4 | ¾" × 3¾" |
| 1 × 6 | ¾" × 5¾" |
| 2 × 4 | 1½" × 3½" |
| 2 × 6 | 1½" × 5½" |
| 2 × 8 | 1½" × 7¼" |
| 2 × 10 | 1½" × 9¼" |
| 2 × 12 | 1½" × 11¼" |
| 4 × 4 | 3½" × 3½" |
| 6 × 6 | 5½" × 5½" |

**Nominal vs. Actual Lumber Dimensions:** When planning a deck, remember that the actual size of lumber is smaller than the nominal size by which lumber is sold. Use the actual dimensions when drawing a deck design plan.

# Span Limit Tables for Deck Lumber

**Recommended Decking Span Between Joists:**
Decking boards can be made from a variety of lumber sizes. For a basic deck use 2 × 4 or 2 × 6 lumber with joists spaced 16" apart.

| Decking Boards | Recommended Span |
|---|---|
| 1 × 4 or 1 × 6, laid straight | 16" |
| 1 × 4 or 1 × 6, laid diagonal | 12" |
| 2 × 4 or 2 × 6, laid straight | 16" |
| 2 × 4 or 2 × 6, laid diagonal | 12" |
| 2 × 4, laid on edge | 24" |

**Maximum Joist Span Between Supports:** Maximum joist span between supports depends on the size of the joists and the spacing between joists. For example, a deck with 2 × 8 joists spaced 16" apart requires supports no more than 12' 10" apart. On a cantilevered deck, the joists may extend past the beam by a distance equal to one-third the total length of the joists.

| Joist Size | Joist Spacing (on center) | | |
|---|---|---|---|
| | 12" | 16" | 24" |
| 2 × 6 | 11' 7" | 9' 9" | 7' 11" |
| 2 × 8 | 15' 0" | 12' 10" | 10' 6" |
| 2 × 10 | 19' 6" | 16' 5" | 13' 4" |

**Maximum Beam Span Between Posts:** Maximum beam span depends on the size of the beams and their spacing. For example, a deck with a 4 × 8 beam, and joists that span 12 feet should have posts that are no more than 7 feet apart.

| Beam Size | Joist Span | | | |
|---|---|---|---|---|
| | 6 ft. | 8 ft. | 10 ft. | 12 ft. |
| 4 × 6 (two 2 × 6s) | 8 ft. | 7 ft. | 6 ft. | 5 ft. |
| 4 × 8 (two 2 × 8s) | 10 ft. | 9 ft. | 8 ft. | 7 ft. |
| 4 × 10 (two 2 × 10s) | 12 ft. | 11 ft. | 10 ft. | 9 ft. |
| 4 × 12 (two 2 × 12s) | 14 ft. | 13 ft. | 12 ft. | 11 ft. |

**Recommended Post Size:** Choose post size by finding the load area for the deck. To find the load area, multiply the distance between beams by the distance between posts. For example, on a deck that has one beam spaced 10 feet from the ledger, with posts spaced 7 feet apart, the load area is 70. If this deck is less than 6 feet high, the recommended post size is 4 × 4.

| Deck Height | Load Area<br>Multiply distance between beams (feet) times the distance between posts (feet). | | | | |
|---|---|---|---|---|---|
| | 48 | 72 | 96 | 120 | 144 |
| Up to 6 ft. | 4 × 4 | 4 × 4 | 6 × 6 | 6 × 6 | 6 × 6 |
| More than 6 ft. | 6 × 6 | 6 × 6 | 6 × 6 | 6 × 6 | 6 × 6 |

**Minimum Stair Stringer Sizes:** Size of stair stringers depends on the span of the stairway. For example, if the bottom of the stairway lies 7 feet from the deck, build the stringers from 2 × 12s.

| Span of Stairway | Stringer Size |
|---|---|
| Up to 6 ft. | 2 × 10 |
| More than 6 ft. | 2 × 12 |

**Recommended Railing Sizes:** Size of posts, rails, and caps depends on the spacing of the railing posts. For example, if railing posts are spaced 6 feet apart, use 4 × 4 posts and 2 × 6 rails and caps.

| Space Between Railing Posts | Post Size | Cap Size | Rail Size |
|---|---|---|---|
| 2 ft. to 3 ft. | 2 × 4 | 2 × 4 | 2 × 4 |
| 3 ft. to 4 ft. | 4 × 4 | 2 × 4 | 2 × 4 |
| 4 ft. to 6 ft. | 4 × 4 | 2 × 6 | 2 × 6 |

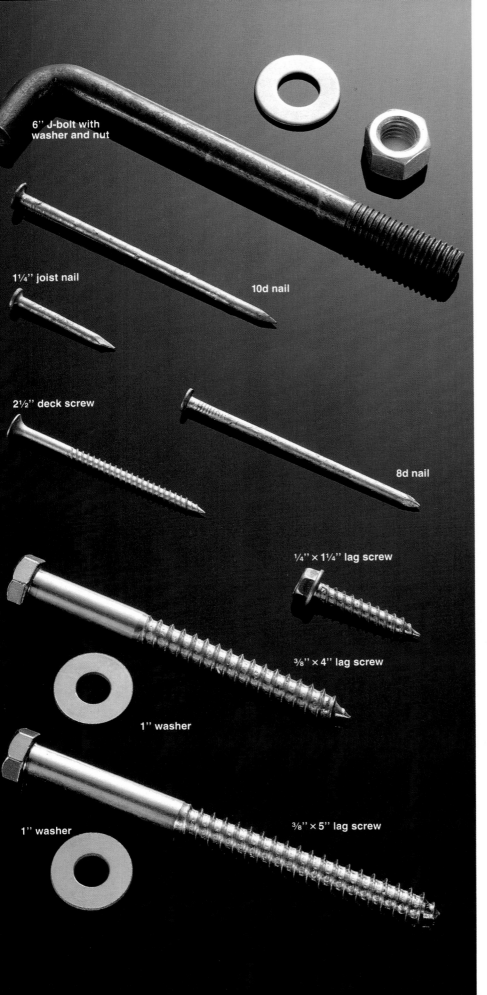

**6" J-bolt with washer and nut**

**1¼" joist nail**

**10d nail**

**2½" deck screw**

**8d nail**

**¼" × 1¼" lag screw**

**⅜" × 4" lag screw**

**1" washer**

**⅜" × 5" lag screw**

**1" washer**

# Hardware & Fasteners

Build your deck with galvanized lumber connectors, nails, and screws. Galvanized metal products resist rust and will not stain the wood.

Metal lumber connectors are used to create strong joints with wood framing members. Post anchors, joist hangers, and brackets are available at lumberyards and home improvement centers.

Seal heads of counterbored screws with silicone caulk to prevent water damage.

**Hot-dipped galvanized nails** (above) have a thick zinc coating and rough surface. Hot-dipped nails will not rust or stain wood.

**Deck fasteners** (left), include 6" J-bolt with nut and washer, 8d and 10d galvanized nails, 1¼" galvanized joist nail, 2½" corrosion-resistant deck screw, ¼" × 1¼" lag screw, ⅜" × 4" lag screw, ⅜" × 5" lag screw, and 1" washer.

**Flashing** fits over ledger to protect wood from moisture damage. Top edge of flashing tucks up under the siding.

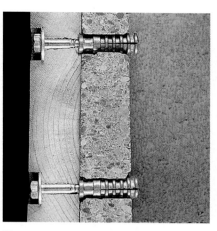

**Masonry anchors** with lag screws hold the ledger to stone, brick, or concrete blocks.

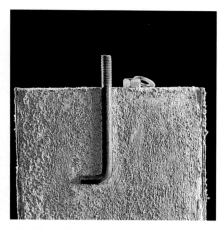

**J-bolts** with nuts and washers hold the post anchors to the concrete footings.

**Post anchors** hold deck posts in place, and raise the base of the posts to help prevent water from entering end grain of wood.

**Angle brackets** help reinforce header and outside joists. Angle brackets are also used to attach stair stringers to the deck.

**Joist hangers** are used to attach joists to the ledger and header joist. Double hanger is used when decking pattern requires a double-width joist.

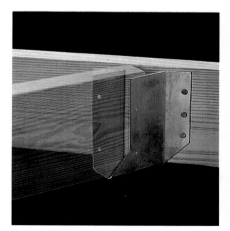

**Angled joist hangers** are used to frame decks that have unusual angles or decking patterns.

**Stair cleats** support the treads of deck steps. Cleats are attached to stair stringers with 1/4" × 1 1/4" galvanized lag screws.

**Silicone caulk** seals lag screw heads and any cracks that may trap water. Choose an exterior-grade caulk rated for lifetime use.

# Concrete

Use concrete to make solid footings that will support the weight of the deck. Concrete for footings is made from a mixture of portland cement, sand, and coarse gravel (¼" to 1½" in diameter). These materials can be purchased separately and mixed at home, or you can buy bags containing the pre-mixed dry ingredients. For larger amounts, buy ready-mixed concrete in trailer loads.

For most deck projects, mixing your own concrete is easy and inexpensive. Mix concrete in a wheelbarrow or with a power mixer, available at tool rental centers.

The estimation charts on the opposite page give approximate volumes of concrete. You may have a small amount of concrete left over after pouring post footings.

**Mix concrete ingredients** in a wheelbarrow. Use a ratio of 1 part portland cement (A), 2 parts sand (B), and 3 parts coarse gravel (C). Or, use the cubic-foot volumes shown in the chart (page opposite).

## Amount of Concrete Needed (cubic feet)

| Number of 8" Diameter Footings | Depth of Footings (feet) | | | |
|---|---|---|---|---|
| | 1 | 2 | 3 | 4 |
| 2 | ¾ | 1½ | 2¼ | 3 |
| 3 | 1 | 2¼ | 3½ | 4½ |
| 4 | 1½ | 3 | 4½ | 6 |
| 5 | 2 | 3¾ | 5¾ | 7½ |

## Concrete Ingredient Amounts

| Amount of Concrete Needed (cubic feet) | Dry Ingredients for Self-mix | | | 60-lb. bags of premixed dry concrete |
|---|---|---|---|---|
| | 94-lb. bags of portland cement | Cubic feet of sand | Cubic feet of gravel | |
| 1 | ⅙ | ⅓ | ½ | 2 |
| 2 | ⅓ | ⅔ | 1 | 4 |
| 3 | ½ | 1½ | 3 | 6 |
| 4 | ¾ | 1¾ | 3½ | 8 |
| 5 | 1 | 2¼ | 4½ | 10 |
| 10 | 2 | 4½ | 9 | 20 |

## Buying & Mixing Concrete

**Buy premixed bags** of dry concrete for small jobs. A 60-lb. bag creates about ½ of a cubic foot of concrete. A 90-lb. bag creates about ⅔ of a cubic foot.

**Rent a power cement mixer** to blend large amounts of cement, gravel, sand, and water quickly.

**Buy ready-mixed concrete** for larger jobs. Trailer loads are available at rental centers, and are sold by the cubic yard. One cubic yard equals 27 cubic feet.

**32-oz. masonry hammer**

**Cat's paw**

**Hoe**

**Shovel**

**Ratchet wrench & socket**

**Trowel**

**22-oz. claw hammer**

**Metal snips**

**50-ft. tape measure**

**16-ft. tape measure**

**Caulk gun**

**Rubber mallet**

**Clamshell posthole digger**

**Combination square**

**Mason's string**

**Compass**

**Plumb bob**

**Flat pry bar**

**Line level**

**Scratch awl**

**Torpedo level**

**Chalk line**

**1" chisel**

**Putty knife**

**Level**

**Framing square**

**Hand tools** for deck building should have heavy-duty construction. Metal tools should be made from high-carbon steel with smoothly finished surfaces. Buy quality hand tools that are well balanced, and that have tight, comfortably molded handles. There is no substitute for quality.

316

# Tool Basics

With a set of basic hand and power tools, you can complete any of the deck projects shown in this book. You may already own many of the tools needed. If you buy new tools, invest in quality, heavy-duty products that will provide long service.

Some specialty tools, like power miter boxes or reciprocating saws, are available at tool rental centers. Or, they can be purchased at home improvement stores.

Always wear eye protection when using tools. Always wear a particle mask and work gloves when sawing or handling pressure-treated lumber, because the chemicals in the wood are toxic.

**Tools for finishing and maintaining** a deck include: rubber gloves (A), shop vacuum (B), 14-gauge extension cord (C), pressure sprayer (D), hydraulic jack and handle (E), eye protection (F), scrub brush (G), paint brush (H), particle mask (I), and orbital sander (J).

**Power tools** include: power miter box (A), circular saw (B) with carbide-tipped blade and Teflon®-coated carbide blade, reciprocating saw (C), ⅜" drill and bits (D), jig saw (E), and screwgun (F). These tools should have heavy-duty motors. Screwgun is designed for driving long deck screws through 2" lumber. Reciprocating saw and power miter box can be purchased at home centers, or leased at tool rental outlets.

**Make a map** of the features of your house and yard. Include any features that might affect how you build and use your deck, like sun and shade patterns, trees, and other landscaping details. For accurate measurements, use a long tape measure and hold it level and perpendicular to the house.

# Creating Site Drawings

Create site drawings of the building area before designing a deck. Show all details that may affect how you build and use the deck.

Building a deck requires two types of site drawings. A **plan view** shows the building site as viewed from directly overhead. An **elevation** shows the vertical details of the site as it is viewed from the side or front.

As you create site drawings, consider how the features of house and yard influence the deck design. Remember that the building site is affected by weather, time of day, and seasonal changes.

For example, if your deck will be used mainly for summertime evening meals, look at the sun, shade, and wind patterns on the site during this time of day.

**Everything You Need:**

Tools: pencil or marker, eraser, 50-ft. tape measure, ruler, compass, line level.

Materials: large sheets of paper.

Supplies: mason's string.

# How to Create Plan-view Site Drawings

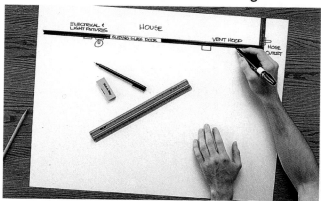

**1** Sketch position of house and yard on a large sheet of paper, using a scale of 1'' equals 1 foot. Show position of doors, windows, and outdoor utilities, like garden hose spigots, or light fixtures.

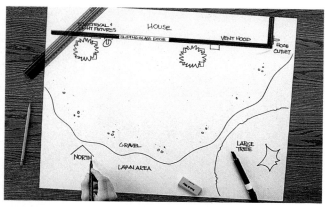

**2** Add a symbol to the site drawing to indicate north. Mark the location of trees, gardening beds or planters, and any other landscaping features. Show any overhead or underground utility lines.

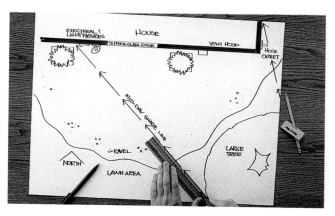

**3** Observe the deck site during the time of day when the deck will be used most often. Outline shade and sun patterns on the site drawing.

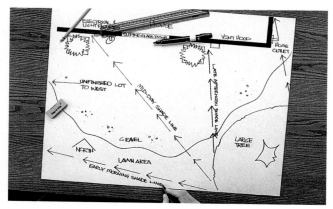

**4** Show how the site changes throughout the day. Outline shade and sun patterns at different times, and quality of nearby view. Note changes in winds, traffic noise, and neighborhood activity.

# How to Create Elevation Site Drawings

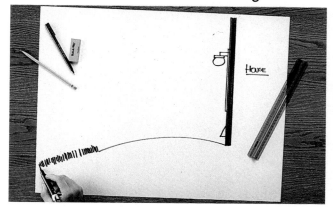

**1** Create a side-view elevation map of your site, showing the slope of the ground and the position of the house. For accuracy, stretch level mason's strings from the house, and use the strings for reference to determine slope of ground.

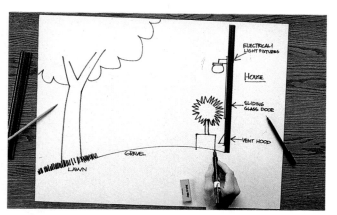

**2** Add any other features that will affect how you build and use the deck, like the height of tree branches or telephone wires, shrubs, flowerbeds, or other landscaping details.

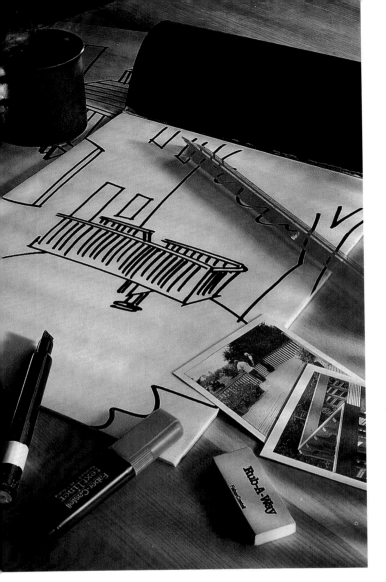

# Drawing Design Plans

Design plans help you estimate lumber and hardware needs, and provide the measurements needed to lay out the deck and cut the lumber. If a work permit is required by local codes, you must have design plans.

You will need two types of design drawings for a deck project. A **plan view** shows the parts of the deck as they are viewed from directly overhead. An **elevation** shows the deck parts as viewed from the side or front.

To avoid confusion, do not try to show all parts of the deck in a single plan view. First, draw one plan that shows the outline of the deck and the pattern of the decking boards. Then make another plan that shows the underlying ledger, joists, beams, and posts.

**Everything You Need:**

Tools: pencil or marker, eraser, ruler.

Materials: site drawing, large sheets of paper, sheets of tissue paper.

## How to Draw Design Plans

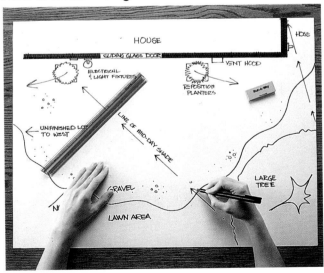

**1** Use the scaled site drawings (pages 318 to 319) to help establish the size and shape of the deck.

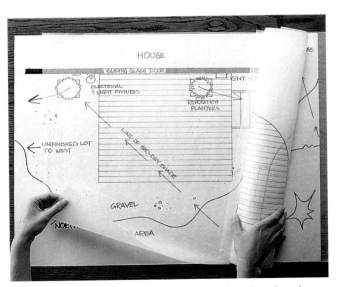

**2** Lay a sheet of tissue paper over the site drawing and tape in position. Experiment with deck ideas by sketching different designs on separate sheets of tissue paper.

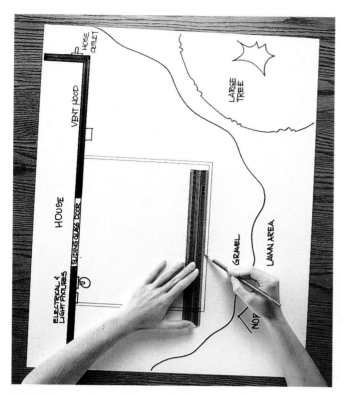

**3** Make copies of the scaled site drawing. Use a ruler and sharp pencil to draw the outline of the deck on one copy of the scaled site drawing.

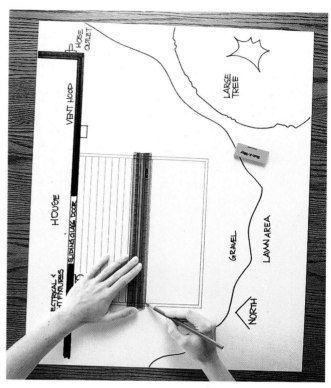

**4** Draw in the decking pattern over the outline. Indicate the size and type of lumber and hardware to be used. Save this plan for reference.

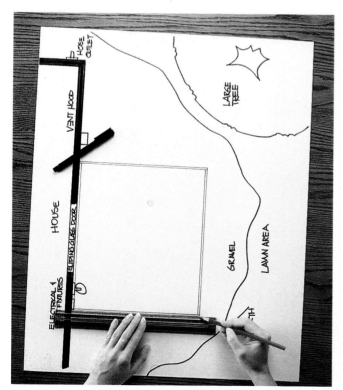

**5** On a second copy of the scaled site drawing, draw another outline of the deck. Draw in the ledger, the outside joists, and the header joist.

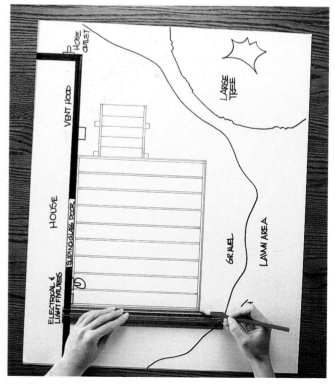

**6** Draw the inner joists, and any blocking. Show any facing boards that will be used. Show the stairway stringers, treads, and posts.

(continued next page)

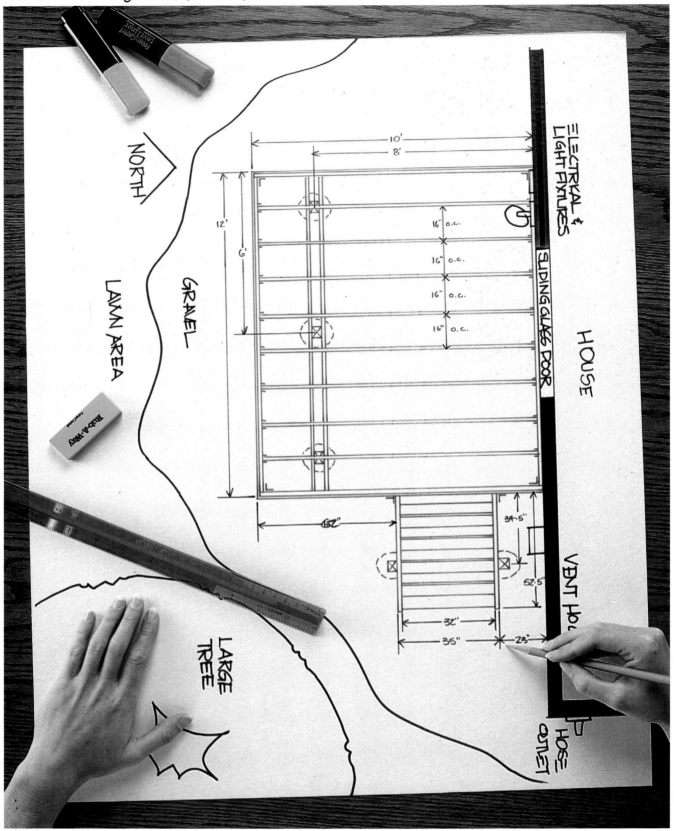

**7** Draw in the deck beam and posts, and show the location of the concrete footings. List all deck dimensions on the plan. Save this drawing for reference when ordering lumber and hardware.

# How to Draw Design Elevations

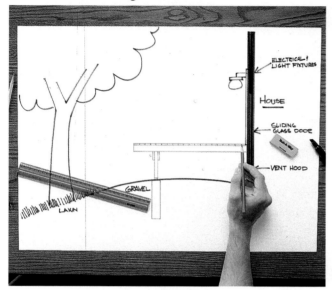

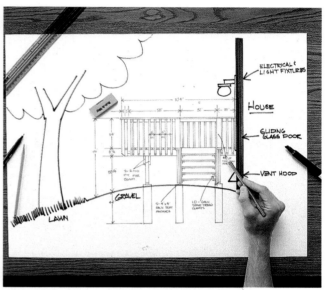

**1** Draw in the basic deck platform on the site elevation drawing (page 319). Draw in the beam and the posts.

**2** Add the stairway to the elevation drawing, then draw in the railing posts, balusters, rails and caps. List all dimensions on the drawing, and indicate size, type, and quantities of lumber and hardware needed. Save this drawing for reference.

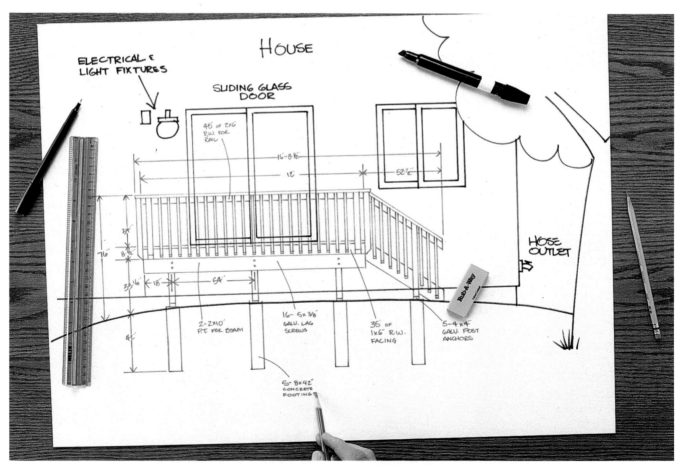

**3** Create another design elevation showing the deck as viewed from the front. Include all deck dimensions, and indicate the size and type of lumber and hardware to be used. Save this drawing for reference.

# Ordering Lumber & Materials

Use the deck design plans and elevations to help make a complete list of the items you will need. For convenience, copy the checklist on the opposite page. Add 10% to lumber and material estimates to compensate for flaws in materials and construction errors.

Most supplies for building a deck are available at lumberyards or home improvement centers. Full-service lumberyards have a complete selection of building materials, but prices may be higher than those at home improvement centers. The quality of lumber at home centers can vary, so inspect the wood and hand-pick the pieces you want.

Order top-quality hardware, caulks, wood sealers, and stains. Save money on nails, screws, and other hardware by buying them in large quantities.

**Buy top-quality** products for a long-lasting deck, including: alkyd-based sealers and stains (A, B, C), galvanized post anchors (D), galvanized nails (E), galvanized joist hangers (F), corrosion-resistant deck screws (G), silicone caulk (H).

# Lumber & Materials Checklist

| Item | Size, type | Quantity | Where to buy | Price each | Total price |
|---|---|---|---|---|---|
| **Lumber** | | | | | |
| Ledger | | | | | |
| Posts | | | | | |
| Beams | | | | | |
| Joists | | | | | |
| Decking | | | | | |
| Stair stringers | | | | | |
| Stair treads | | | | | |
| Railing posts | | | | | |
| Balusters or rails | | | | | |
| **Hardware** | | | | | |
| Flashing | | | | | |
| Galvanized nails | | | | | |
| 1¼″ joist nails | | | | | |
| Post anchors | | | | | |
| Lag screws | | | | | |
| Deck screws | | | | | |
| Joist hangers | | | | | |
| Joist angle brackets | | | | | |
| Metal stair cleats | | | | | |
| **Concrete** | | | | | |
| Concrete forms | | | | | |
| Portland cement | | | | | |
| Sand | | | | | |
| Gravel | | | | | |
| **Miscellaneous** | | | | | |
| Silicone caulk | | | | | |
| Sealer/stain | | | | | |
| **Equipment rental** | | | | | |
| | | | | | |
| | | | | | |
| **Tools to buy** | | | | | |
| | | | | | |

Photocopy this checklist for reference when ordering lumber and materials.

# Building Decks:
# A Step-by-Step Overview

Review the design plan (pages 320 to 323) and the directions on pages 328 to 377 before beginning deck construction. Build the deck in several stages, and gather tools and materials for each stage before beginning. Arrange to have a helper for the more difficult stages.

Check with local utilities for the location of underground electrical, telephone, or water lines. Apply for a building permit, where required, and make sure a building inspector has approved the deck design before beginning work.

The time it takes to build a deck depends on the size and complexity of the design. A rectangular deck, about 10 ft. × 14 ft., can be completed in two or three weekends.

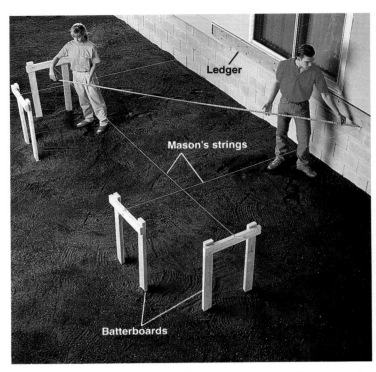

**1** Install a ledger to anchor the deck to the house and to serve as reference for laying out footings (pages 328 to 333). Use batterboards and mason's strings to locate footings, and check for square by measuring diagonals (pages 334 to 339).

**4** Install metal joist hangers on the ledger and header joist, then hang the remaining joists (pages 356 to 359). Most decking patterns require joists that are spaced 16" on center.

**5** Lay decking boards, and trim them with a circular saw (pages 360 to 363). If desired for appearance, cover pressure-treated header and outside joists with redwood or cedar facing boards (page 363).

**2** Pour concrete post footings (pages 340 to 343), and install metal post anchors (pages 345 to 346). Set and brace the posts, attach them to the post anchors, and mark posts to show where beam will be attached (pages 346 to 349).

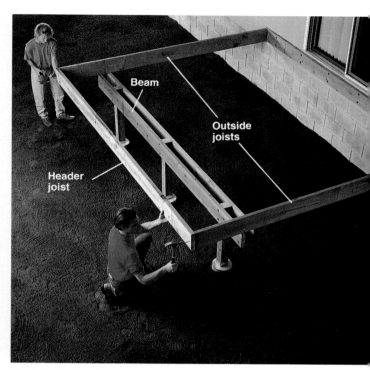

**3** Attach the beam to the posts (pages 350 to 353). Install the outside joists and header joist, using galvanized nails (pages 354 to 355).

**6** Build deck stairs (pages 364 to 369). Stairs provide access to the deck and establish traffic patterns.

**7** Install a railing around the deck and stairway (pages 370 to 377). A railing adds a decorative touch, and may be required on any deck that is more than 24" above the ground.

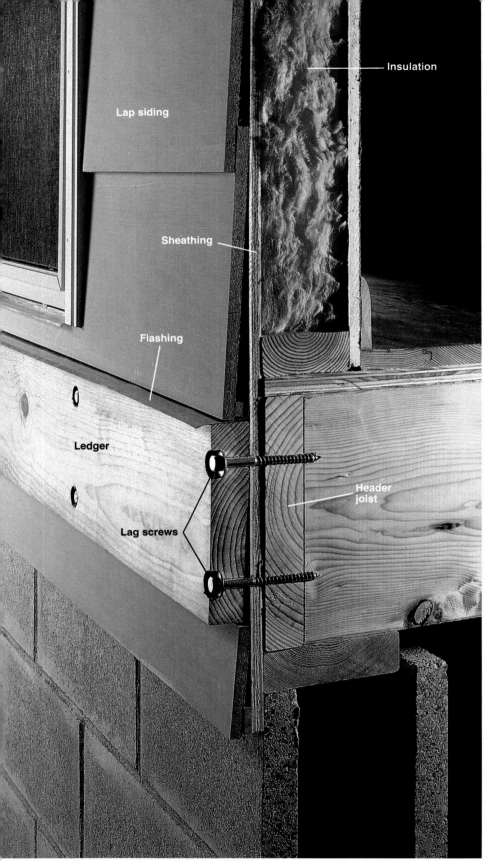

# Installing a Ledger

The first step in building an attached deck is to fasten the ledger to the house. The ledger anchors the deck and establishes a reference point for building the deck square and level. The ledger also supports one end of all the deck joists, so it must be attached securely to the framing members of the house.

Install the ledger so that the surface of the decking boards will be 1" below the indoor floor level. This height difference prevents rainwater or melted snow from seeping into the house.

### Everything You Need:

Tools (page 316): pencil, level, circular saw with carbide blade, chisel, hammer, metal snips, caulk gun, drill and bits (1/4" twist, 1" spade, 3/8" and 5/8" masonry), ratchet wrench, awl, rubber mallet.

Materials: pressure-treated lumber, galvanized flashing, 8d galvanized common nails, silicone caulk, 3/8" × 4" lag screws and 1" washers, lead masonry anchors for 3/8" lag screws (for brick walls).

Supplies: 2 × 4s for braces.

**Ledger (shown in cross section)** is made from pressure-treated lumber. Lap siding is cut away to expose sheathing and to provide a flat surface for attaching the ledger. Galvanized flashing tucked under siding prevents moisture damage to wood. Countersunk 3/8" × 4" lag screws hold ledger to header joist inside house.

## How to Attach a Ledger to Lap Siding

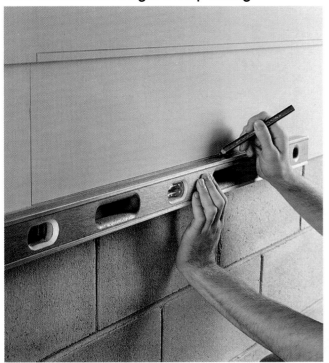

**1** Draw an outline showing where the deck will fit against the house, using a level as a guide. Include the thickness of the outside joists and any decorative facing boards that will be installed.

**2** Cut out siding along outline, using a circular saw. Set blade depth to same thickness as siding, so that blade does not cut into sheathing.

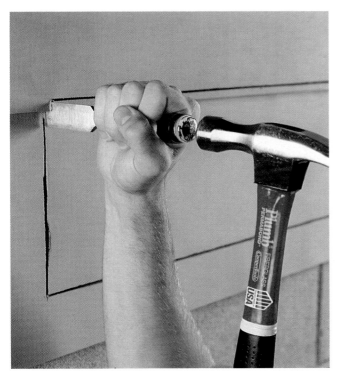

**3** Use a chisel to finish the cutout where circular saw blade does not reach. Hold the chisel with the bevel-side in.

**4** Measure and cut ledger from pressure-treated lumber. Remember that ledger will be shorter than overall length of cutout.

(continued next page)

**5** Cut galvanized flashing to length of cutout, using metal snips. Slide flashing up under siding.

**6** Center the ledger in the cutout, underneath the flashing. Brace in position, and tack ledger into place with 8d galvanized nails. Apply a thick bead of silicone caulk to crack between siding and flashing.

**7** Drill pairs of ¼" pilot holes spaced every 2 feet, through the ledger and sheathing and into the header joist.

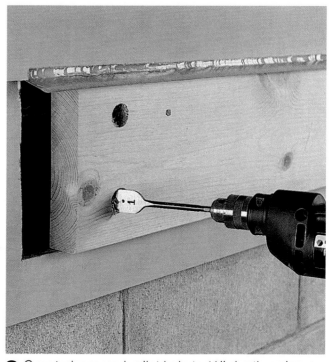

**8** Counterbore each pilot hole to ½" depth, using a 1" spade bit.

**9** Attach ledger to wall with ⅜" × 4" lag screws and washers, using a ratchet wrench.

**10** Seal lag screw heads with silicone caulk. Seal the crack between the wall and the sides and bottom of the ledger.

## How to Attach a Ledger to Masonry

**1** Measure and cut ledger. Ledger will be shorter than overall length of cutout. Drill pairs of ¼" pilot holes every 2 feet in ledger. Counterbore each pilot hole to ½" depth, using a 1" spade bit.

**2** Draw an outline of the deck on the wall, using a level as a guide. Center ledger in outline on wall, and brace in position. Mark the pilot hole locations on wall, using an awl or nail. Remove ledger.

(continued next page)

**3** Drill anchor holes 3" deep into masonry, using a ⅝" masonry bit.

**4** Drive lead masonry anchors for ⅜" lag screws into drilled holes, using a rubber mallet.

**5** Attach ledger to wall with ⅜" × 4" lag screws and washers, using a ratchet wrench. Tighten screws firmly, but do not overtighten.

**6** Seal the cracks between the wall and ledger with silicone caulk. Also seal the lag screw heads.

## How to Attach a Ledger to Stucco

**1** Draw outline of deck on wall, using a level as a guide. Measure and cut ledger, and drill pilot holes (page 331, step 1). Brace ledger against wall, and mark hole locations, using a nail or awl.

**2** Remove ledger. Drill pilot holes through stucco layer of wall, using a ⅜" masonry bit.

**3** Extend each pilot hole through the sheathing and into the header joist, using a ¼" bit. Reposition ledger and brace in place.

**4** Attach ledger to wall with ⅜" × 4" lag screws and washers, using a ratchet wrench. Seal the lag screw heads and the cracks between the wall and ledger with silicone caulk.

**Mason's strings** stretched between ledger and batterboards are used to position footings for deck posts. Use a plumb bob and stakes to mark the ground at the exact centerpoints of footings.

# Locating Post Footings

Establish the exact locations of all concrete footings by stretching mason's strings across the site. Use the ledger board as a starting point. These perpendicular layout strings will be used to locate holes for concrete footings, and to position metal post anchors on the finished footings. Anchor the layout strings with temporary 2 × 4 supports, often called batterboards.

**Everything You Need:**

Tools: tape measure, felt-tipped pen, circular saw, screwgun, framing square, masonry hammer, claw hammer, line level, plumb bob.

Supplies: 2 × 4s, 10d nails, 2½" wallboard screws, mason's strings, masking tape.

## How to Locate Post Footings

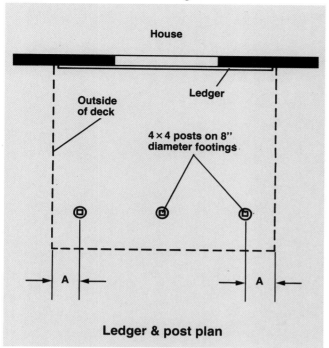

**House**

**Ledger**

**Outside of deck**

**4 × 4 posts on 8" diameter footings**

A

A

**Ledger & post plan**

**1** Use the design plan (page 322) to find distance (A). Measure from the side of the deck to the center of each outside post. Use the elevation drawings (page 323) to find the height of each deck post.

**2** Cut 2 × 4 stakes for batterboards, each about 8" longer than post height. Trim one end of each stake to a point, using a circular saw. Cut 2 × 4 crosspieces, each about 2 feet long.

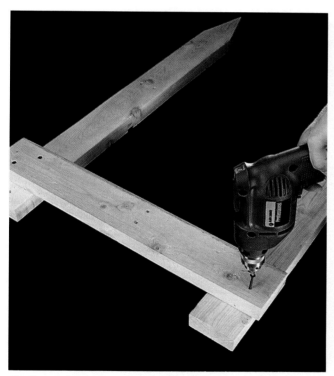

**3** Assemble batterboards by attaching crosspieces to stakes with 2½" wallboard screws. Crosspieces should be about 2" below tops of stakes.

**4** Transfer measurement A (step 1) to ledger, and mark reference points at each end of ledger. String lines will be stretched from these points on ledger. When measuring, remember to allow for outside joists and facing that will be butted to the ends of the ledger.

(continued next page)

**5** Drive a batterboard 6" into the ground, about 2 feet past the post location. Crosspiece of batterboard should be parallel to the ledger.

**6** Drive a 10d nail into bottom of ledger at reference point (step 4). Attach a mason's string to nail.

**7** Extend the mason's string so that it is taut and perpendicular to the ledger. Use a framing square as a guide. Secure the string temporarily by wrapping it several times around the batterboard.

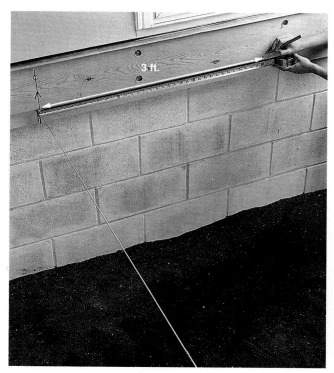

**8** Check the mason's string for square using "3-4-5 carpenter's triangle." First, measure along the ledger 3 feet from the mason's string and mark a point, using a felt-tipped pen.

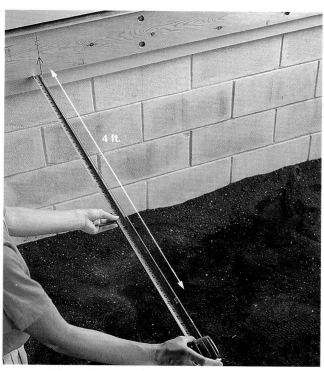

**9** Measure mason's string 4 feet from edge of ledger, and mark with masking tape.

**10** Measure distance between marks. If string is perpendicular to ledger, the distance will be exactly 5 feet. If necessary, move string left or right on batterboard until distance between marks is 5 feet.

**11** Drive a 10d nail into top of batterboard at string location. Leave about 2" of nail exposed. Tie string to nail.

(continued next page)

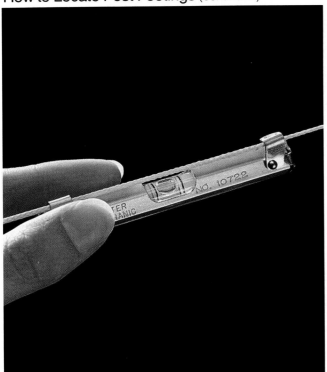

**12** Hang a line level on the mason's string. Raise or lower string until it is level. Locate other outside post footing, repeating steps 5 to 12.

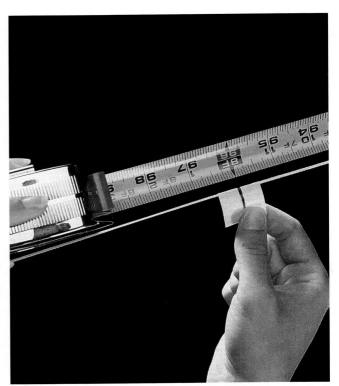

**13** Measure along mason's strings from ledger to find centerpoint of posts. Mark centerpoints on strings, using masking tape.

**14** Drive additional batterboards into ground, about 2 feet outside mason's strings and lined up with post centerpoint marks (step 13).

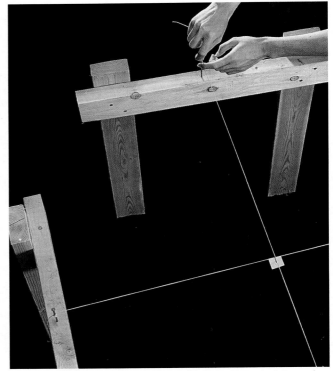

**15** Align a third cross string with the centerpoint marks on the first strings. Drive 10d nails in new batterboards, and tie off cross string on nails. Cross string should be close to, but not touching, the first strings.

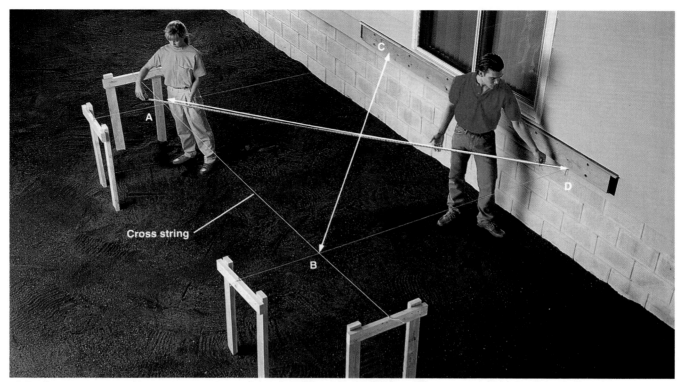

**16** Check strings for square by measuring distances A-B and C-D. Measure diagonals A-D and B-C from edge of ledger to opposite corners. If strings are square, measurement A-B will be same as C-D, and diagonal A-D will be same as B-C. If necessary, adjust strings on batterboards until square.

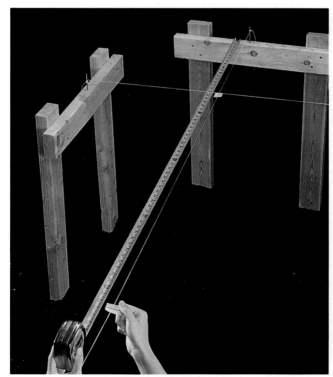

**17** Measure along the cross string and mark center-points of any posts that will be installed between the outside posts.

**18** Use a plumb bob to mark post centerpoints on the ground, directly under the marks on the mason's strings. Drive a stake into ground at each point. Remove mason's strings before digging footings.

# Digging & Pouring Footings

Concrete footings hold deck posts in place and support the weight of the deck. Check local codes to determine the size and depth of footings required for your area. In cold climates, footings must be deeper than the soil frost line.

To help protect posts from water damage, each footing should be poured so that it is 2" above ground level. Tube-shaped forms let you extend the footings above ground level.

It is easy and inexpensive to mix your own concrete by combining portland cement, sand, gravel, and water. See pages 314 to 315 for more information on buying and mixing concrete.

Before digging, consult local utilities for location of any underground electrical, telephone, or water lines that might interfere with footings.

## Everything You Need:

Tools (Page 316): power auger or clamshell posthole digger, tape measure, pruning saw, shovel, reciprocating saw or handsaw, torpedo level, hoe, trowel, shovel, old toothbrush, plumb bob, utility knife.

Materials: 8" concrete tube forms, portland cement, sand, gravel, J-bolts.

Supplies: wheelbarrow, scrap 2×4.

**Power augers** quickly dig holes for post footings. They are available at rental centers. Some models can be operated by one person, while others require two people.

## How to Dig & Pour Post Footings

**1** Dig holes for post footings with a clamshell digger or power auger, centering the holes on the layout stakes. For holes deeper than 35", use a power auger to dig post-hole footings.

**2** Measure hole depth. Local building codes specify depth of footings. Cut away tree roots, if necessary, using a pruning saw.

**3** Pour 2" to 3" of loose gravel in the bottom of each footing hole. Gravel will provide drainage under concrete footings.

**4** Add 2" to hole depth so that footings will be above ground level. Cut concrete tube forms to length, using a reciprocating saw or handsaw. Make sure cut is straight.

**5** Insert tubes into footing holes, leaving about 2" of tube above ground level. Use a level to make sure tops of tubes are level. Pack soil around tubes to hold them in place.

(continued next page)

**6** Mix dry ingredients for concrete in a wheelbarrow, using a hoe.

**7** Form a hollow in center of dry concrete mixture. Slowly pour a small amount of water into hollow, and blend in dry mixture with a hoe.

**8** Add more water gradually, mixing thoroughly until concrete is firm enough to hold its shape when sliced with a trowel.

**9** Pour concrete slowly into tube form, guiding concrete from wheelbarrow with a shovel. Use a long stick to tamp the concrete, filling any air gaps in the footing.

**10** Level the concrete by pulling a 2 × 4 across the top of the tube form, using a sawing motion. Add concrete to any low spots. Retie the mason's strings on the batterboards, and recheck measurements.

342

**11** Insert a J-bolt at an angle into the wet concrete at center of the footing.

**12** Lower the J-bolt slowly into the concrete, wiggling it slightly to eliminate any air gaps.

**13** Set the J-bolt so ¾" to 1" is exposed above concrete. Brush away any wet concrete on bolt threads with an old toothbrush.

**14** Use a plumb bob to make sure the J-bolt is positioned exactly at center of post location.

**15** Use a torpedo level to make sure the J-bolt is plumb. If necessary, adjust the bolt and re-pack concrete. Let concrete cure, then cut away exposed portion of tube with a utility knife.

# Setting Posts

Posts support the deck beams and transfer the weight of the deck to the concrete footings. For maximum strength, the posts must be plumb.

To prevent rot or insect damage, use pressure-treated lumber for posts, and make sure the factory-treated end faces down.

Use metal post anchors to attach the posts to the concrete footings. Post anchors have drainage holes and pedestals that raise the ends of the wood posts above the concrete footings.

## Everything You Need:

Tools (Page 316): pencil, framing square, ratchet wrench, tape measure, power miter box or circular saw, hammer, screwgun, level, combination square.

Materials: metal post anchors, nuts for J-bolts, lumber for posts, 6d galvanized common nails, 2" wallboard screws.

Supplies: long, straight 2 × 4; 1 × 4s; pointed 2 × 2 stakes.

## How to Attach Post Anchors

**1** Mark the top of each footing as a reference line for installing post anchors. Lay a long, straight 2 × 4 flat across two or three concrete footings, parallel to the ledger, with one edge tight against the J-bolts.

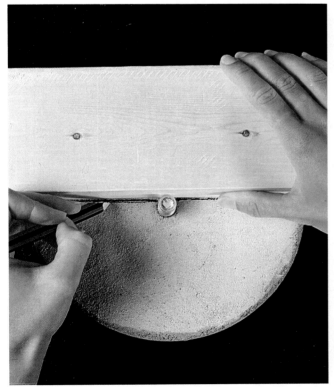

**2** Draw a reference line across each concrete footing, using the edge of the 2 × 4 as a guide. Remove the 2 × 4.

**3** Place a metal post anchor on each concrete footing, and center it over the J-bolt.

(continued next page)

## How to Attach Post Anchors (continued)

**4** Use a framing square to make sure the post anchor is positioned square to the reference line drawn on the footing.

**5** Thread a nut over each J-bolt, and tighten it securely with a ratchet wrench.

## How to Set Posts

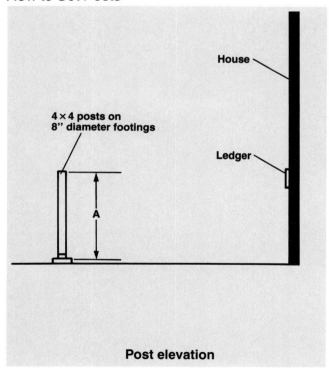

**House**

**4 × 4 posts on 8" diameter footings**

**Ledger**

**A**

**Post elevation**

**1** Use the elevation drawing from the design plan (page 323) to find the length of each post (A). Add 6" for a cutting margin.

**2** Cut posts with power miter box or circular saw. Make sure factory-treated ends of posts are square. If necessary, square them by trimming with a power miter box or circular saw.

**3** Place post in anchor, and tack into place with a single 6d galvanized common nail.

**4** Brace post with a 1 × 4. Place the 1 × 4 flat across post, so that it crosses the post at a 45° angle about halfway up.

**5** Attach the brace to the post temporarily with a single 2'' wallboard screw.

**6** Drive a pointed 2 × 2 stake into the ground next to the end of the brace.

(continued next page)

**7** Use a level to make sure the post is plumb. Adjust the post, if necessary.

**8** Attach the brace to the stake with two 2" wallboard screws.

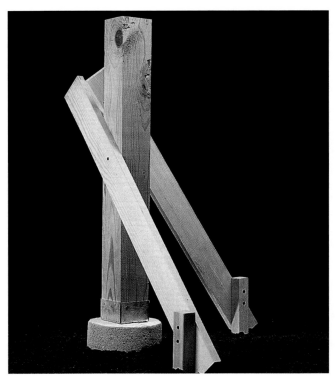

**9** Plumb and brace the post on the side perpendicular to the first brace.

**10** Attach the post to the post anchor with 6d galvanized common nails.

**11** Position a straight 2 × 4 with one end on ledger and other end across face of post. Level the 2 × 4, then lower its post end ¼" for every 3 ft. between ledger and post (for water runoff) Draw a line on the post along the bottom of the 2 × 4. For cantilevered construction (pages 350 to 352), this line indicates the top of the joists. For corner-post construction (page 353), this line indicates the top of the beam.

**12** For cantilevered construction, draw a line as shown in step 11. Then measure down a distance equal to width of joists, and mark the post.

**13** Use a square to draw a line completely around the post. This line indicates the top of the canti-lever beam.

# Installing a Beam

A deck beam is attached to the posts, and helps support the weight of the joists and decking. The method for installing the beam depends on whether the deck is a cantilevered or corner-post design.

A **cantilevered deck** has posts and one or more beams that are set back from the edge of the deck. The advantage is a neater and more attractive appearance. In cantilevered construction, the joists run across and extend past the beam. The general rule is the overhanging, or cantilevered, portion of the deck may be one-third the total length of the joists.

A **corner-post deck** has posts that are set at the edge of the deck. Because joists butt into the beam, rather than run across the top, corner-post construction is ideal for low decks.

## How to Install a Beam for a Cantilevered Deck

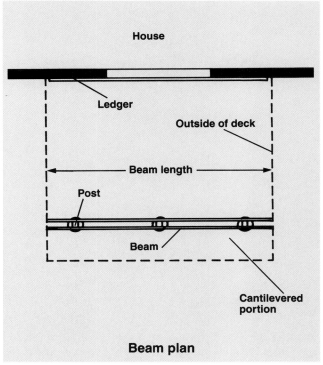

**Beam plan**

**1** Use the deck design plan (page 322) to find the beam length. In plan shown above, the cantilever beam is cut to match overall width of deck.

**2** Measure and mark two straight pressure-treated boards to length. Cut boards with a circular saw. Seal cut ends with clear sealer-preservative.

**3** Hold beam boards together. Measure and mark the post locations on the tops and sides of boards, using a combination square as a guide.

**4** Position one beam board against the sides of the posts with crown side up. Marks on the board should be aligned with beam height marks on posts. Hold board in position with 2½'' deck screws.

(continued next page)

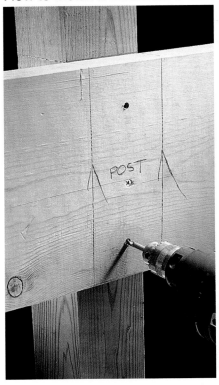

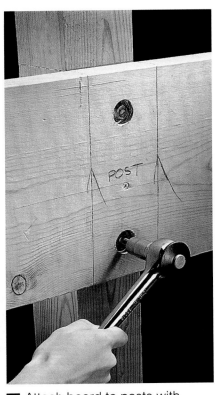

**5** Drill two ¼'' pilot holes through the beam board and into each of the posts.

**6** Counterbore each pilot hole to ½'' depth, using 1'' spade bit.

**7** Attach board to posts with ⅜'' × 4'' lag screws and washers, using a ratchet wrench.

**8** Attach the remaining beam board to the opposite sides of the posts, repeating steps 4 to 7. Seal screw heads with silicone caulk.

**9** Cut tops of posts flush with top edge of beam, using a reciprocating saw or handsaw. Seal cut ends of posts with clear sealer-preservative.

## How to Install a Beam for a Corner-post Deck

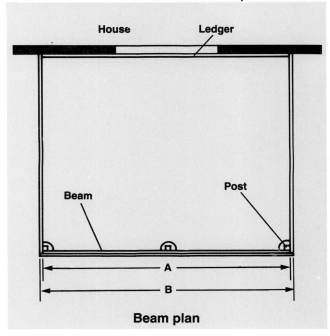

**Beam plan**

(labels in diagram: House, Ledger, Beam, Post, A, B)

**1** Use deck design plan (page 322) to find length of beam. Measure distance (A) between outside edges of corner posts. Mark pressure-treated board to length and cut with circular saw. Cut a second beam board (B), 3" longer than first board. Seal cut ends with clear sealer-preservative.

**2** Position shorter beam board against outside of posts so that ends are flush with post edges. Top edge of board should be flush with beam height marks on posts. Drill ⅛" pilot holes, and hold beam board in position with 2½" deck screws.

**3** Position the longer beam board against outside of the first board, so that ends overhang by 1½" to allow for outside joists. Fasten boards together with a pair of 2½" deck screws driven every 2 feet.

**4** Drill two ¼" pilot holes through both beam boards and into each post. Counterbore each pilot hole to ½" depth, using a 1" spade bit. Secure boards to posts with ⅜" × 5" lag screws and washers, using a ratchet wrench. Seal screw heads and crack between boards with silicone caulk.

# Hanging Joists

Joists provide support for the decking boards. In cantilever construction, joists are attached to the ledger and header joist with galvanized metal joist hangers, and are nailed to the top of the beam. In corner-post construction, joists are attached to the ledger and inside of the beam with galvanized joist hangers.

For strength and durability, use pressure-treated lumber for all joists. The exposed outside joists and header joist can be faced with redwood or cedar boards for a more attractive appearance (page 363).

### Everything You Need:

Tools (page 316): tape measure, pencil, hammer, combination square, circular saw, paint brush, drill, twist bits (1/16", 1/4"), 1" spade bit.

Materials: pressure-treated lumber, clear sealer-preservative, 10d galvanized common nails, 1¼" joist nails, joist angle brackets, galvanized metal joist hangers, ⅜" × 4" lag screws and 1" washers.

## How to Hang Joists

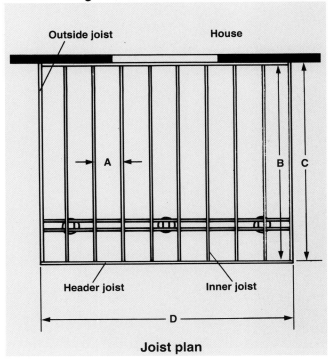

**Joist plan**

**1** Use the design plan (page 322) to find the spacing (A) between joists, and the length of inner joists (B), outside joists (C), and header joist (D). Measure and mark lumber for outside joists, using a combination square as a guide. Cut joists with a circular saw. Seal cut ends with clear sealer-preservative.

**2** Drill three 1/16" pilot holes, spaced about 3" apart, through one end of each outside joist.

**3** Hold the outside joists in position at ends of ledger with 10d nails driven into the ledger.

**4** Attach the outside joists to the top of the beam by toenailing them with 10d nails.

(continued next page)

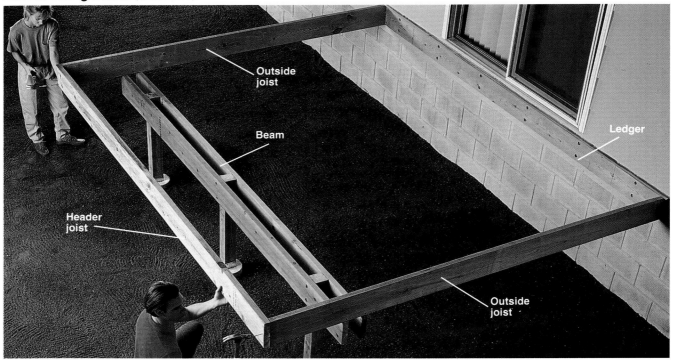

Outside joist

Beam

Ledger

Header joist

Outside joist

**5** Measure and cut header joist. Seal cut ends with clear sealer-preservative. Drill ¹⁄₁₆" pilot holes at each end of header joist. Attach header to ends of outside joists with 10d galvanized nails.

**6** Strengthen each inside corner of the deck frame with an angle bracket. Attach the brackets with 1¼" joist nails.

**Alternate for corner-post deck:** Position outside joist against post, flush with end of beam. Drill ¼" pilot holes through end of joist, into post. Counterbore pilot holes to depth of ½", using 1" spade bit. Attach with ⅜" × 4" lag screws and washers. Cut off posts flush with top of beam, using a reciprocating saw or handsaw.

**7** Measure along ledger from edge of outside joist, and mark where joists will be attached to ledger.

**8** Draw the outline of each joist on the ledger, using a combination square as a guide.

**9** Measure along the beam from outside joist and mark where joists will cross beam. Draw the outlines across top of both beam boards.

**10** Measure along the header joist from the outside joist, and mark where joists will be attached to header joist. Draw the outlines on the inside of the header, using a combination square as a guide.

(continued next page)

**11** Attach joist hangers to the ledger and to the header joist. Position each hanger so that one of the flanges is against the joist outline. Nail flange to framing member with 1¼" joist nails.

**12** Cut a scrap board to use as a spacer. Hold spacer inside each joist hanger, then close the hanger around the spacer.

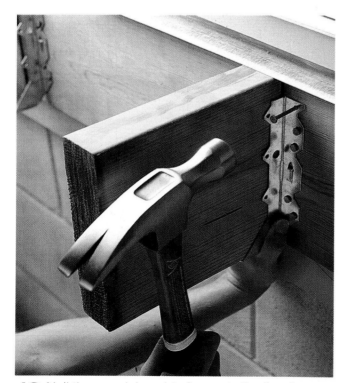

**13** Nail the remaining side flange to the framing member with 1¼" joist nails. Remove spacer.

**14** Measure and mark lumber for joists, using a combination square as a guide. Cut joists with a circular saw.

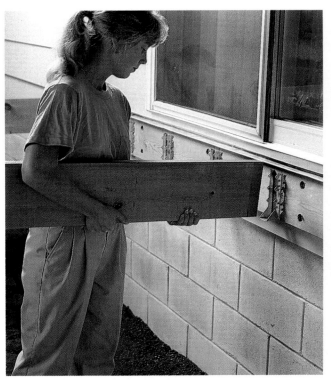

**15** Seal cut ends with clear sealer-preservative. Place joists in hangers with crowned side up.

**16** Attach the ledger joist hangers to the joists with 1¼" joist nails. Drive nails into both sides of each joist.

**17** Align the joists with the outlines drawn on the top of the beam. Anchor the joists to the beam by toe-nailing from both sides with 10d galvanized nails.

**18** Attach the joists to the header joist hangers with 1¼" joist nails. Drive nails into both sides of each joist.

# Laying Decking

Buy decking boards that are long enough to span the width of the deck, if possible. If boards must be butted end-to-end, make sure to stagger the joints so they do not overlap from row to row. Predrill the ends of boards to prevent screws or nails from splitting the wood.

Install decking so that there is a 1/8" gap between boards to provide drainage. Boards naturally "cup" as they age (page 307). Lay boards with the bark side facing down, so that the cupped surface cannot hold standing water.

## Everything You Need:

Tools (page 316): tape measure, circular saw, screwgun, hammer, drill, 1/8" twist bit, pry bar, chalk line, jig saw or handsaw.

Materials: decking boards, 2½" corrosion-resistant deck screws, galvanized common nails (8d, 10d), redwood or cedar facing boards.

## How to Lay Decking

**1** Position the first row of decking flush against the house. First decking board should be perfectly straight, and should be precut to proper length. Attach the first decking board by driving a pair of 2½" corrosion-resistant deck screws into each joist.

**2** Position remaining decking boards so that ends overhang outside joists. Space boards about 1/8" apart. Attach boards to each joist with a pair of 2½' deck screws driven into each joist.

**Alternate method:** Attach decking boards with 10d galvanized common nails. Angle the nails toward each other to improve holding power.

(continued next page)

**3** If boards are bowed, use a pry bar to lever them into position while fastening.

**4** Drill ⅛" pilot holes in ends of boards before attaching them to outside joists. Pilot holes prevent screws from splitting decking boards at ends.

**5** After every few rows of decking are installed, measure from edge of the decking board to edge of header joist. If measurements show that the last board will not fit flush against the edge of the deck, adjust board spacing.

**6** Adjust board spacing by changing the gaps between boards by a small amount over three or four rows of boards. Very small spacing changes will not be obvious to the eye.

**7** Use a chalk line to mark the edge of decking flush with the outside edge of deck. Cut off decking with a circular saw. Set saw blade ⅛" deeper than thickness of decking so that saw will not cut side of deck. At areas where circular saw cannot reach, finish cutoff with a jig saw or handsaw.

**8** For a more attractive appearance, face the deck with redwood or cedar facing boards. Miter-cut corners, and attach boards with deck screws or 8d galvanized nails.

**Alternate facing technique:** Attach facing boards so that edges of decking overhang facing.

# Building Stairs

Building deck stairs requires four calculations.

**Number of steps** depends on the vertical drop of the deck. The vertical drop is the distance from the surface of the deck to the ground.

**Rise** is the vertical space between treads. Building codes require that the rise measurement be about 7''.

**Run** is the depth of the treads. A convenient way to build deck stairs is to use a pair of 2 × 6s for each tread.

**Span** is figured by multiplying the run by the number of treads. The span lets you locate the end of the stairway, and position support posts.

### Everything You Need:

Tools (page 316): tape measure, pencil, framing square, level, plumb bob, posthole digger, wheelbarrow, hoe, circular saw, hammer, drill, 1/8" twist bit, 1" spade bit, ratchet wrench, caulk gun.

Materials: sand, portland cement, gravel, J-bolts, metal post anchors, 2 × 12 lumber, metal cleats, ¼" × 1¼" lag screws, joist angle brackets, 1¼" galvanized joist nails, ⅜" × 4" lag screws and 1" washers, 2 × 6 lumber, 16d nails, silicone caulk.

Supplies: long, straight 2 × 4; pointed stakes; masking tape.

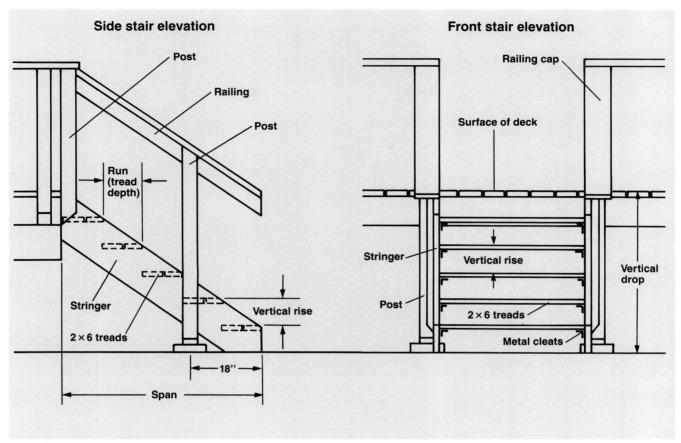

| Side stair elevation | Front stair elevation |
|---|---|

**Side stair elevation** labels: Post, Railing, Post, Run (tread depth), Stringer, 2 × 6 treads, Vertical rise, 18", Span

**Front stair elevation** labels: Railing cap, Surface of deck, Stringer, Vertical rise, Post, 2 × 6 treads, Metal cleats, Vertical drop

**A deck stairway** is made from two 2 × 12 stringers, and a series of treads attached with metal cleats. Posts set 18" back from the end of the stairway help to anchor the stringers and the railings. Calculations needed to build stairs include the **number of steps**, the **rise** of each step, the **run** of each step, and the stairway **span**.

## How to Find Measurements for Stairway Layout

Sample Measurements<br>(39" High Deck)

| | | | | |
|---|---|---|---|---|
| **1. Find the number of steps:** Measure vertical drop from deck surface to ground. Divide by 7. Round off to nearest whole number. | Vertical drop: | | | 39" |
| | ÷ 7 = | | | 5.57" |
| | Number of steps: | = | = | 6 |
| **2. Find step rise:** Divide the vertical drop by the number of steps. | Vertical drop: | | | 39" |
| | Number of steps: | ÷ | ÷ | 6 |
| | Rise: | = | = | 6.5" |
| **3. Find step run:** Typical treads made from two 2 × 6s have a run of 11¼". If your design is different, find run by measuring depth of tread, including any space between boards. | Run: | | | 11¼" |
| **4. Find stairway span:** Multiply the run by the number of treads. (Number of treads is always one less than number of steps.) | Run: | | | 11¼" |
| | Number of treads: | × | × | 5 |
| | Span: | = | = | 56¼" |

## How to Build Deck Stairs

**1** Use the stairway elevation drawings (page 365) to find measurements for stair stringers and posts. Use a pencil and framing square to outline where stair stringers will be attached to the side of the deck.

**2** Locate the post footings so they are 18" back from the end of stairway span. Lay a straight 2 × 4 on the deck so that it is level and square to side of deck. Use a plumb bob to mark the ground at centerpoints of footings.

**3** Dig holes and pour footings for posts (pages 340 to 343). Attach metal post anchors to footings and install 4 × 4 posts (pages 344 to 349).

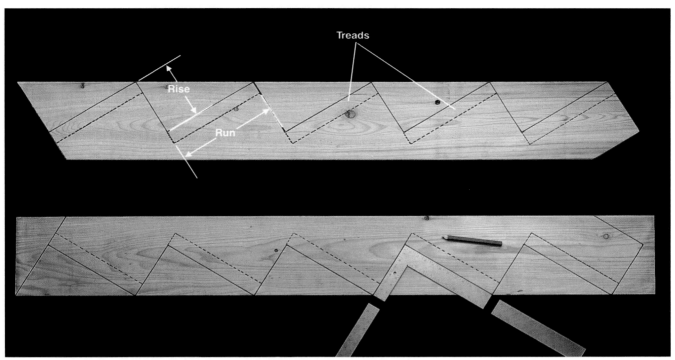

**4** Lay out stair stringers. Use tape to mark the rise measurement on one leg of a framing square, and the run measurement on the other leg. Beginning at one end of stringer, position the square with tape marks flush to edge of board, and outline the rise and run for each step. Then draw in the tread outline against the bottom of each run line. Use a circular saw to trim ends of stringers as shown.

**5** Attach metal tread cleats flush with bottom of each tread outline, using 1/4" × 1 1/4" lag screws. Drill 1/8" pilot holes to prevent the screws from splitting the wood.

**6** Attach angle brackets to upper ends of stringers, using 1 1/4" joist nails. Brackets should be flush with cut ends of stringers.

(continued next page)

## How to Build Deck Stairs (continued)

**7** Position the stair stringers against side of deck, over the stringer outlines. Align top point of stringer flush with the surface of the deck. Attach stringers by nailing the angle brackets to the deck with 1¼" joist nails.

**8** Drill two ¼" pilot holes through each stringer and into each adjacent post. Counterbore each hole to depth of ½", using a 1" spade bit. Attach stringers to posts with ⅜" × 4" lag screws and washers, using a ratchet wrench. Seal screw heads with silicone caulk.

**9** Measure width of stair treads. Cut two 2 × 6s for each tread, using a circular saw.

**10** For each step, position the front 2 × 6 on the tread cleat, so that the front edge is flush with the tread outline on the stringers.

**11** Drill ⅛" pilot holes, then attach the front 2 × 6s to the cleats with ¼" × 1¼" lag screws.

**12** Position the rear 2 × 6s on the cleats, allowing a small space between boards. Use a 16d nail as a spacing guide. Drill ⅛" pilot holes, and attach 2 × 6s to cleats with ¼" × 1¼" lag screws.

## Stair Variations

**Hardware option:** Metal step brackets can be attached to tops of stringers. This method allows the treads to overhang at the sides.

**Notched stringers** made of pressure-treated wood are available precut at building centers. Edges of cut-out areas should be coated with sealer-preservative to prevent rot.

# Installing a Deck Railing

Railings must be sturdy, and should be firmly attached to the framing members of the deck. Never attach railing posts to the surface decking. Check local building codes for guidelines regarding railing construction. Most codes require that railings be at least 34" above decking. Vertical balusters should be spaced less than 6" apart.

### Everything You Need:

Tools (page 316): tape measure, pencil, power miter box, drill, twist bits ($1/8$", $1/4$"), 1" spade bit, combination square, awl, ratchet wrench, caulk gun, level, reciprocating saw or circular saw, jig saw with wood-cutting blade.

Materials: railing lumber (4 × 4s, 2 × 6s, 2 × 4s, 2 × 2s), clear sealer-preservative, $3/8$" × 4" lag screws and 1" washers, silicone caulk, $2\frac{1}{2}$" corrosion-resistant deck screws, 10d galvanized common nails.

## How to Install a Deck Railing

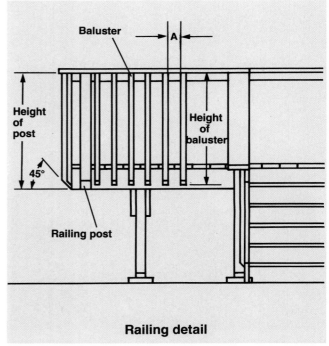

**Railing detail**

**1** Refer to the deck design plan (pages 322 to 323) for spacing (A) and length of railing posts and balusters. Posts should be spaced no more than 6 feet apart.

370

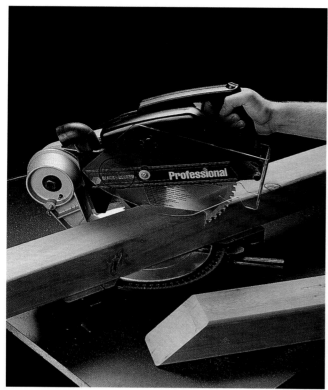

**2** Measure and cut 4 × 4 posts, using a power miter box or circular saw. Cut off tops of the posts square, and cut the bottoms at 45° angle. Seal cut ends of lumber with clear sealer-preservative.

**3** Measure and cut balusters for main deck, using a power miter box or circular saw. Cut off tops of the balusters square, and cut bottoms at 45° angle. Seal cut ends of lumber with clear sealer-preservative.

**4** Drill two ¼'' pilot holes through bottom end of each post, spaced 4'' apart. Counterbore each pilot hole to ½'' depth, using a 1'' spade bit.

**5** Drill two ⅛'' pilot holes near bottom end of each baluster, spaced 4'' apart. Drill two ⅛'' pilot holes at top of each baluster, spaced 1½'' apart.

(continued next page)

**6** Measure and mark position of posts around the outside of the deck, using a combination square as a guide. Plan to install a post on outside edge of each stair stringer.

**7** Position each post with beveled end flush with bottom of deck. Plumb post with a level. Insert a screwdriver or nail into pilot holes and mark side of deck.

**8** Remove post and drill ¼" pilot holes into side of deck.

**9** Attach railing posts to side of deck with ⅜" × 4" lag screws and washers, using a ratchet wrench. Seal screw heads with silicone caulk.

**10** Measure and cut 2 × 4 side rails. Position rails with edges flush to tops of posts, and attach to posts with 2½" corrosion-resistant deck screws.

**11** Join 2 × 4s for long rails by cutting ends at 45° angle. Drill ¹⁄₁₆'' pilot holes to prevent nails from splitting end grain, and attach rails with 10d galvanized nails. (Screws may split mitered ends.)

**12** Attach ends of rails to stairway posts, flush with edges of posts, as shown. Drill ⅛'' pilot holes, and attach rails with 2½'' deck screws.

**13** At stairway, measure from surface of decking to the top of the upper stairway post (A).

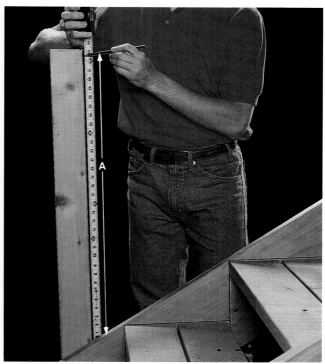

**14** Transfer measurement A to lower stairway post, measuring from the edge of the stair stringer.

(continued next page)

# How to Install a Deck Railing (continued)

**15** Position 2 × 4 rail against inside of stairway posts. Align rail with top rear corner of top post, and with the pencil mark on the lower post. Have a helper attach rail temporarily with 2½" deck screws.

**16** Mark the outline of the post and the deck rail on the back side of the stairway rail.

**17** Mark the outline of the stairway rail on the lower stairway post.

**18** Use a level to mark a plumb cutoff line at the bottom end of the stairway rail. Remove the rail.

**19** Extend the pencil lines across both sides of the stairway post, using a combination square as a guide.

**20** Cut off lower stairway post along diagonal cutoff line, using a reciprocating saw or circular saw.

**21** Use a jig saw to cut the stairway rail along the marked outlines.

**22** Position the stairway rail flush against top edge of posts. Drill ⅛" pilot holes, then attach rail to posts with 2½" deck screws.

(continued next page)

## How to Install a Deck Railing (continued)

**23** Use a spacer block to ensure equal spacing between balusters. Beginning next to a plumb railing post, position each baluster tight against spacer block, with top of baluster flush to top of rail. Attach each baluster with 2½'' deck screws.

**24** For stairway, position baluster against stringer and rail, and adjust for plumb. Draw diagonal cutoff line on top of baluster, using top of stair rail as a guide. Cut baluster on marked line, using power miter box. Seal ends with clear sealer-preservative.

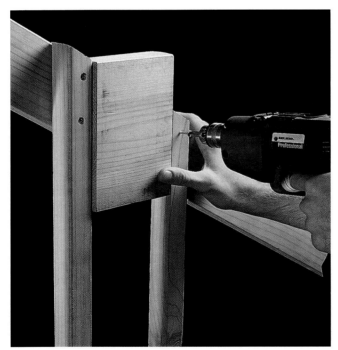

**25** Beginning next to upper stairway post, position each baluster tight against spacer block, with top flush to top of stair rail. Attach baluster with 2½'' deck screws.

**26** Position 2 × 6 cap so edge is flush with inside edge of rail. Drill ⅛'' pilot holes, and attach cap to rail with 2½'' deck screws driven every 12''. Also drive screws into each post and into every third baluster. For long caps, bevel ends at 45°. Drill 1/16'' pilot holes, and attach at post using 10d nails.

**27** At corners, miter ends of railing cap at 45°. Drill ⅛" pilot holes, and attach cap to post with 2½" deck screws.

**28** At top of stairs, cut cap so that it is flush with stairway rail. Drill ⅛" pilot holes and attach cap with 2½" deck screws.

**29** Measure and cut cap for stairway rail. Mark outline of post on side of cap, and bevel-cut the ends of the cap.

**30** Position cap over the stairway rail and balusters so that edge of cap is flush with inside edge of rail. Drill ⅛" pilot holes, and attach cap to rail with 2½" deck screws driven every 12". Also drive screws through cap into stair post and into every third baluster.

# Platform Deck

A platform deck is built low to the ground, so it is ideal for a flat, level yard, and when the height of the interior floor is close to the surface of the yard.

Because it is low to the ground, a platform deck does not require railings or stairs. It has an open, airy feeling that makes it an ideal place for sunning or entertaining.

The platform deck shown at left adds visual interest with a second level and redwood decking laid on the diagonal. The decking is a mix of cream-colored sapwood, and reddish heartwood that is rot-resistant. Always treat sapwood with a clear sealer-preservative.

A redwood facing board runs around the edges of this deck. Redwood that comes in contact with the ground or with grass should be treated with a clear sealer-preservative before installation.

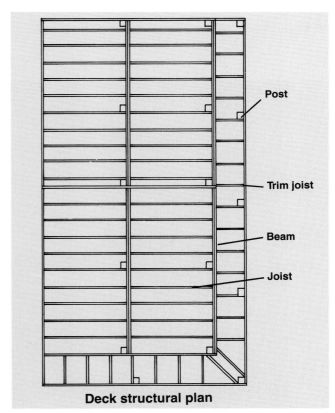

**Deck structural plan**

**Low platform deck** uses 2 × 6 joists and corner-post beams that require closely spaced posts for extra support. Joists for interior portion of deck are spaced 12" on-center to support longer spans of diagonal decking. Short joists (called trim joists) around the perimeter of the deck support the border decking boards.

**1** Attach 2 × 6 pressure-treated ledgers to house with 3/8" × 4" lag screws (pages 328 to 333). Pour footings and install 4 × 4 pressure-treated posts (pages 340 to 349). Mark posts to indicate tops of beams.

**2** Build each beam from a pair of pressure-treated 2 × 6s (pages 350 to 353). Hold 2 × 6s together with 2½" corrosion-resistant deck screws driven every 18". Drill counterbored pilot holes and attach beams to posts with 3/8" × 5" lag screws. Cut all post tops flush with tops of beams.

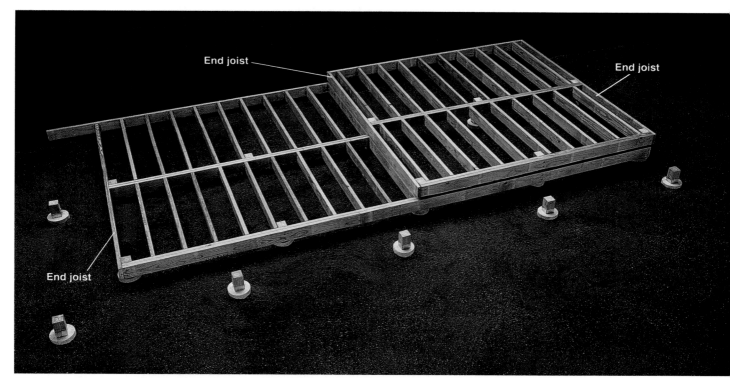

**3** Hang pressure-treated joists (pages 354 to 359). Lay out interior joists at 12" on-center. Install all joists with galvanized joist hangers and joist nails. Attach end joists to posts, not beams, with 2½" deck screws. End grain has little holding power.

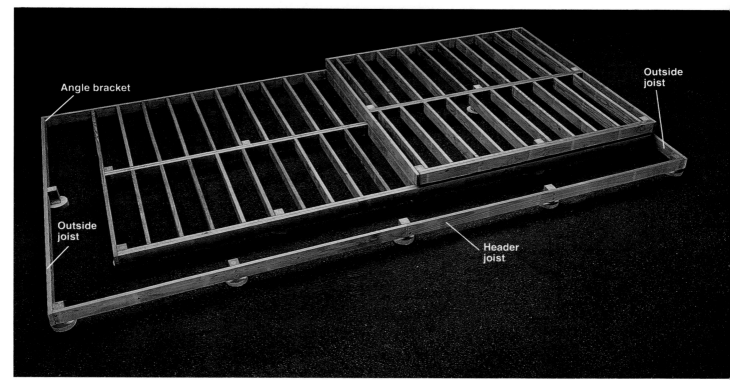

**4** Attach 2 × 6 pressure-treated outside joists and header joist to posts, using ³/8" × 3" lag screws (pages 355 to 356). Counterbore pilot holes so that facing boards can be installed. Reinforce inside corners of outside joists with angle brackets. Cut off all post tops flush with tops of header and outside joists.

(continued next page)

# How to Build a Platform Deck (continued)

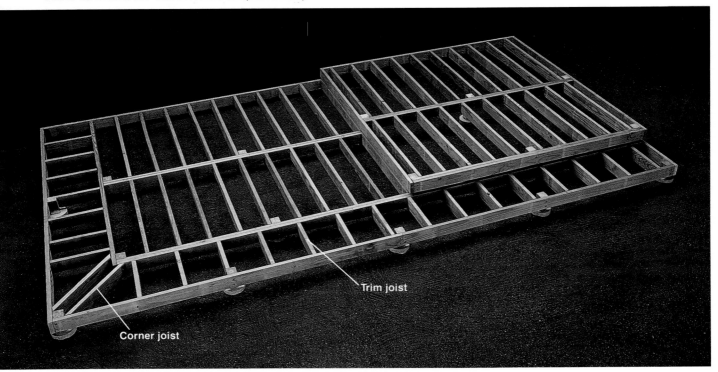

**5** Lay out trim joists at 16" on-center. Attach the trim joists with galvanized joist hangers and joist nails. Cut the ends of the diagonal corner joists at a 45° angle, and install with angled joist hangers.

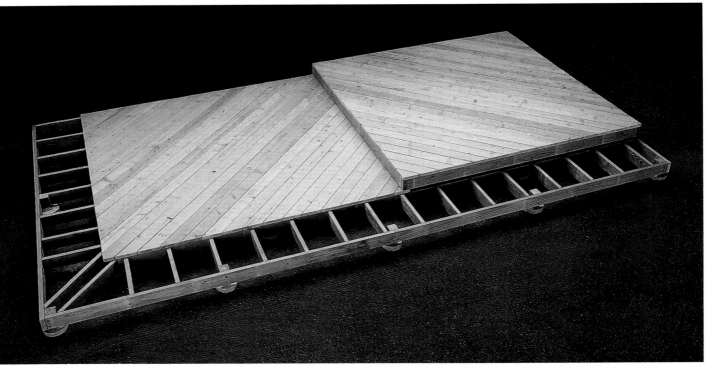

**6** Install all diagonal decking (pages 360 to 363). Decking boards that will butt against the house should be premitered at 45°. Use a chalk line to snap a cutoff line across the overhanging decking, flush with outside edges of beams and end joists. Cut off decking with circular saw with blade depth set to match thickness of decking.

**Herringbone pattern**

**7** Install the decking border. Begin with board against diagonal pattern, and work toward outside edge of deck. Adjust spacing between decking so that the edge of the last board is exactly flush with edge of header or outside joist (page 362). Stagger the ends of the boards at corner to create a herringbone pattern, as shown.

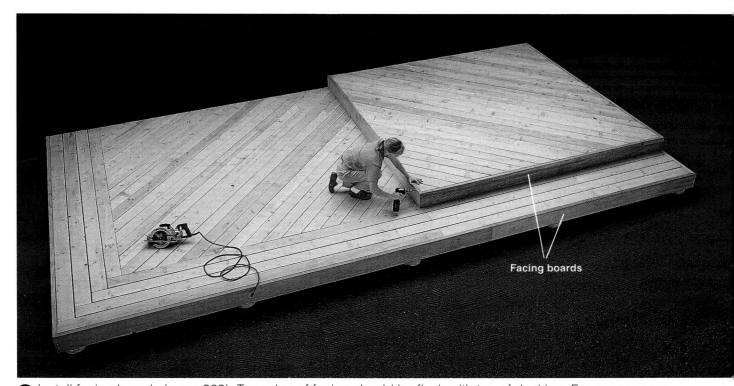

**Facing boards**

**8** Install facing boards (page 363). Top edge of facing should be flush with top of decking. For appearance, choose top-grade lumber for facing. Miter the corners at 45°, and fasten facing boards with 2½" corrosion-resistant deck screws driven every 18".

# Diamond-pattern Deck

Give your deck a distinct look with an unusual decking pattern. The visual appeal of a deck can be improved by using a diagonal or diamond-shaped decking pattern, like the one at left.

Install double joists or a row of double blocking for extra strength and stability wherever ends of decking boards butt together. Space the joists at 12'' on-center to support the diagonal decking.

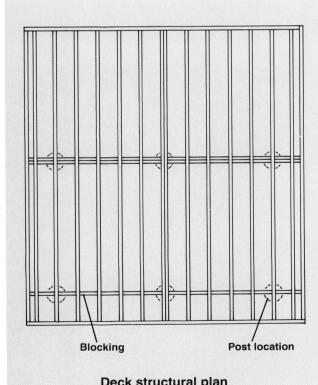

**Blocking**          **Post location**

**Deck structural plan**

**Diamond-pattern deck** has blocking added to provide surface for attaching ends of decking. Joist spacing on diagonal decking pattern is 12'' on-center.

## How to Build a Diamond-pattern Deck

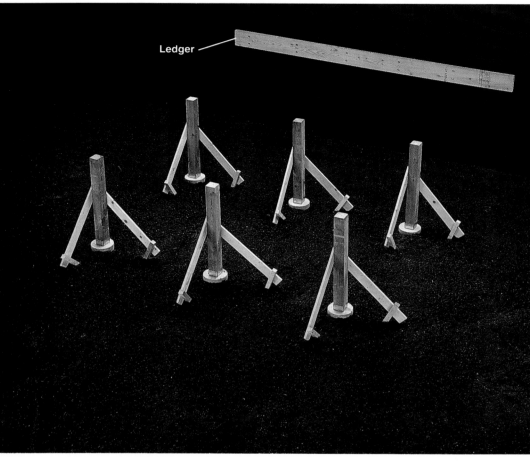

**1** Install pressure-treated ledger (pages 328 to 333).

Pour post footings and install 4 × 4 pressure-treated posts (pages 340 to 349). Seal all cut ends of lumber with sealer-preservative.

Brace all posts longer than 2 feet (pages 347 to 348).

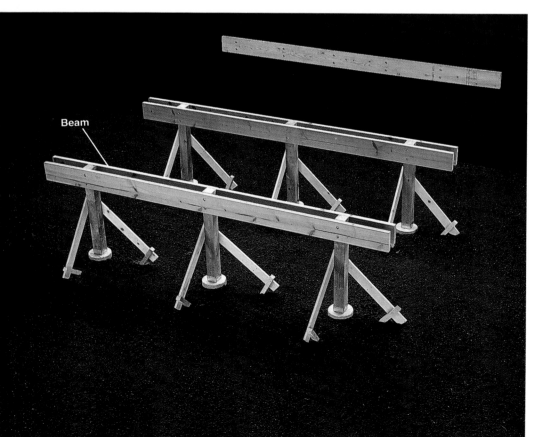

**2** Build each deck beam from pressure-treated lumber (pages 350 to 353). Position the boards against the row of posts, and drill a pair of 1/4" pilot holes through boards and into each post. Attach the beam to the posts with 3/8" × 4" galvanized lag screws and washers.

Cut off all post tops flush with the top edges of the beams, using a reciprocating saw or handsaw.

**3** Cut the header and outside joists from pressure-treated lumber.

Attach the outside joists to the ledger and to the tops of the beams, using 10d galvanized nails.

Attach the header joist to the ends of the outside joists, using 10d nails, then reinforce inside corners with angle brackets (page 356).

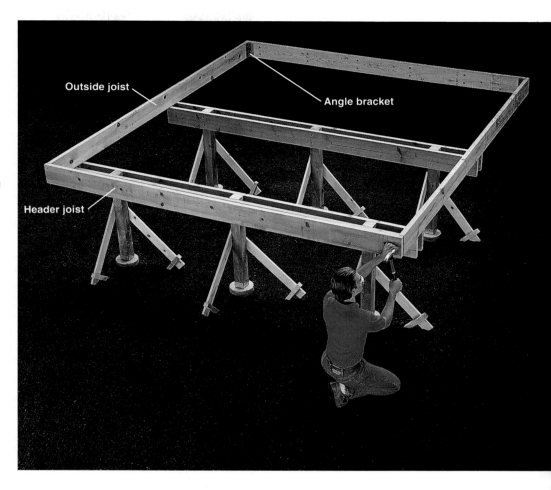

Outside joist

Angle bracket

Header joist

**4** Hang the inside joists (pages 354 to 359).

Attach the joists to the ledger and header joist with galvanized metal joist hangers.

Install a double joist at the center of the framework to provide extra support where the ends of the decking boards will butt together.

Toenail all joists to the tops of the beams with 10d galvanized nails. Seal seam between double joists with silicone caulk.

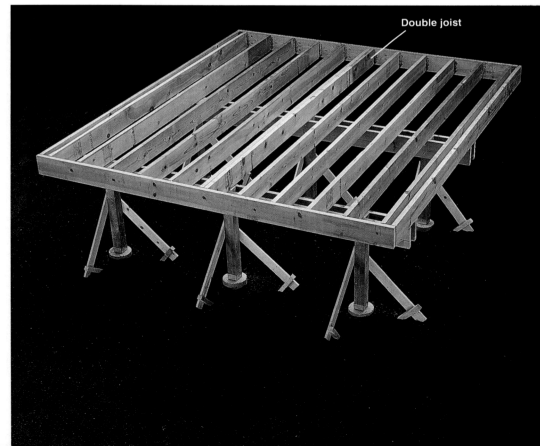

Double joist

(continued next page)

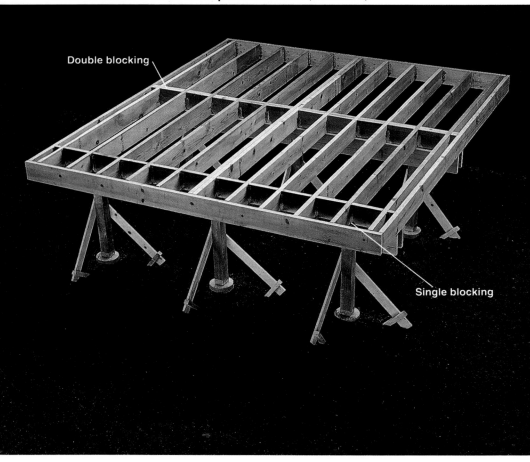

Double blocking

Single blocking

**5** Install a row of double blocking between each pair of joists at the center of the diamond pattern, using galvanized joist hangers.

Install a row of single blocking at the end of the diamond pattern joist, using galvanized joist hangers. Blocking provides support where the ends of the diagonal decking boards form a continuous line.

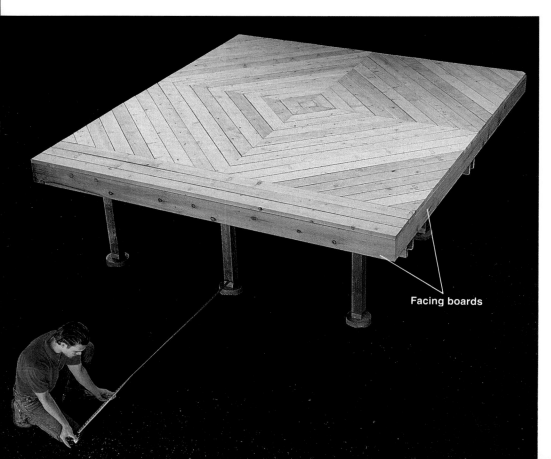

Facing boards

**6** Face the header and outside joists with high-quality boards (page 363). Miter the corners of the boards at 45°, and attach with 8d galvanized nails.

Lay 2 × 6 redwood decking (pages 360 to 363). Use a combination square to mark the ends of angled boards at 45°, and cut with a circular saw or a power miter box.

Lay out the deck stairs (pages 364 to 365).

**7** Pour stairway footings, and install post anchors and 4 × 4 posts.

Build the deck stairs (pages 364 to 369). The 2 × 10 stringers are attached to side of deck with ⅜" × 4" lag screws driven through back of header joist, and are anchored to the stairway posts with ⅜" × 4" lag screws.

Attach the stair treads to the stringers with metal cleats and lag screws.

**8** Build post-and-baluster railing for the deck and stairway (pages 370 to 377).

Attach the 4 × 4 posts to the deck with ⅜" × 6" lag screws. Attach the 2 × 4 horizontal rails, the rail cap, and 2 × 2 balusters with 2½" corrosion-resistant deck screws. For a decorative detail, let posts and balusters extend below facing boards.

# Island Deck

Build an island deck to create a sitting or dining area anywhere in your yard. Because an island deck is not attached to your house, it can be constructed to take advantage of afternoon shade patterns or scenic views.

Create visual interest with an octagonal deck. A short platform, or "gangway," gives access to the deck from three directions. An island deck may include pathways of brick or crushed rock that lead to the house.

Careful planning is usually required for decks with odd shapes, like an octagon. The eight-sided portion of the deck shown at right uses eight posts and four beams for complete stability.

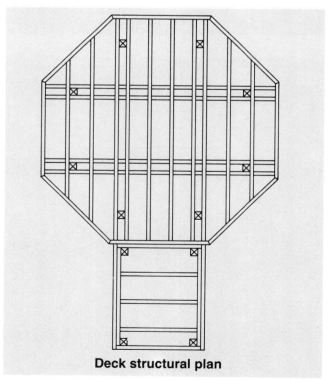

**Deck structural plan**

**Island deck** has four beams and eight posts to create the support system for octagonal shape. Joists run at right angles to the decking. Outside joists are mitered at 22½° on an octagonal deck. Gangway platform is built using corner-post construction.

**1** Pour post footings and install 4 × 4 pressure-treated posts (pages 340 to 349).

Plan deck layout so that there are eight posts for the main deck and four additional posts for the gangway.

The main portion of the deck uses cantilevered construction. Because the gangway is built low to the ground, use corner-post construction for this portion of the deck.

Posts longer than 2 feet should be braced plumb.

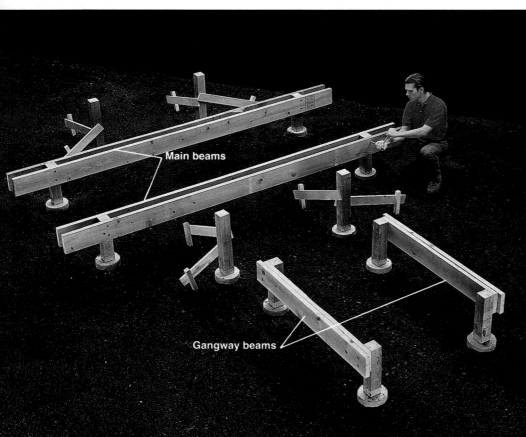

Main beams

Gangway beams

**2** Build main beams from pressure-treated lumber (pages 350 to 353).

The two main beams for the octagonal deck run in the same direction as the decking boards. Build the beams for gangway using corner-post construction.

Attach the beams to the posts with ⅜'' × 4'' galvanized lag screws and washers.

Cut off the posts flush with the tops of the beams. Seal the cut ends with clear sealer-preservative.

**3** Install two additional 2 × 8 beams across the main beams.

These beams are on the same level as the joists. Because they are attached directly to posts, these beams function as structural beams.

Cut off posts flush with the tops of the beams, and seal the ends with clear sealer-preservative.

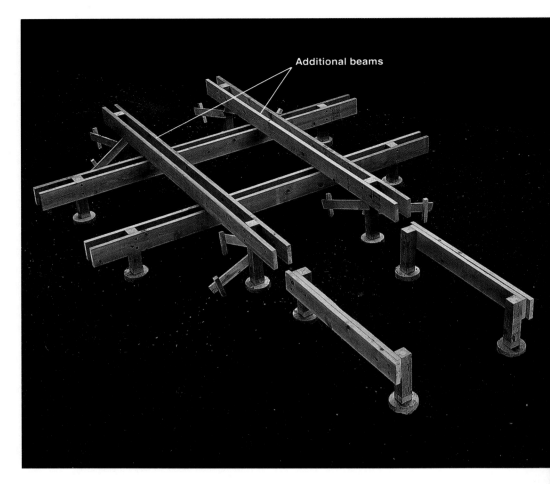

Additional beams

**4** Attach all outside joists (page 356). The cutting angle for the ends of outside joists is 22¹/₂° on an octagonal deck.

Attach the outside joists to the additional beams with galvanized metal joist hangers.

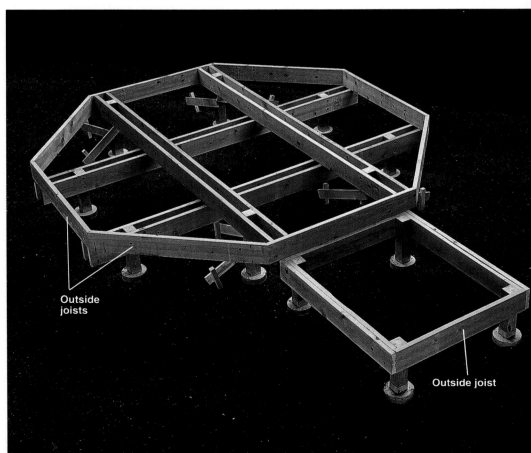

Outside joists

Outside joist

(continued next page)

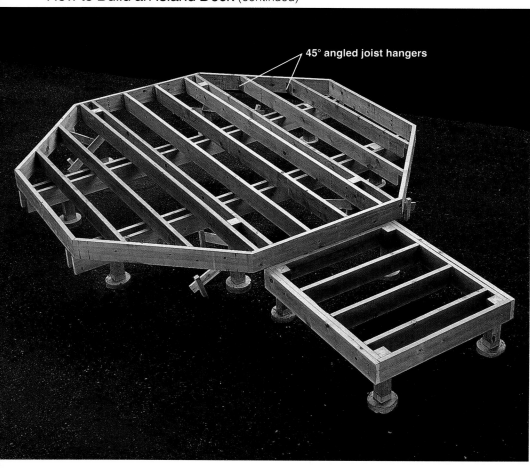

45° angled joist hangers

**5** Hang pressure-treated inside joists (pages 357 to 359).

Install the joists parallel to the additional beams, using galvanized metal joist hangers.

Use 45° joist hangers for installing joists to angled outside joists.

Remove all post bracing.

**6** Install all the decking using 2¹/2" corrosion-resistant deck screws (pages 360 to 363). Run the ends of the decking boards past all outside joists.

Use a chalk line to snap a cutting line on the decking, flush with the edges of the outside joists.

Cut decking using a circular saw with blade depth set to match thickness of the decking.

**7** Face the outside edges of the deck with high-quality lumber for appearance.

Build deck stairs (pages 364 to 369). For stairways with three steps or less, railings may not be required. Consult local building codes.

The ends of stairway stringers may rest directly on a concrete sidewalk, patio paths, or the ground.

Seal all parts of the stairway with a clear sealer-preservative to prevent rot.

**Facing boards**

**Facing boards**

**8** Install the post-and-baluster railings (pages 370 to 377). To support the handrail of an octagonal deck, use pairs of 2 × 4s at the corners instead of 4 × 4s. Use 2 × 2s for the balusters.

Install the 2 × 4s on edge, using ⅜'' × 5'' galvanized lag screws. The spacing between the 2 × 4s should be the same as that used between the 2 × 2 balusters.

2 × 4

2 × 2       2 × 4

# Deck Finishing & Repair

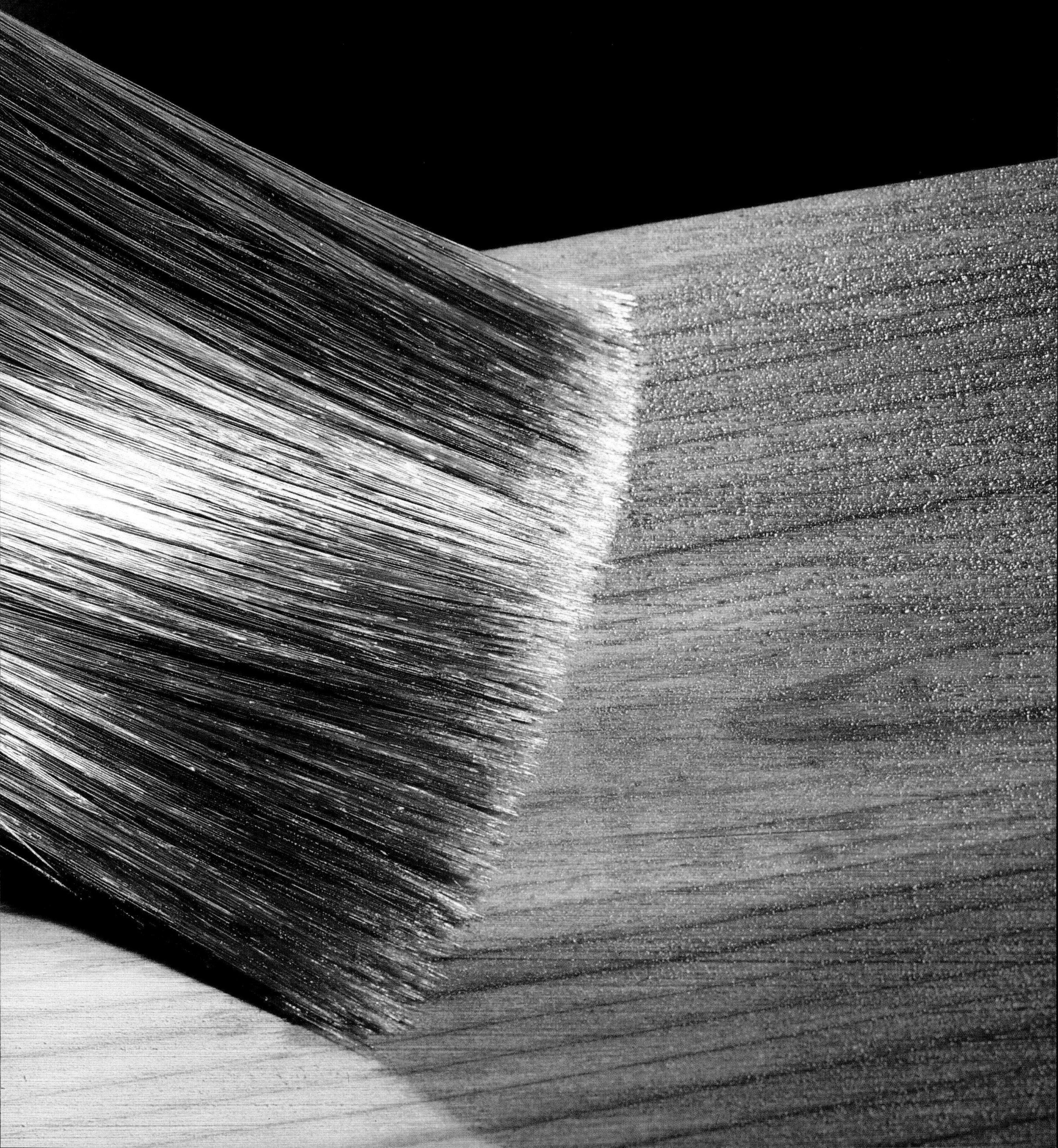

# Finishing a New Deck

Finish a deck with clear sealer-preservative or staining sealer. Sealer-preservatives protect wood from water and rot, and are often used on cedar or redwood, because they preserve the original color of the wood. If you want the wood to look weathered, wait several months before applying sealer-preservative.

Staining sealers, sometimes called toners, are often applied to pressure-treated lumber to give it the look of redwood or cedar. Staining sealers are available in a variety of colors.

For best protection, use finishing products with an alkyd base. Apply fresh finish each year.

## Everything You Need:

Tools: orbital sander, sandpaper, shop vacuum, pressure sprayer, eye protection, paint brush.

Materials: clear sealer-preservative or staining sealer.

**Use an orbital sander** to smooth out any rough areas before applying finish to decking boards, railings, or stair treads.

## How to Finish a Redwood or Cedar Deck

**1** Test wood surface by sprinkling water on it. If wood absorbs water quickly, it is ready to be sealed. If wood does not absorb water, let it dry for several weeks before sealing.

**2** Sand rough areas and vacuum deck. Apply clear sealer to all wood surfaces, using a pressure sprayer. If possible, apply sealer to underside of decking and to joists, beams, and posts.

**3** Use a paint brush to work sealer into cracks and narrow areas that could trap water.

## How to Finish a Pressure-treated Deck

**1** Sand rough areas and vacuum the deck. Apply a staining sealer (toner) to all deck wood, using a pressure sprayer.

**2** Use a paint brush to smooth out drips and runs. Porous wood may require a second coat of staining sealer for even coverage.

Inspect hidden areas regularly for signs of rotted or damaged wood. Apply a fresh coat of finish yearly.

# Maintaining a Deck

Inspect your deck once each year. Replace loose or rusting hardware or fasteners, and apply fresh finish to prevent water damage.

Look carefully for areas that show signs of damage. Replace or reinforce damaged wood as soon as possible (pages 404 to 407).

Restore an older, weathered deck to the original wood color with a deck-brightening solution. Brighteners are available at any home improvement store.

### Everything You Need:

Tools: flashlight, awl or screwdriver, screwgun, putty knife, scrub brush, rubber gloves, eye protection, pressure sprayer.

Materials: 2½" corrosion-resistant deck screws, deck brightener.

## Tips for Maintaining an Older Deck

Use an awl or screwdriver to check deck for soft, rotted wood. Replace or reinforce damaged wood (pages 404 to 407).

## How to Renew a Deck

**1** Mix deck-brightening solution as directed by manufacturer. Apply solution with pressure sprayer. Let solution set for 10 minutes.

**Clean debris from cracks** between decking boards with a putty knife. Debris traps moisture, and can cause wood to rot.

**Drive new fasteners** to secure loose decking to joists. If using the old nail or screw holes, new fasteners should be slightly longer than the originals.

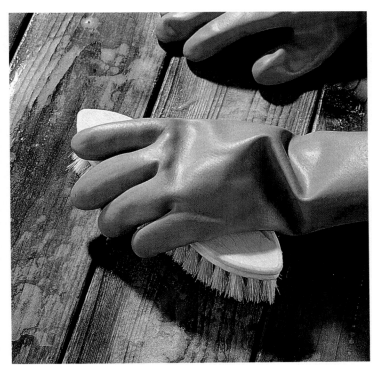

**2** Scrub deck thoroughly with a stiff scrub brush. Wear rubber gloves and eye protection.

**3** Rinse deck with clear water. If necessary, apply a second coat of brightener to extremely dirty or stained areas. Rinse and let dry. Apply a fresh coat of sealer or stain (pages 400 to 401).

# Repairing a Deck

Replace or reinforce damaged deck wood as soon as possible. Wood rot can spread and weaken solid wood.

After replacing or reinforcing the rotted wood, clean the entire deck and apply a fresh coat of clear sealer-preservative or staining sealer. Apply a fresh coat of finish each year to prevent future water damage.

### Everything You Need:

Tools: cat's paw or flat pry bar, screwgun, awl or screwdriver, hammer, chisel, eye protection, pressure-sprayer, circular saw, scrub brush, paint brush, hydraulic jack, drill or hammer drill, ⅝" masonry bit, level, ratchet wrench.

Materials: sealer-preservative or staining sealer, galvanized nails (6d, 10d), deck lumber, baking soda, corrosion-resistant deck screws, ⅝" masonry anchor, ⅜" lag screw.

Supplies: rubber gloves, bucket, concrete block, scrap plywood.

## How to Repair Damaged Decking & Joists

**1** Remove nails or screws from the damaged decking board, using a cat's paw or screwgun. Remove the damaged board.

**4** Apply a thick coat of sealer-preservative to damaged joist. Let dry, then apply a second coat of sealer. Cut a reinforcing joist (sister joist) from pressure-treated lumber.

**5** Treat all sides of sister joist with clear sealer-preservative, and let dry. Position sister joist tightly against the damaged joist, and attach with 10d nails driven every 2 feet.

**2** Inspect the underlying joists for signs of rotted wood. Joists with discolored, soft areas should be repaired and reinforced.

**3** Use a hammer and chisel to remove any rotted portions of joist.

**6** Attach sister joist to ledger and header joist by toenailing with 10d nails. Cut replacement decking boards from matching lumber, using a circular saw.

**7** If the existing decking is gray, "weather" the new decking by scrubbing with a solution made from 1 cup baking soda and 1 gallon warm water. Rinse and let dry.

(continued next page)

## How to Repair Damaged Decking & Joists (continued)

**8** Apply a coat of sealer-preservative or staining sealer to all sides of the new decking board.

**9** Position the new decking and attach to joists with galvanized deck screws or nails. Make sure space between boards matches that of existing decking.

## How to Replace a Post on an Older Deck

**1** Build a support, using plywood scraps, a concrete block, and a hydraulic jack. Place 1½" layer of plywood between head of jack and beam. Apply just enough pressure to lift the beam slightly.

Anchor pad

**2** Remove the nails or lag screws holding the damaged post to the anchor pad and to the beam. Remove the damaged post and the wood anchor pad on the concrete pier.

**3** Drill a hole in the middle of the concrete pier, using a hammer drill and a ⅝" masonry bit. Insert ⅝" masonry anchor into hole.

**4** Position galvanized post anchor on pier block, and thread a ⅜" lag screw with washer through the hole in the anchor and into the masonry anchor. Tighten the screw with a ratchet wrench.

**5** Cut new post from pressure-treated lumber, and treat cut ends with sealer-preservative. Position post and make sure it is plumb.

**6** Attach the bottom of the post to the post anchor, using 6d galvanized nails. Attach the post to the beam by redriving the lag screws, using a ratchet wrench. Release the pressure on the jack and remove the support.

# Index

## For Product Information:

If you have difficulty finding any of the following materials featured in this book, call the manufacturers and ask for the name of the nearest sales representatives. The representatives can direct you to local retailers that stock these useful products.

**Bay window accessories (page 169)**
Flintwood Products (roof skirt, skirt trim boards, metal braces)
telephone: 1-800-728-4365

**Brick pavers (pages 268, 271)**
Uni-Group U. S. A.
telephone: 1-407-626-4666
Pine Hall Brick
telephone: 1-919-721-7500

**Computer software for remodelers (page 92)**
Expert Software (Home Design)
telephone: 1-800-759-2562

**Garden pond liners, shells & aquatic plants (page 287)**
Lilypons Water Gardens
telephone: 1-800-765-5459

**Interlocking concrete block (pages 228 to 233)**
Anchor Wall Systems (Diamond Block™ and Windsor Stone™)
telephone: 1-800-473-4452

**Landscape fabric (pages 218, 230, 248, 266)**
Easy Garden Weedblock™
telephone: 1-817-753-5353

**Manufactured framing members (page 125)**
Trusjoist-MacMillan (MicroLam®)
telephone: 1-800-338-0515

**Metal connectors (pages 219, 244, 273, 345 to 349, 354 to 369)**
Kant-Sag (a division of United Steel Products)
telephone: 1-800-328-5934

**Natural cut stone (page 236)**
Buechel Stone Corporation
telephone: 1-414-849-9361

**Perforated drain pipe (pages 225, 229 to 237)**
Wisconsin Tubing
telephone: 1-800-242-828

**Remodeler's blade for circular saws (page 95)**
Vermont American Corporation
telephone: 1-800-742-3869

**Rigid plastic edging (pages 248, 263, 267)**
Pave Tech Inc. (Pave Edge™)
telephone: 1-612-881-5773

**Storm doors (page 144)**
Cole Sewell Corporation
telephone: 1-800-328-6596

**Stone veneer (pages 238, 245)**
Stucco Stone Products, Inc.
telephone: 1-800-225-6462

**Windows and patio doors (pages 136, 143)**
Marvin Windows
telephone: 1-800-246-5128